# Language Technology for Closely Related Languages and Language Variants Workshop 2014

# (LT4CloseLang 2014)



**Held at the Conference on Empirical Methods in Natural Language Processing (EMNLP 2014)**

## Doha, Qatar
## 29 October 2014

ISBN: 978-1-63439-484-0

**Printed from e-media with permission by:**

Curran Associates, Inc.
57 Morehouse Lane
Red Hook, NY 12571

CURRAN ASSOCIATES INC. proceedings.com

**Some format issues inherent in the e-media version may also appear in this print version.**



Printed by Curran Associates, Inc. (2014)



Association for Computational Linguistics
209 N. Eighth Street
Stroudsburg, Pennsylvania 18360

Phone: 1-570-476-8006
Fax: 1-570-476-0860

acl@aclweb.org

**Additional copies of this publication are available from:**

Curran Associates, Inc.
57 Morehouse Lane
Red Hook, NY 12571 USA
Phone: 845-758-0400
Fax: 845-758-2634
Email: curran@proceedings.com
Web: www.proceedings.com

# Introduction

Recent initiatives in language technology have led to the development of at least minimal language processing toolkits for all EU-official languages as well as for languages with a large number of speakers worldwide such as Chinese and Arabic. This is a big step towards the automatic processing and/or extraction of information, especially from official documents and newspapers, where the standard, literary language is used.

Apart from those official languages, a large number of dialects or closely-related language variants are in daily use, not only as spoken colloquial languages but also in some written media, e.g., in SMS, chats, and social networks. Building language resources and tools for them from scratch is expensive, but the efforts can often be reduced by making use of pre-existing resources and tools for related, resource-richer languages.

Examples of closely-related language variants include the different variants of Spanish in Latin America, the Arabic dialects in North Africa and the Middle East, German in Germany, Austria and Switzerland, French in France and in Belgium, Dutch in the Netherlands and Flemish in Belgium, etc. Examples of pairs of related languages include Swedish-Norwegian, Bulgarian-Macedonian, Serbian-Bosnian, Spanish-Catalan, Russian-Ukrainian, Irish-Gaelic Scottish, Malay-Indonesian, Turkish–Azerbaijani, Mandarin-Cantonese, Hindi–Urdu, and many other.

The workshop aims to bring together researchers interested in building language technology applications that make use of language closeness to exploit existing resources in a related language or a language variant. A previous version of this workshop, organised at RANLP 2013, attracted a lot of research interest, showing the need for further activities.

We received 20 submissions and we selected 11 papers for presentation. The papers cover the following general NLP topics: Parsing, Variety and Adaptation, and Machine Translation.

We would like to thank our reviewers for the professional and in-time reviewing!

Preslav Nakov, Petya Osenova and Cristina Vertan

**Program Co-Chairs and Organizers:**

Preslav Nakov, Qatar Computing Research Institute
Petya Osenova, Sofia University and Bulgarian Academy of Sciences
Cristina Vertan, University of Hamburg

**Program Committee:**

Laura Alonso y Alemany (University of Cordoba, Argentina)
César Antonio Aguilar (Pontificia Universidad Católica de Chile, Santiago de Chile, Chile)
José Castaño (University of Buenos Aires, Argentina)
David Chiang (University of Southern California, USA)
Marta Costa-Jussà (Institute for Infocomm Research, Singapore)
Walter Daelemans (University of Antwerp, Belgium)
Kareem Darwish (Qatar Computing Research Institute, Qatar)
Tomaz Erjavec (Jozef Stefan Institute, Slovenia)
Maria Gavrilidou (ILSP, Greece)
Francisco Guzman (Qatar Computing Research Institute, Qatar)
Barry Haddow (University of Edinburgh, UK)
Nizar Habash (Columbia University, USA)
Walther v. Hahn (University of Hamburg,Germany)
Cvetana Krstev (University of Belgrade, Serbia)
Vladislav Kubon (Charles University Prague, Czech Republic)
Thang Luong Minh (Stanford University, USA)
John Nerbonne (University of Groningen, Netherlands)
Graham Neubig (Nara Institute of Science and Technology, Japan)
Kemal Oflazer (Carnegie-Mellon University, Qatar)
Maciej Ogrodniczuk (IPAN, Polish Academy of Sciences, Poland)
Slav Petrov (Google, New York, USA)
Stefan Riezler (University of Heidelberg, Germany)
Laurent Romary (INRIA, France)
Hassan Sajjad (Qatar Computing Research Institute, Qatar)
Kiril Simov (Bulgarian Academy of Sciences)
Milena Slavcheva (Bulgarian Academy of Sciences)
Marco Tadic (University of Zagreb, Croatia)
Jörg Tiedemann (Uppsala University, Sweden)
Dusko Vitas (University of Belgrade, Serbia)
Stephan Vogel (Qatar Computing Research Institute, Qatar)
Pidong Wang (National University of Singapore, Singapore)
Taro Watanabe (NICT, Japan)

**Keynote Speakers:**

Nizar Habash (New York University Abu Dhabi, UAE)
Slav Petrov (Google, USA)

**Panelists:**

Houda Bouamor (Carnegie Mellon University, Qatar)
Kareem Darwish (Qatar Computing Research Institute, Qatar)
Vladislav Kubon (Charles University in Prague, Czech Republic)
Wolfgang Maier (University of Dusseldorf, Germany)
Kemal Oflazer (Carnegie Mellon University, Qatar)

# Table of Contents

# Conference Program

**Wednesday, October 29, 2014**

**Opening Session and Invited Talk 1**

8:50–9:00 *Opening Remarks*
The organizers

9:00–10:00 *INVITED TALK 1: Computational Processing of Arabic Dialects*
Nizar Habash

**Session 1: Parsing**

10:00–10:20 *Learning from a Neighbor: Adapting a Japanese Parser for Korean Through Feature Transfer Learning*
Hiroshi Kanayama, Youngja Park, Yuta Tsuboi and Dongmook Yi

10:20–10:40 *Cross-lingual Dependency Parsing of Related Languages with Rich Morphosyntactic Tagsets*
Željko Agić, Jörg Tiedemann, Danijela Merkler, Simon Krek, Kaja Dobrovoljc and Sara Moze

**10:40–11:00** ***Coffee Break***

**Session 2: Variety and Adaptation**

11:00–11:20 *Language variety identification in Spanish tweets*
Wolfgang Maier and Carlos Gómez-Rodríguez

11:20–11:40 *Exploiting Language Variants Via Grammar Parsing Having Morphologically Rich Information*
Qaiser Abbas

11:40–12:00 *Adapting Predicate Frames for Urdu PropBanking*
Riyaz Ahmad Bhat, Naman Jain, Ashwini Vaidya, Martha Palmer, Tafseer Ahmed Khan, Dipti Misra Sharma and James Babani

12:00–12:20 *Measuring Language Closeness by Modeling Regularity*
Javad Nouri and Roman Yangarber

**12:20–14:00** ***Lunch***

**Wednesday, October 29, 2014 (continued)**

**Invited Talk 2**

14:00–15:00 *INVITED TALK 2: Towards Universal Syntactic Processing of Natural Language*
Slav Petrov

**Session 3: Machine Translation I**

15:00–15:20 *Proper Name Machine Translation from Japanese to Japanese Sign Language*
Taro Miyazaki, Naoto Kato, Seiki Inoue, Shuichi Umeda, Makiko Azuma, Nobuyuki Hiruma and Yuji Nagashima

15:20–15:40 *Exploring cross-language statistical machine translation for closely related South Slavic languages*
Maja Popović and Nikola Ljubešić

**15:40–16:00** ***Coffee Break***

**Session 4: Machine Translation II**

16:00–16:20 *Exploring System Combination approaches for Indo-Aryan MT Systems*
Karan Singla, Anupam Singh, Nishkarsh Shastri, Megha Jhunjhunwala, Srinivas Bangalore and Dipti Misra Sharma

16:20–16:40 *A Comparison of MT Methods for Closely Related Languages: a Case Study on Czech - Slovak Language Pair*
Vladislav Kubon and Jernej Vicic

16:40–17:00 *Handling OOV Words in Dialectal Arabic to English Machine Translation*
Maryam Aminian, Mahmoud Ghoneim and Mona Diab

**Wednesday, October 29, 2014 (continued)**

**Closing Session**

17:00–18:00 *Panel*
Panelists: Houda Bouamor, Kareem Darwish, Vladislav Kubon, Wolfgang Maier, Kemal Oflazer

18:00–18:10 *Closing Remarks*
The organizers

# Computational Processing of Arabic Dialects (invited talk)

**Nizar Habash**
Computer Science Department
New York University Abu Dhabi
nizar.habash@nyu.edu

## 1 Abstract

The Arabic language is a collection of variants among which Modern Standard Arabic (MSA) has a special status as the formal written standard of the media, culture and education across the Arab World. The other variants are informal spoken dialects that are the media of communication for daily life. As expected, most of the natural language processing resources and research in Arabic focuses on MSA. However, there is more work now on Arabic dialects, which includes efforts to build resources as well as exploit existing resources from MSA. In this talk, we present the challenges of processing Arabic dialects and the current advances in that area, with special emphasis on directions that exploit existing MSA (and other dialect) resources.

## 2 Author's Biography

Nizar Habash is an Associate Professor of Computer Science at New York University Abu Dhabi. He received his Ph.D. in 2003 from the Computer Science Department, University of Maryland College Park. He later joined Columbia University's Center for Computational Learning Systems where he co-founded in 2005 the Columbia Arabic Dialect Modeling group (CADIM) with Mona Diab and Owen Rambow. His research includes work on machine translation, morphological analysis, generation and disambiguation, and computational modeling of Arabic and its dialects. Professor Habash has over 100 publications including a book entitled "Introduction to Arabic Natural Language Processing". His website is http://www.nizarhabash.com.



*Language Technology for Closely Related Languages and Language Variants (LT4CloseLang)*, page 1,
October 29, 2014, Doha, Qatar. 

# Learning from a Neighbor: Adapting a Japanese Parser for Korean through Feature Transfer Learning

**Hiroshi Kanayama**
IBM Research - Tokyo
Koto-ku, Tokyo, Japan
hkana@jp.ibm.com

**Youngja Park**
IBM Research - T.J.Watson Research Center
Yorktown Heights, NY, USA
young_park@us.ibm.com

**Yuta Tsuboi**
IBM Research - Tokyo
Koto-ku, Tokyo, Japan
yutat@jp.ibm.com

**Dongmook Yi**
Korea Software Solutions Laboratory, IBM Korea
Gangnam-gu, Seoul, Korea
dmyi@kr.ibm.com

## Abstract

We present a new dependency parsing method for Korean applying cross-lingual transfer learning and domain adaptation techniques. Unlike existing transfer learning methods relying on aligned corpora or bilingual lexicons, we propose a *feature transfer* learning method with minimal supervision, which adapts an existing parser to the target language by transferring the features for the source language to the target language. Specifically, we utilize the *Triplet/Quadruplet Model*, a hybrid parsing algorithm for Japanese, and apply a delexicalized feature transfer for Korean. Experiments with *Penn Korean Treebank* show that even using only the transferred features from Japanese achieves a high accuracy (81.6%) for Korean dependency parsing. Further improvements were obtained when a small annotated Korean corpus was combined with the Japanese training corpus, confirming that efficient cross-lingual transfer learning can be achieved without expensive linguistic resources.

## 1 Introduction

Motivated by increasing demands for advanced natural language processing (NLP) applications such as sentiment analysis (Pang et al., 2002; Nasukawa and Yi, 2003) and question answering (Kwok et al., 2001; Ferrucci et al., 2010), there is a growing need for accurate syntactic parsing and semantic analysis of languages, especially for non-English languages with limited linguistic resources. In this paper, we propose a new dependency parsing method for Korean which requires minimal human supervision. Dependency parsing can handle long-distance relationships and coordination phenomena very well, and has proven to be very effective for parsing free-order languages such as Korean and Japanese (Kübler et al., 2009).

Most statistical parsing methods rely on annotated corpora labeled with phrase structures or dependency relationships, but it is very expensive to create a large number of consistent annotations. Recently, treebanks have become available for many languages such as English, German, Arabic, and Chinese. However, the parsing results on these treebanks vary a lot depending on the size of annotated sentences and the type of annotations (Levy and Manning, 2003; McDonald et al., 2013). Further, many languages lack annotated corpus, or the size of the annotated corpus is too small to develop a reliable statistical method. To address these problems, there have been several attempts at unsupervised parsing (Seginer, 2007; Spitkovsky et al., 2011), grammar induction (Klein and Manning, 2004; Naseem et al., 2010), and cross-lingual transfer learning using annotated corpora of other languages (McDonald et al., 2011). However, the accuracies of unsupervised methods are unacceptably low, and results from cross-lingual transfer learning show different outcomes for different pairs of languages, but, in most cases, the parsing accuracy is still low for practical purposes. A recent study by McDonald *et al.* (2013) concludes that cross-lingual transfer learning is beneficial when the source and target languages were similar. In particular, it reports that Korean is an outlier with the lowest scores (42% or less in UAS) when a model was trained from European languages.

In this paper, we present a new cross-lingual



*Language Technology for Closely Related Languages and Language Variants (LT4CloseLang)*, pages 2–12,
October 29, 2014, Doha, Qatar. 

transfer learning method that learns a new model for the target language by transferring the features for the source language. Unlike other approaches which rely on aligned corpora or a bilingual lexicon, we learn a parsing model for Korean by reusing the features and annotated data used in the Japanese dependency parsing, the *Triplet/Quadruplet Model* (Kanayama et al., 2000), which is a hybrid approach utilizing both grammatical knowledge and statistics.

We exploit many similarities between the two languages, such as the head-final structure, the noun to verb modification via case and topic markers, and the similar word-order constraints. It was reported that the mapping of the grammar formalism in the language pair was relatively easy (Kim et al., 2003b; Kim et al., 2003a). However, as the two languages are classified into independent language families (Gordon and Grimes, 2005), there are many significant differences in their morphology and grammar (especially in the writing systems), so it is not trivial to handle the two languages in a uniform way.

We show the *Triplet/Quadruplet Model* is suitable for bilingual transfer learning, because the grammar rules and heuristics reduce the number of modification candidates and can mitigate the differences between two languages efficiently. In addition, this model can handle the relationships among the candidates as a richer feature space, making the model less dependent upon the lexical features of the content words that are difficult to align between the two languages. Similarly to the delexicalized parsing model in (McDonald et al., 2011), we transfer only part-of-speech information of the features for the content words. We create new mapping rules to extract syntactic features for Korean parsing from the Japanese annotated corpus and refine the grammar rules to get closer modification distributions in two languages.

Our experiments with Penn Korean Treebank (Han et al., 2002) confirm that the *Triplet/Quadruplet Model* adapted for Korean outperforms a distance-based dependency parsing method, achieving 81.6% accuracy when no annotated Korean corpus was used. Further performance improvements were obtained when a small size of annotated Korean corpus was added, confirming that our algorithm can be applied without more expensive linguistic resources such as an aligned corpora or bilingual lexicons. Moreover, the delexicalized feature transfer method enables the algorithm applicable to any two languages that have similar syntactic structures.

## 2 Related Work

### 2.1 Parsing for Korean

Since Korean is a morphologically-rich language, many efforts for Korean parsing have focused on automatically extracting rich lexical information such as the use of case frame patterns for the verbs (Lee et al., 2007), the acquisition of case frames and nominal phrases from raw corpora (Park et al., 2013), and effective features from phrases and their neighboring contexts (Choi and Palmer, 2011). Recently, Choi et al. (2012) discussed the transformation of *eojeol*-based Korean treebank to entity-based treebank to effectively train probabilistic CFG parsers. We apply similar techniques as in (Choi et al., 2012) to mitigate the differences between Korean and Japanese syntactic structures.

Chung and Rim (2003) applied the *Triplet/Quadruplet Model* for Korean parsing as done in our work. They reported that the model performed well for long-distance dependencies, but, in their experiments, the number of modification candidates was not effectively reduced (only 91.5% of phrases were in one of the three positions, while it was 98.6% in Kanayama's work for Japanese). In this paper, we introduce more sophisticated grammatical knowledge and heuristics to have similar dependency distributions in the two languages. Smith and Smith (2004) attempted a bilingual parsing for English and Korean by combining statistical dependency parsers, probabilistic context-free grammars, and word translation models into a unified framework that jointly searches for the best English parse, Korean parse and word alignment. However, we utilize an existing parser and align the features from the source language to the features for the target language, and, thus, our method is applicable to situations where there is no aligned corpora or word translation models.

### 2.2 Transfer learning and domain adaptation

Recently, transfer learning has attracted much attention, as it can overcome the lack of training data for new languages or new domains for both classification and regression tasks (Pan and Yang, 2010). Transfer learning has also been applied to

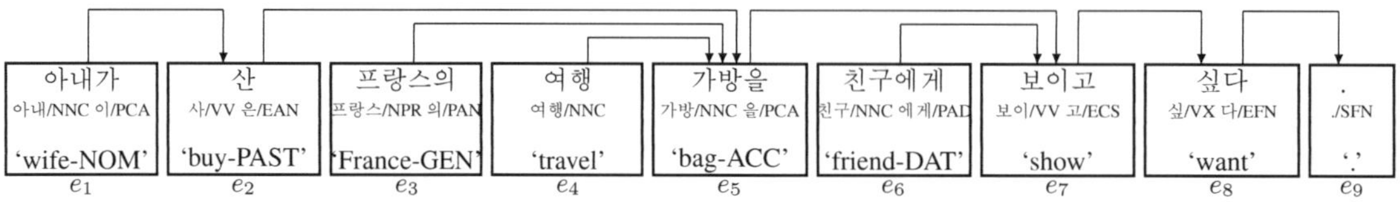


Figure 1: An example of dependency structures of a Korean sentence "아내가 산 프랑스의 여행 가방을 친구에게 보이고 싶다." ('(I) want to show the French travel bag which (my) wife bought to (my) friend'). Each box corresponds to a Korean phrasal unit *eojeol*.

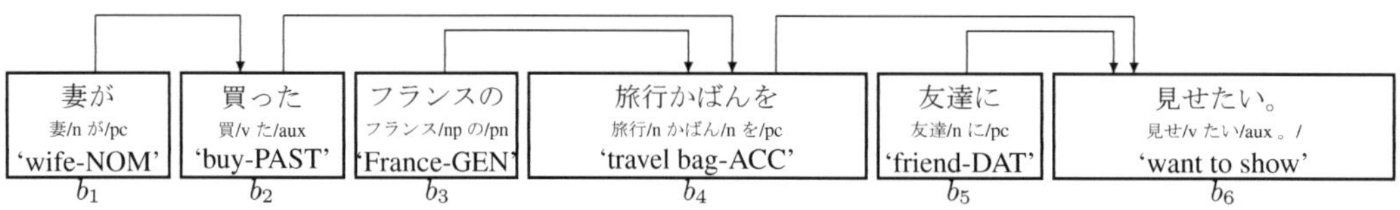


Figure 2: A dependency structure of a Japanese sentence which corresponds to the Korean sentence in Figure 1, "妻が買ったフランスの旅行かばんを友達に見せたい。". Each box corresponds to a Japanese phrasal unit *bunsetsu*.

syntactic parsing, where a parsing model for a target language is learned from linguistic resources in one or more different languages (Hwa et al., 2005; Zeman and Resnik, 2008; McDonald et al., 2011; Durrett et al., 2012; Georgi et al., 2012; Naseem et al., 2012). McDonald et al. (2011) proposed a delexicalized parsing model for cross-lingual dependency parsing and demonstrated that a high accuracy parsing was achieved for Indo-European languages where significant amount of parallel texts exist. However, in more recent work, McDonald et al. (2013) showed that, unlike transfer learning within close language families, building a Korean parser from European languages was not successful with a very low accuracy. Durrett et al. (2012) and Georgi et al. (2012) show that transfer parsing can be improved when additional bilingual resources are available, such as bilingual dictionaries and parallel corpora of glossed texts respectively.

Our method does not require such resources and does not have restrictions on the sentence type that can be parsed. Instead, we use a mixture of a small corpus in a target language (i.e., Korean) and a larger corpus of a source language (Japanese). This task is similar to domain adaptation, and our objective is to outperform the training model built on each language separately. To avoid the loss of accuracy due to the differences between two domains, we apply the domain adaptation technique proposed by Daumé III (2007) which duplicates the feature space into three categories with each of the features trained by source, by target, and by combined domains.

## 3 Dependency Structures of Korean and Japanese

A dependency structure in Korean is typically analyzed in terms of *eojeol* units, a basic phrase that consists of a content word agglutinated with optional functional morphemes such as postpositional particles or endings for verbs. Figure 1 shows an example Korean sentence with the dependencies between the *eojeol*s indicated by arrows. Figure 2 illustrates the dependency structure between the *bunsetsu*s in Japanese that corresponds to the Korean structure in Figure 1. As these figures show, the syntactic structures are quite similar in these languages: All of the dependencies are directed from left to right, and the postpositional particles determine if the content word modifies a verb ("가" in $e_1$ and "が" in $b_1$) or a noun ("의" in $e_3$ and "の" in $b_3$). The *eojeol*s in Korean roughly correspond to the *bunsetsu*s in Japanese. In the remainder of this paper, we denote both an *eojeol* or a *bunsetsu* as a '*PU*' (phrasal unit) when distinction is not needed.

While Korean and Japanese have similar syntactic structures, the two languages have many differences. The *eojeol*s in Korean are separated by white space, while the *bunsetsu*s in Japanese are not. Further, the statistics show several differences in the two languages. Table 1 compares a Korean corpus, *Penn Korean Treebank* (henceforth KTB)

Table 1: Statistics of Korean and Japanese corpora.

| | KTB (Korean) | EDR (Japanese) |
|---|---|---|
| Average number of characters (except for whitespace) per sentence | 73.7 | 28.0 |
| Average number of PUs per sentence | 25.5 | 8.53 |
| Average number of morphemes per PU | 1.83 | 2.86 |
| Ratio of modification to the next PU | 70.0% | 61.8% |

Table 2: Simplified examples of Japanese grammar rules.

| Rightmost morpheme of the modifier PU | Conditions for the modified PUs |
|---|---|
| postpositional "を" *wo* (accusative) | verb, adjective |
| postpositional "の" *no* (genitive, nominative) | noun, verb, adjective |
| postpositional "と" *to* (conjunctive) | noun, verb, adjective, adverb "一緒に" *isshoni* ('together') |
| adverb | verb, adjective, adverb, copula |

(Han et al., 2002), and a Japanese corpus, *EDR Corpus* (EDR, 1996). Both corpora consist of word-level bracketed constituents, so they are converted into PU-level dependency structures using the method described in Choi and Palmer (2011). Though both corpora consist mainly of newspaper or magazine articles, the sentences are not aligned with each other, so the statistics show the comparisons of the two corpora, rather than the theoretical comparisons of the two languages. However, we can see that Korean sentences tend to be longer than Japanese sentences both in terms of the number of characters and PUs. More *eojeol*s modify an adjacent *eojeol* in Korean than in Japanese. For instance, $e_1$, $e_4$, $e_6$, $e_7$, and $e_8$ modify the next *eojeol* in Figure 1, but only $b_1$, $b_3$, and $b_5$ modify the next *bunsetsu* in Figure 2. Those differences suggest some of the difficulties in applying the Japanese dependency model to Korean. The Japanese parsing method that will be described in the next section exploits these characteristics, which we apply to Korean parsing.

## 4 Triplet/Quadruplet Model

This section describes the *Triplet/Quadruplet Model* (Kanayama et al., 2000) which was originally designed for Japanese parsing. First, we review the two main ideas of the model – restriction of modification candidates and feature selection for probability calculation. Then, we describe how we apply the *Triplet/Quadruplet Model* to Korean parsing in Section 4.3.

### 4.1 Restriction of modification candidates

The *Triplet/Quadruplet Model* utilizes a small number (about 50) of hand-crafted grammar rules that determine whether a PU can modify each PU to its right in a sentence. The main goal of the grammar rules is to maximize the coverage, and the rules are simple describing high-level syntactic dependencies, and, thus, the rules can be easily created without worrying about the precision or contradictory rules. The statistical information is later used to select the right rules for a given sentence to produce an accurate parsing result. Table 2 shows several grammar rules for Japanese, in which the modified PUs are determined depending on the conditions of the rightmost morpheme in the modifier PU.

An analysis of the EDR corpus shows that 98.6% of the correct dependencies are either the nearest PU, the second nearest PU, or the farthest PU from the modifier (more details in Table 4(a)). Therefore, the model can be simplified by restricting the candidates to these three candidates and by ignoring the other PUs with a small sacrifice (1.4%) of parsing accuracy.

### 4.2 Calculation of modification probabilities

Let $u$ be a modifier PU in question, $c_{un}$ the $u$'s $n$-th modification candidate PU, $\Phi_u$ and $\Psi_{c_{un}}$ the attributes of $u$ and $c_{un}$, respectively. Then the probability that $u$ modifies its $n$-th candidate is calculated by the triplet equation (1) or the quadruplet equation (2) when $u$ has two or three candidates, respectively [1].

$$P(u \rightarrow c_{un}) = P(n \mid \Phi_u, \Psi_{c_{u1}}, \Psi_{c_{u2}}) \quad (1)$$

$$P(u \rightarrow c_{un}) = P(n \mid \Phi_u, \Psi_{c_{u1}}, \Psi_{c_{u2}}, \Psi_{c_{u3}}) \quad (2)$$

[1] It is trivial to show that $P(u \rightarrow cu_1) = 1$, when $u$ has only one candidate.

Table 3: Simplified examples of Korean grammar rules.

| Rightmost morpheme of the modifier PU | Conditions for the modified PUs |
|---|---|
| PCA,PCJ,PAD,PAU (postpositional particles) | V* (verb, adjective or auxiliary), CO (copula) |
| EAN (nominal verb ending *e.g.* "은" *eun*) | N* (noun) |
| ADV (adverb), ADC (conjunction) | N* (noun), V* (verb, adjective or auxiliary), ADV (adverb), ADC (conjunction) |
| postpositional "과" *gwa* (conjunctive) | N* (noun), V* (verb, adjective or aux), adverb "함께" *hamkke* ('together') |
| N* (noun) | N* (noun), V* (verb, adjective or auxiliary) |

Table 4: Distribution (percentage) of the position of the correct modified PU among the candidate PUs selected by the initial grammar rules. The column 'Sum' shows the coverage of the 1st, 2nd and last PUs. The EDR corpus was used for Japanese, and the KTB was used for Korean in this analysis.

(a) Japanese

| # of Candidates | Ratio | 1st | 2nd | Last | Sum |
|---|---|---|---|---|---|
| 1 | 32.7 | 100.0 | – | – | 100.0 |
| 2 | 28.1 | 74.3 | 26.7 | – | 100.0 |
| 3 | 17.5 | 70.6 | 12.6 | 16.8 | 100.0 |
| 4 | 9.9 | 70.4 | 11.1 | 13.8 | 95.3 |
| ≥5 | 11.8 | 70.2 | 11.1 | 10.5 | 91.9 |
| Total | 100 | – | – | – | 98.6 |

(b) Korean (with the initial grammar)

| # of Candidates | Ratio | 1st | 2nd | Last | Sum |
|---|---|---|---|---|---|
| 1 | 10.5 | 100.0 | – | – | 100.0 |
| 2 | 11.4 | 85.9 | 14.1 | – | 100.0 |
| 3 | 10.4 | 76.2 | 13.4 | 10.4 | 100.0 |
| 4 | 9.3 | 74.7 | 11.3 | 8.0 | 93.9 |
| ≥5 | 58.4 | 75.5 | 10.0 | 4.9 | 90.5 |
| Total | 100 | – | – | – | 93.9 |

These probabilities are estimated by the maximum entropy method with a feature set to express $\Phi$ and $\Psi$. Assuming the independence of those modifications, the probability of the dependency tree for an entire sentence $P(T)$ is calculated as the product of the probabilities of all of the dependencies in the sentence using beam search to maximize $P(T)$ under the constraints of the projected structure.

$$P(T) \simeq \prod_{u} P(u \to c_{un}) \tag{3}$$

In comparison, a traditional statistical parser (Collins, 1997) uses Equation (4) to calculate the probability of $u$ modifying $t$.

$$P(u \to t) = P(True \mid \Phi_u, \Psi_t, \Delta_{u,t}) \tag{4}$$

We call the model based on Equation (4) the *Distance Model*, since $\Delta_{u,t}$ (the distance between $u$ and $t$) is typically used as the key feature. Though other contextual information, in addition to the attributes of $u$ and $t$, can be added, the model calculates the probabilities of the dependencies between $u$ and $t$ independently and thus often fails to incorporate appropriate contextual information.

Equations (1) and (2) have two major advantages over the *Distance Model*: First, all the attributes of the modifier and its candidates can be handled simultaneously. The combination of those attributes helps the model to express the context of the modifications. Second, the probability of each modification is calculated based on the relative positions of the candidates, instead of the distance from the modifier PU in the surface sentence, and, thus, the model is more robust.

### 4.3 Korean dependency parsing with the *Triplet/Quadruplet Model*

We design the Korean parser by adapting the *Triplet/Quadruplet Model* based on the analogous characteristics of Japanese and Korean. First, we created the Korean grammar rules for generating candidate modified PUs by modifying the rules for Japanese shown in Table 2 for Korean. The rule set, containing fewer than 50 rules, is simple enough to be created manually, because the rules simply describe possible dependencies, and Japanese phenomena are good hints for Korean phenomena. Table 3 shows some examples of the rules for Korean based on the POS schema used in the KTB corpus. We did not automatically extract the rules from the annotated corpora so that the rules are general and independent of the training corpus. Nonetheless, 96.6% of the dependencies in KTB are covered by the grammar rules. The remaining dependencies (3.4%) not covered by the rule set are mainly due to rare modifications and may indicate inconsistencies in the annotations, so we do not seek any grammar rules to achieve nearly 100%.

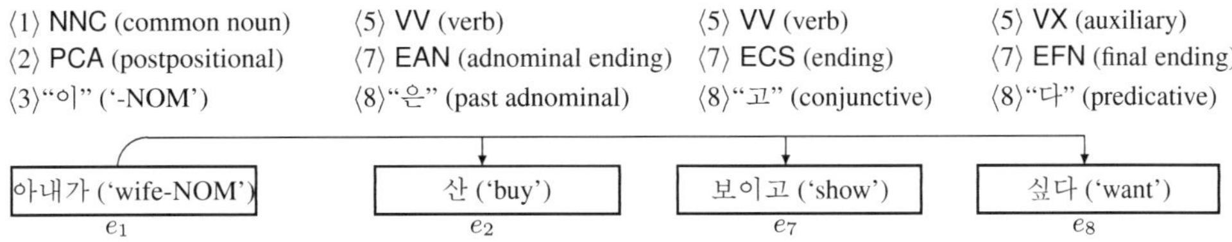


Figure 3: The features used to select the modified PU of $e_1$ among its three candidates. The full sentence of this example is shown in Figure 1. The numbers in brackets correspond to the feature IDs in Table 5.

Table 5: The features to express attributes of a modifier and modification candidates.

| Feature set ID | Description |
|---|---|
| ⟨1⟩ | PoS of the head morpheme of the modifier |
| ⟨2⟩ | PoS of the last morpheme of the modifier |
| ⟨3⟩ | Lex of the postpositional or endings of the modifier |
| ⟨4⟩ | Lex of the adverb of the modifier |
| ⟨5⟩ | PoS of the head morpheme of the modification candidate |
| ⟨6⟩ | Lex of the head morpheme of the modification candidate |
| ⟨7⟩ | PoS of the last morpheme of the modification candidate |
| ⟨8⟩ | Lex of the postpositional or endings of the modification candidate |
| ⟨9⟩ | Existence of a quotation expression "다고" *dago* or "라고" *rago* |
| ⟨10⟩ | Number of "은" *eun* (TOPIC marker) between the modifier and modification candidate |
| ⟨11⟩ | Number of commas between the modifier and modification candidate |
| combination | ⟨1⟩ × ⟨5⟩ / ⟨2⟩ × ⟨5⟩ / ⟨2⟩ × ⟨7⟩ / ⟨3⟩ × ⟨5⟩ / ⟨3⟩ × ⟨8⟩ |

Table 4(a) and (b) show the distribution of the numbers of candidate PUs and the position of the correct modified PUs obtained from the analysis of the EDR corpus and the KTB corpus respectively. As we can see, the first candidate is preferred in both languages, but the preference of the nearer candidate is stronger in Korean. For instance, when there are more than one candidates, the probability that the first candidate is the correct one is 78% for Korean but 71% for Japanese. Further, when there are more than 2 candidates, Japanese prefers the last candidate, while Korean prefers the second candidate. Based on the analysis results, the number of modification candidates is restricted to at most three (the first, second and last candidates) for Korean as well.

The next step is to design $\Phi_u$ and $\Psi_{c_{un}}$, which are required in Equations (1) and (2) to choose the correct modified PU. We converted the feature set from the Japanese study to get the Korean features as listed in Table 5. For example, to find the modified PU of $e_1$ "아내가" *anae-ga* ('wife-NOM') in the sentence shown in Figure 1, the attributes of $e_1$ and the attributes of the three candidates, $e_2$, $e_7$, and $e_8$, are extracted as shown in Figure 3, and their attributes are used to estimate the probability of each candidate in Equation (2).

## 5 Adaptation for Bilingual Transfer Learning

In Section 4.3, we explained how the *Triplet/Quadruplet Model* can be used for Korean. In this section, we describe the feature adaption techniques in more detail and investigate if the new model with transferred features works well when a small amount of annotated corpus for the target language is provided. Further, we study if we can leverage the annotated corpus for the source language in addition to the parsing model and train a model for the target language using the training data for the source language.

### 5.1 Feature Transfer

With the assumption that Korean and Japanese have similar syntactic dependencies, we adopt the delexicalized parsing model presented in McDonald et al. (2011). We transfer the part-of-speech (POS) in the Japanese features to the POS scheme in the KTB corpus, and translate Japanese functional words to the corresponding functional words in Korean. This transfer process is mandatory because we use the language specific POS systems to capture language-specific dependency phenomena, unlike other works using language universal but coarser POS systems.

We do not transfer lexical knowledge on con-

Table 6: Example of mapping rules for parts-of-speech and functional words.

| Japanese PoS | | Korean PoS |
|---|---|---|
| common noun | | NNC |
| verb | | VV |
| adjective | | VJ |
| nominal suffix | | XSF |
| case particle | "で","に","へ","から" | PAD |
| | others | PCA |

| Japanese particle | | Korean particle |
|---|---|---|
| "を" *wo* ('-ACC') | | "을" *eul* |
| "より" *yori* ('from') | | "부터" *buteo* |
| "は" *ha* ('-TOPIC') | | "은" *eun* |
| "も" *mo* ('too') | | "도" *do* |
| "が" *ga* | case particle ('-NOM') | "이" *i* |
| | conjunctive particle ('but') | "지만" *jiman* |

tent words and exceptional cases, so feature sets ⟨4⟩ and ⟨6⟩ are not transferred. Table 6 shows some examples of the feature transfer which handle POS tags and functional words. We note that the Korean features shown in Figure 3 are directly extracted from Japanese corpus using those rules.

### 5.2 Adaptation of parsing rules

While Japanese and Korean are similar in terms of syntactic dependencies, there are significant differences between the two languages in the distribution of modification as shown in the Table 4(a) and (b): In Korean, more than half of modifiers have 5 or more candidates, while only 12% of Japanese modifiers do. In Japanese, 98.6% of correct modified PUs are located in one of the three positions (1st, 2nd or last), but, in Korean, the ratio falls to 93.9% as shown in Table 4. Another major difference of the two languages is the different average numbers of PUs per sentence as shown in Table 1. Korean has 25.5 PUs per sentence, while the number is only 8.5 in Japanese. This is mainly caused by the difference between *eojeol* in Korean and *bunsetsu* in Japanese. In Japanese, compound nouns and verb phrases with an auxiliary verb are likely to form a single *bunsetsu*, while, in Korean, they are split into multiple *eojeol*s with a whitespace in-between.

These differences significantly reduce the effect of transfer learning. To address these problems, we further refine the grammar rules as in the following. We added heuristic rules for the Korean model to effectively reduce the number of candidates in compound nouns which consist of a noun sequence in multiple *eojeol*s, and verbs or adjectives followed by auxiliary verbs. Figure 4 shows an algorithm to reduce the number of modified PUs considering the structure of compound nouns. In this example, both PUs $e_4$ ("travel") and $e_5$ ("bag-ACC") can be candidate PUs for *eojeol* $e_3$. However, based on the rule in Figure 4, $e_4$ and $e_5$ are considered as a compound noun (line 1), and $e_4$ is determined to modify $e_5$ (line 3). Subsequently, $e_3$'s modifiability to $e_4$ is rejected (line 5), and, thus, the correct modified PU of $e_3$ is determined as $e_5$. After refining the rules for compound nouns and auxiliary verbs, the probability of the correct modified PU being the 1st, 2nd or last candidate PU increases from 93.9% to 96.3% as shown in Table 7, and the distribution of the candidate's positions for Korean became closer to the Japanese distribution shown in Table 4(a).

### 5.3 Learning from heterogeneous bilingual corpora

The feature transfer and rule adaptation methods described in previous sections generate a very accurate Korean parser using only a Japanese corpus as shown in the first row in Table 8. The next question is if we can leverage bilingual corpora to further improve the accuracy, when annotated corpus for the target language (Korean) is available. We note that the two corpora do not need to be aligned and can come from different domains. To mitigate the side effects of merging heterogeneous training data in different languages, we apply the domain adaptation method proposed by Daumé III (2007) and augment the feature set to a source language-specific version, a target-specific version and a general version. Specifically, a feature set $\boldsymbol{x}$ in Table 5 is expanded as follows:

$$\boldsymbol{x}_K = < \boldsymbol{x}, \mathbf{0}, \boldsymbol{x} > \tag{5}$$

$$\boldsymbol{x}_J = < \mathbf{0}, \boldsymbol{x}, \boldsymbol{x} > \tag{6}$$

where $\boldsymbol{x}_K$ and $\boldsymbol{x}_J$ denote the feature sets extracted from the Korean corpus and the Japanese corpus respectively. Then, the features specific to Korean and Japanese get higher weights for the first part or the second part respectively, and the characteristics existing in both languages influence the last part.

**if** PoS of $u_i$'s last morpheme is N* **and** PoS of $u_{i+1}$'s first morpheme is N*
**then**
$u_i$ must modify $u_{i+1}$
**if** $u_{i-1}$'s last morpheme is **not** "의" **then** $u_{i-1}$ cannot modify $u_{i+1}$
**else** $u_{i-1}$ cannot modify $u_i$
$u_1$ to $u_{i-2}$ cannot modify $u_i$

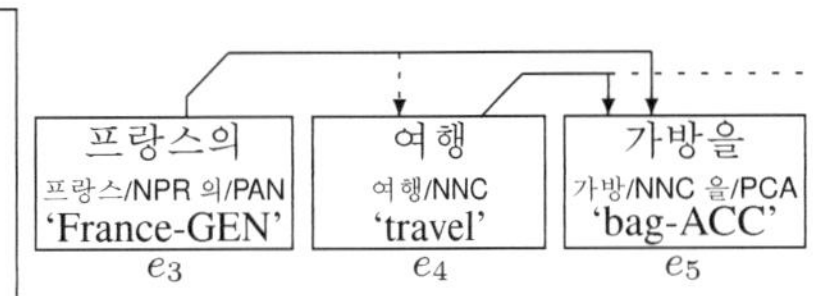


Figure 4: Heuristic rules to reduce the number of modification candidates surrounding compound nouns in Korean. The example in the right figure shows that candidates in the dotted lines are removed by the heuristics.

Table 7: Distribution of the position of correct modified PU for Korean after the refinement of the Korean grammar rules.

| # of candidates | Ratio | 1st | 2nd | Last | Sum |
|---|---|---|---|---|---|
| 1 | 46.4% | 100.0% | – | – | 100.0% |
| 2 | 9.8% | 79.0% | 21.0% | – | 100.0% |
| 3 | 9.2% | 75.5% | 12.7% | 11.8% | 100.0% |
| 4 | 8.0% | 71.0% | 11.8% | 9.6% | 92.4% |
| $\geq 5$ | 26.6% | 70.4% | 10.1% | 7.8% | 88.3% |
| Total | 100% | – | – | – | 96.3% |

## 6 Experiments

In this section, we validate the effectiveness of learning a Korean parser using the feature transfer learning from the Japanese parser and compare the Korean model with other baseline cases. We also compare the parsing results when various sizes of bilingual corpora were used to train the Korean model.

### 6.1 Korean parsing using the *Triplet/Quadruplet Model*

First, to validate the effectiveness of the *Triplet/Quadruplet Model* for parsing Korean, we built eight Korean dependency parsing models using different numbers of training sentences for Korean. The KTB corpus Version 2.0 (Han et al., 2002) containing 5,010 annotated sentences was used in this study. We first divide the corpus into 5 subsets by putting each sentence into its (sentence ID mod 5)-th group. We use sentences from the first subgroup for estimating the parameters, sentences from the second subgroup for testing, and use the remaining three subgroups for training. We built 8 models in total, using from 0 sentence up to 3,006 sentences selected from the training set. The number of training sentences in each model is shown in the first column in Table 8. The parameters were estimated by the maximum entropy method, and the most preferable tree is selected using each dependency probability and the beam search. The test data set contains 1,043 sentences.

We compare the *Triplet/Quadruplet Model*-based models with the Distance Model. For the Distance Model, we used the same feature set as in Table 5, and added the distance feature ($\Delta_{u,t}$) by grouping the distance between two PUs into 3 categories (1, 2 to 5, and 6 or more). The performances are measured by UAS (unlabeled attachment score), and the results of the two methods are shown in the second column, where Japanese Corpus Size=0, in Table 8 (a) and (b) respectively. The top leftmost cells (80.61% and 71.63%) show the parsing accuracies without any training corpora. In these cases the nearest candidate PU is selected as the modified PU. The difference between two models suggests the effect of restriction of modification candidates by the grammar rules. We note that the *Triplet/Quadruplet Model* produces more accurate results and outperforms the Distance Model by more than 2 percentage points in all cases. The results confirm that the method for Japanese parsing is suitable for Korean parsing.

### 6.2 Results of bilingual transfer learning

Next, we evaluate the transfer learning when annotated sentences for Japanese were also added. Table 8(a) shows the accuracies of our model when various numbers of training sentences from Korean and Japanese are used. The first row shows the accuracies of Korean parsing when the models were trained only with the Japanese corpus, and

Table 8: The accuracy of Korean dependency parsing with various numbers of annotated sentences in the two languages. † denotes that the mixture of bilingual corpora significantly outperformed ($p < .05$) the parser trained with only the Korean corpus without Japanese corpus.

(a) Triplet/Quadruplet Model

| | | Japanese Corpus Size | | | |
|---|---|---|---|---|---|
| | | 0 | 2,500 | 5,000 | 10,000 |
| Korean Corpus Size | 0 | 80.61% | 80.78% | 81.23% † | 81.58% † |
| | 50 | 82.21% | 82.32% | 82.40% † | 82.43% † |
| | 98 | 82.36% | 82.66% † | 82.69% † | 82.70% † |
| | 197 | 83.13% | 83.18% | 83.30% † | 83.28% |
| | 383 | 83.62% | 83.92% † | 83.94% † | 83.91% † |
| | 750 | 84.03% | 84.00% | 84.06% | 84.06% |
| | 1,502 | 84.41% | 84.34% | 84.32% | 84.28% |
| | 3,006 | 84.77% | 84.64% | 84.64% | 84.65% |

(b) Distance Model

| | | Japanese Corpus Size | | |
|---|---|---|---|---|
| | | 0 | 2,500 | 5,000 |
| Korean Corpus Size | 0 | 71.63% | 62.42% | 54.92% |
| | 50 | 79.31% | 79.55% † | 79.54% † |
| | 98 | 80.53% | 80.63% † | 80.72% † |
| | 197 | 80.91% | 80.84% | 80.85% |
| | 383 | 81.86% | 81.75% | 81.76% |
| | 750 | 82.10% | 81.92% | 81.94% |
| | 1,502 | 82.50% | 82.48% | 82.50% |
| | 3,006 | 82.66% | 82.57% | 82.54% |

other rows show the results when the Korean and Japanese corpora were mixed using the method described in Section 5.3.

As we can see from the results, the benefit of transfer learning is larger when the size of the annotated corpus for Korean (*i.e.*, target language) is smaller. In our experiments with Triplet/Quadruplet Model, positive results were obtained by the mixture of the two languages when the Korean corpus is less than 500 sentences, that is, the annotations in the source language successfully compensated the small corpus of the target language. When the size of the Korean corpus is relatively large ($\geq 1,500$ sentences), adding the Japanese corpus decreased the accuracy slightly, due to syntactic differences between the two languages. Also the effect of the corpus from the source language tends to saturate as the size of the source corpus, when the target corpus is larger. This is mainly because our mapping rules ignore lexical features, so few new features found in the larger corpus were incorrectly processed.

When merging the corpus in two languages, if we simply concatenate the transferred features from the source language and the features from the target language (instead of using the duplicated features shown in Equations (5) and (6)), the accuracy dropped from 82.70% to 82.26% when the Korean corpus size was 98 and Japanese corpus size was 10,000, and from 83.91% to 83.40% when Korean=383. These results support that there are significant differences in the dependencies between two languages even if we have improved the feature mapping, and our approach with the domain adaptation technique (Daumé III, 2007) successfully solved the difficulty.

Table 8(b) shows the results of the Distance Model. As we can see from the first row, using only the Japanese corpus did not help the Distance Model at all in this case. The Distance Model was not able to mitigate the differences between the two languages, because it does not use any grammatical rules to control the modifiability. This demonstrates that the hybrid parsing method with the grammar rules makes the transfer learning more effective. On the other hand, the domain adaptation method described in (5) and (6) successfully counteracted the contradictory phenomena in the two languages and increased the accuracy when the size of the Korean corpus was small (size=50 and 98). This is because the interactions among multiple candidates which cannot be captured from the small Korean corpus were provided by the Japanese corpus.

Some of previous work reported the parsing accuracy with the same KTB corpus; 81% with trained grammar (Chung et al., 2010) and 83% with Stanford parser after corpus transformation (Choi et al., 2012), but as Choi et al. (2012) noted it is difficult to directly compare the accuracies.

### 6.3 Discussion

The analysis of $e_2$'s dependency in Figure 1 is a good example to illustrate how the *Triplet/Quadruplet Model* and the Japanese corpus help Korean parsing. *Eojeol* $e_2$ has three modification candidates, $e_3$, $e_5$, and $e_6$. In the

Distance Model, $e_3$ is chosen because the distance between the two *eojeols* ($\Delta_{e_2,e_3}$) was 1, which is a very strong clue for dependency. Also, in the *Triplet/Quadruplet Model* trained only with a small Korean corpus, $e_3$ received a higher probability than $e_5$ and $e_6$. However, when a larger Japanese corpus was combined with the Korean corpus, $e_5$ was correctly selected as the Japanese corpus provided more samples of the dependency relation of "verb-PAST" ($e_2$) and "common noun-ACC (을)" ($e_5$) than that of "verb-PAST" and "proper noun-GEN (의)" ($e_3$).

As we can notice, larger contextual information is required to make the right decision for this case, which may not exist sufficiently in a small corpus due to data sparseness. The grammar rules in the *Triplet/Quadruplet Model* can effectively capture such contextual knowledge even from a relatively small corpus. Further, since the grammar rules are based only on part-of-speech tags and a small number of functional words, they are similar to the delexicalized parser (McDonald et al., 2011). These delexicalized rules are more robust to linguistic idiosyncrasies, and, thus, are more effective for transfer learning.

## 7 Conclusion

We presented a new dependency parsing algorithm for Korean by applying transfer learning from an existing parser for Japanese. Unlike other transfer learning methods relying on aligned corpora or bilingual lexical resources, we proposed a *feature transfer* method utilizing a small number of hand-crafted grammar rules that exploit syntactic similarities of the source and target languages. Experimental results confirm that the features learned from the Japanese training corpus were successfully applied for parsing Korean sentences and mitigated the data sparseness problem. The grammar rules are mostly delexicalized comprising only POS tags and a few functional words (*e.g.*, case markers), and some techniques to reduce the syntactic difference between two languages makes the transfer learning more effective. This methodology is expected to be applied to any two languages that have similar syntactic structures, and it is especially useful when the target language is a low-resource language.

## References


Jinho D. Choi and Martha Palmer. 2011. Statistical dependency parsing in Korean: From corpus generation to automatic parsing. In *Proceedings of the Second Workshop on Statistical Parsing of Morphologically Rich Languages*, pages 1–11.

DongHyun Choi, Jungyeul Park, and Key-Sun Choi. 2012. Korean treebank transformation for parser training. In *Proceedings of the ACL 2012 Joint Workshop on Statistical Parsing and Semantic Processing of Morphologically Rich Languages*, pages 78–88.

Hoojung Chung and Heechang Rim. 2003. A new probabilistic dependency parsing model for head-final, free word order languages. *IEICE TRANSACTIONS on Information and Systems*, E86-1(11):2490–2493.

Tagyoung Chung, Matt Post, and Daniel Gildea. 2010. Factors affecting the accuracy of korean parsing. In *Proceedings of the NAACL HLT 2010 First Workshop on Statistical Parsing of Morphologically-Rich Languages*, pages 49–57.

Michael Collins. 1997. Three generative, lexicalised models for statistical parsing. In *Proceedings of the 35th Annual Meeting of the Association for Computational Linguistics and Eighth Conference of the European Chapter of the Association for Computational Linguistics. Association for Computational Linguistics.*

Hal Daumé III. 2007. Frustratingly easy domain adaptation. In *Proceedings of the 45th Annual Meeting of the Association of Computational Linguistics*, pages 256–263.

Greg Durrett, Adam Pauls, and Dan Klein. 2012. Syntactic transfer using a bilingual lexicon. In *Proceedings of the 2012 Joint Conference on Empirical Methods in Natural Language Processing and Computational Natural Language Learning*, pages 1–11.

EDR. 1996. EDR (Japan Electronic Dictionary Research Institute, Ltd.) electronic dictionary version 1.5 technical guide.

David A. Ferrucci, Eric W. Brown, Jennifer Chu-Carroll, James Fan, David Gondek, Aditya Kalyanpur, Adam Lally, J. William Murdock, Eric Nyberg, John M. Prager, Nico Schlaefer, and Christopher A. Welty. 2010. Building Watson: An overview of the DeepQA project. *AI Magazine*, 31(3):59–79.

Ryan Georgi, Fei Xia, and William D Lewis. 2012. Improving dependency parsing with interlinear glossed text and syntactic projection. In *Proceedings of COLING 2012*, pages 371–380.

Raymond G Gordon and Barbara F Grimes. 2005. *Ethnologue: Languages of the world*, volume 15. SIL international Dallas, TX.

Chung-hye Han, Na-Rae Han, Eon-Suk Ko, Heejong Yi, and Martha Palmer. 2002. Penn Korean treebank: Development and evaluation. In *Proc. Pacific Asian Conf. Language and Comp.*

Rebecca Hwa, Philip Resnik, and Amy Weinberg. 2005. Breaking the resource bottleneck for multilingual parsing. Technical report, DTIC Document.

Hiroshi Kanayama, Kentaro Torisawa, Yutaka Mitsuishi, and Jun'ichi Tsujii. 2000. A hybrid Japanese parser with hand-crafted grammar and statistics. In *Proceedings of the 18th International Conference on Computational Linguistics*, pages 411–417.

Roger Kim, Mary Dalrymple, Ronald M Kaplan, and Tracy Holloway King. 2003a. Porting grammars between typologically similar languages: Japanese to korean. In *Proceedings of the 17th Pacific Asia Conference on Language, Information.*

Roger Kim, Mary Dalrymple, Ronald M Kaplan, Tracy Holloway King, Hiroshi Masuichi, and Tomoko Ohkuma. 2003b. Multilingual grammar development via grammar porting. In *ESSLLI 2003 Workshop on Ideas and Strategies for Multilingual Grammar Development*, pages 49–56.

Dan Klein and Christopher D Manning. 2004. Corpus-based induction of syntactic structure: Models of dependency and constituency. In *Proceedings of the 42nd Annual Meeting on Association for Computational Linguistics*, pages 478–487.

Sandra Kübler, Ryan McDonald, and Joakim Nivre. 2009. Dependency parsing. *Synthesis Lectures on Human Language Technologies*, 1(1):1–127.

Cody Kwok, Oren Etzioni, and Daniel S Weld. 2001. Scaling question answering to the web. *ACM Transactions on Information Systems (TOIS)*, 19(3):242–262.

Hyeon-Yeong Lee, Yi-Gyu Hwang, and Yong-Seok Lee. 2007. Parsing of Korean based on CFG using sentence pattern information. *International Journal of Computer Science and Network Security*, 7(7).

Roger Levy and Christopher Manning. 2003. Is it harder to parse chinese, or the chinese treebank? In *Proceedings of the 41st Annual Meeting on Association for Computational Linguistics*, ACL, pages 439–446.

Ryan McDonald, Slav Petrov, and Keith Hall. 2011. Multi-source transfer of delexicalized dependency parsers. In *Proceedings of the Conference on Empirical Methods in Natural Language Processing*, pages 62–72.

Ryan McDonald, Joakim Nivre, Yvonne Quirmbach-Brundage, Yoav Goldberg, Dipanjan Das, Kuzman Ganchev, Keith Hall, Slav Petrov, Hao Zhang, Oscar Täckström, et al. 2013. Universal dependency annotation for multilingual parsing. In *Proceedings of ACL 2013.*

Tahira Naseem, Harr Chen, Regina Barzilay, and Mark Johnson. 2010. Using universal linguistic knowledge to guide grammar induction. In *Proceedings of the 2010 Conference on Empirical Methods in Natural Language Processing*, pages 1234–1244.

Tahira Naseem, Regina Barzilay, and Amir Globerson. 2012. Selective sharing for multilingual dependency parsing. In *Proceedings of the 50th Annual Meeting of the Association for Computational Linguistics: Long Papers-Volume 1*, pages 629–637.

Tetsuya Nasukawa and Jeonghee Yi. 2003. Sentiment analysis: Capturing favorability using natural language processing. In *Proceedings of the Second International Conferences on Knowledge Capture*, pages 70–77.

Sinno Jialin Pan and Qiang Yang. 2010. A survey on transfer learning. *Knowledge and Data Engineering, IEEE Transactions on*, 22(10):1345–1359.

Bo Pang, Lillian Lee, and Shivakumar Vaithyanathan. 2002. Thumbs up? Sentiment classification using machine learning techniques. In *Proceedings of the ACL-02 conference on Empirical methods in natural language processing (EMNLP)*, pages 79–86, Philadelphia, Pennsylvania.

Jungyeul Park, Daisuke Kawahara, Sadao Kurohashi, and Key-Sun Choi. 2013. Towards fully lexicalized dependency parsing for Korean. In *Proceedings of The 13th International Conference on Parsing Technologies.*

Yoav Seginer. 2007. Fast unsupervised incremental parsing. In *Proceedings of the 45th Annual Meeting of the Association of Computational Linguistics*, pages 384–391.

David A. Smith and Noah A. Smith. 2004. Bilingual parsing with factored estimation: Using English to parse Korean. In *Proceedings of the 2004 Conference on Empirical Methods in Natural Language Processing*, pages 49–56.

Valentin I Spitkovsky, Hiyan Alshawi, Angel X Chang, and Daniel Jurafsky. 2011. Unsupervised dependency parsing without gold part-of-speech tags. In *Proceedings of the Conference on Empirical Methods in Natural Language Processing*, pages 1281–1290.

Daniel Zeman and Philip Resnik. 2008. Cross-language parser adaptation between related languages. In *IJCNLP*, pages 35–42.

# Cross-lingual Dependency Parsing of Related Languages with Rich Morphosyntactic Tagsets

**Željko Agić**
zagic@uni-potsdam.de

**Jörg Tiedemann**
jorg.tiedemann@lingfil.uu.se

**Kaja Dobrovoljc**
kaja.dobrovoljc@trojina.si

**Simon Krek**
simon.krek@ijs.si

**Danijela Merkler**
dmerkler@ffzg.hr

**Sara Može**
s.moze@wlv.ac.uk

## Abstract

This paper addresses cross-lingual dependency parsing using rich morphosyntactic tagsets. In our case study, we experiment with three related Slavic languages: Croatian, Serbian and Slovene. Four different dependency treebanks are used for monolingual parsing, direct cross-lingual parsing, and a recently introduced cross-lingual parsing approach that utilizes statistical machine translation and annotation projection. We argue for the benefits of using rich morphosyntactic tagsets in cross-lingual parsing and empirically support the claim by showing large improvements over an impoverished common feature representation in form of a reduced part-of-speech tagset. In the process, we improve over the previous state-of-the-art scores in dependency parsing for all three languages.

## 1 Introduction

A large majority of human languages are under-resourced in terms of text corpora and tools available for applications in natural language processing (NLP). According to recent surveys (Bender, 2011; Uszkoreit and Rehm, 2012; Bender, 2013), this is especially apparent with syntactically annotated corpora, i.e., treebanks – both dependency-based ones and others. In this paper, we focus on dependency parsing (Kübler et al., 2009), but the claims should hold in general. The lack of dependency treebanks is due to the fact that they are expensive and time-consuming to construct (Abeillé, 2003). Since dependency parsing of under-resourced languages nonetheless draws substantial interest in the NLP research community, over time, we have seen a number of research efforts directed towards their processing despite the absence of training data for supervised learning of parsing models. We give a brief overview of the major research directions in the following subsection. Here, we focus on supervised learning of dependency parsers, as the performance of unsupervised approaches still falls far behind the state of the art in supervised parser induction.

### 1.1 Related Work

There are two basic strategies for data-driven parsing of languages with no dependency treebanks: annotation projection and model transfer. Both fall into the general category of cross-lingual dependency parsing as they attempt to utilize existing dependency treebanks or parsers from a resource-rich language *(source)* for parsing the under-resourced *(target)* language.

**Annotation projection:** In this approach, dependency trees are projected from a source language to a target language using word alignments in parallel corpora. It is based on a presumption that source-target parallel corpora are more readily available than dependency treebanks. The approach comes in two varieties. In the first one, parallel corpora are exploited by applying the available state-of-the-art parsers on the source side and subsequent projection to the target side using word alignments and heuristics for resolving possible link ambiguities (Yarowsky et al., 2001; Hwa et al., 2005). Since dependency parsers typically make heavy use of various morphological and other features, the apparent benefit of this approach is the possibility of straightforward projection of these features, resulting in a feature-rich representation for the target language. On the downside, the annotation projection noise adds up to dependency parsing noise and errors in word alignment, influencing the quality of the resulting target language parser.

The other variety is rare, since it relies on parallel corpora in which the source side is a depen-



*Language Technology for Closely Related Languages and Language Variants (LT4CloseLang)*, pages 13–24,
October 29, 2014, Doha, Qatar. 

dency treebank, i.e., it is already manually annotated for syntactic dependencies (Agić et al., 2012). This removes the automatic parsing noise, while the issues with word alignment and annotation heuristics still remain.

**Model transfer:** In its simplest form, transferring a model amounts to training a source language parser and running it directly on the target language. It is usually coupled with delexicalization, i.e., removing all lexical features from the source treebank for training the parser (Zeman and Resnik, 2008; McDonald et al., 2013). This in turn relies on the same underlying feature model, typically drawing from a shared part-of-speech (POS) representation such as the Universal POS Tagset of Petrov et al. (2012). Negative effects of using such an impoverished shared representation are typically addressed by adapting the model to better fit the target language. This includes selecting source language data points appropriate for the target language (Søgaard, 2011; Täckström et al., 2013), transferring from multiple sources (McDonald et al., 2011) and using cross-lingual word clusters (Täckström et al., 2012). These approaches need no projection and enable the usage of source-side gold standard annotations, but they all rely on a shared feature representation across languages, which can be seen as a strong bottleneck. Also, while most of the earlier research made use of heterogenous treebanks and thus yielded linguistically implausible observations, research stemming from an uniform dependency scheme across languages (De Marneffe and Manning, 2008; McDonald et al., 2013) made it possible to perform more consistent experiments and to assess the accuracy of dependency labels.

**Other approaches:** More recently, Durrett et al. (2012) suggested a hybrid approach that involves bilingual lexica in cross-lingual phrase-based parsing. In their approach, a source-side treebank is adapted to a target language by "translating" the source words to target words through a bilingual lexicon. This approach is advanced by Tiedemann et al. (2014), who utilize full-scale statistical machine translation (SMT) systems for generating synthetic target language treebanks. This approach relates to annotation projection, while bypassing the issue of dependency parsing noise as gold standard annotations are projected. The SMT noise is in turn mitigated by better word alignment quality for synthetic data. The influence of various projection algorithms in this approach is further investigated by Tiedemann (2014). This line of cross-lingual parsing research substantially improves over previous work.

### 1.2 Paper Overview

All lines of previous cross-lingual parsing research left the topics of related languages and shared rich feature representations largely unaddressed, with the exception of Zeman and Resnik (2008), who deal with phrase-based parsing test-cased on Danish and Swedish treebanks, utilizing a mapping over relatively small POS tagsets.

In our contribution, the goal is to observe the properties of cross-lingual parsing in an environment of relatively free-word-order languages, which are related and characterized by rich morphology and very large morphosyntactic tagsets. We experiment with four different small- and medium-size dependency treebanks of Croatian and Slovene, and cross-lingually parse into Croatian, Serbian and Slovene. Along with monolingual and direct transfer parsing, we make use of the SMT framework of Tiedemann et al. (2014). We are motivated by:

- observing the performance of various approaches to cross-lingual dependency parsing for closely related languages, including the very recent treebank translation approach by Tiedemann et al. (2014);
- doing so by using rich morphosyntactic tagsets, in contrast to virtually all other recent cross-lingual dependency parsing experiments, which mainly utilize the Universal POS tagset of Petrov et al. (2012);
- reliably testing for labeled parsing accuracy in an environment with heterogenous dependency annotation schemes; and
- improving the state of the art for Croatian, Slovene and Serbian dependency parsing across these heterogenous schemes.

In Section 2, we describe the language resources used: treebanks, tagsets and test sets. Section 3 describes the experimental setup, which includes a description of parsing, machine translation and annotation projection. In Section 4, we discuss the results of the experiments, and we conclude the discussion by sketching the possible directions for future research in Section 5.

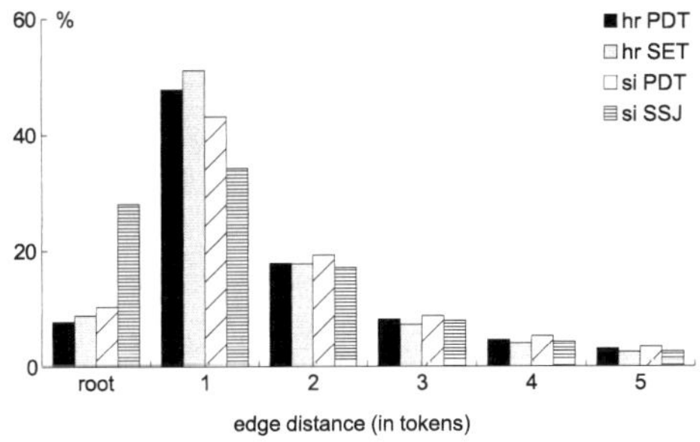


Figure 1: Histogram of edge distances in the treebanks. Edge distance is measured in tokens between heads and dependents. Distance of 1 denotes adjacent tokens.

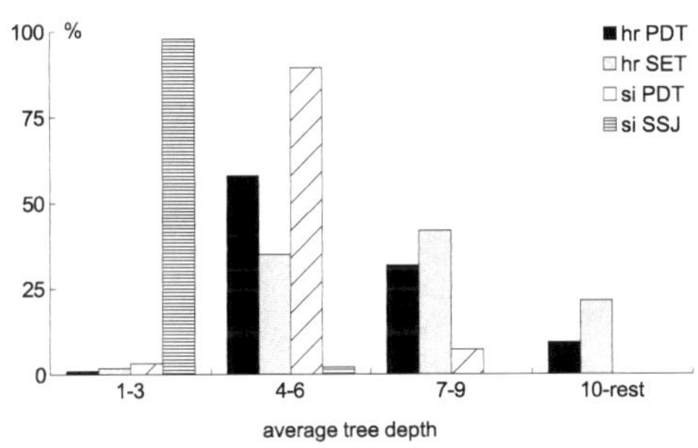


Figure 2: Histogram of average tree depths.

| Feature | *hr* PDT | *hr* SET | *sl* PDT | *sl* SSJ |
|---|---|---|---|---|
| Sentences | 4,626 | 8,655 | 1,534 | 11,217 |
| Tokens | 117,369 | 192,924 | 28,750 | 232,241 |
| Types | 25,038 | 37,749 | 7,128 | 48,234 |
| Parts of speech | 13 | 13 | 12 | 13 |
| MSDs | 821 | 685 | 725 | 1,142 |
| Syntactic tags | 26 | 15 | 26 | 10 |

Table 1: Basic treebank statistics.

## 2 Resources

We make use of the publicly available language resources for Croatian, Serbian and Slovene. These include dependency treebanks, test sets annotated for morphology and dependency syntax, and a morphosyntactic feature representation drawing from the Multext East project (Erjavec, 2012). A detailed assessment of the current state of development for morphosyntactic and syntactic processing of these languages is given by Agić et al. (2013) and Uszkoreit and Rehm (2012). Here, we provide only a short description.

### 2.1 Treebanks

We use two Croatian and two Slovene dependency treebanks.[1] One for each language is based on the Prague Dependency Treebank (PDT) (Böhmová et al., 2003) annotation scheme, while the other two introduced novel and more simplified syntactic tagsets. All four treebanks use adaptations of the Multext East version 4 tagset (Erjavec, 2012) for the underlying morphological annotation layer, which we shortly describe further down. Basic statistics for the treebanks are given in Table 1.

***hr* PDT:** This treebank is natively referred to as the Croatian Dependency Treebank (HOBS) (Tadić, 2007; Berović et al., 2012). Its most recent instance, HOBS 2.0 (Agić et al., 2014) slightly departs from the PDT scheme. Thus, in this experiment, we use the older version, HOBS 1.0, and henceforth refer to it as *hr* PDT for consistency and more clear reference to its annotation.[2]

***hr* SET:** The SETIMES.HR dependency treebank of Croatian has a 15-tag scheme. It is targeted towards high parsing accuracy, while maintaining a clear distinction between all basic grammatical categories of Croatian. Its publicly available 1.0 release consists of approximately 2,500 sentences (Agić and Merkler, 2013), while release 2.0 has just under 4,000 sentences (Agić and Ljubešić, 2014) of newspaper text. Here, we use an even newer, recently developed version with more than 8,500 sentences from multiple domains.[3]

***sl* PDT:** The PDT-based Slovene Dependency Treebank (Džeroski et al., 2006) is built on top of a rather small portion of Orwell's novel *1984* from the Multext East project (Erjavec, 2012). Even if the project was discontinued, it is still heavily used as part of the venerable CoNLL 2006 and 2007 shared task datasets (Buchholz and Marsi, 2006; Nivre et al., 2007).[4]

***sl* SSJ:** The Slovene take on simplifying syntactic annotations resulted in the 10-tag strong JOS Corpus of Slovene (Erjavec et al., 2010). Similar to *hr* SET, this new annotation scheme is loosely

[1]No treebanks of Serbian were publicly available at the time of conducting this experiment.

[2]HOBS is available through META-SHARE (Tadić and Váradi, 2012).

[3]`http://nlp.ffzg.hr/resources/corpora/setimes-hr/`

[4]`http://nl.ijs.si/sdt/`

PDT-based, but considerably reduced to facilitate manual annotation. The initial 100,000 token corpus has recently doubled in size, as described by Dobrovoljc et al. (2012). We use the latter version in our experiment.[5]

The statistics in Table 1 show a variety of treebank sizes and annotations. Figure 1 illustrates the structural complexity of the treebanks by providing a histogram of egdes by token distance. While adjacent edges expectedly dominate the distributions, it is interesting to see that almost 30% of all edges in *sl* SSJ attach to root, resulting in an easily parsable flattened tree structure. Knowing that relations denoting attributes account for more than one third of all non-root dependents in the remainder, one can expect dependency parsing performance comparable to CoNLL-style chunking (Tjong Kim Sang and Buchholz, 2000). This is further supported by the distributions of sentences in the four treebanks by average tree depth in Figure 2. We can see that virtually all *sl* SSJ trees have average depths of 1 to 3, while the other treebanks exhibit the more common structural properties of dependency trees.

In these terms of complexity, the Croatian treebanks are richer than their Slovene counterparts. In *sl* SSJ, attributes and edges to root account for more than 60% of all dependencies. Even in the other three treebanks, 20-30% of the edges are labeled as attributes, while the rest is spread more evenly between the basic syntactic categories such as predicates, subject and objects. More detailed and more linguistically motivated comparisons of the three annotation guidelines fall outside the scope of our paper. Instead, we refer to the previously noted publications on the respective treebanks, and to (Agić and Merkler, 2013; Agić et al., 2013) for comparisons between PDT and SET in parsing Croatian and Serbian.

### 2.2 Morphosyntactic Tagset

All four treebanks were manually created: they are sentence- and token-split, lemmatized, morphosyntactically tagged and syntactically annotated. In morphosyntactic annotation, they all make use of the Multext East version 4 (MTE 4) guidelines (Erjavec, 2012).[6] MTE 4 is a positional tagset in which morphosyntactic descriptors of word forms are captured by a morphosyntactic tag (MSD) created by merging atomic attributes in the predefined positions. This is illustrated in Table 2 through an example verb tag. The first character of the tag denotes the part of speech (POS), while each of the following characters encodes a specific attribute in a specific position. Both the positions and the attributes are language-dependent in MTE 4, but the attributes are still largely shared between these three languages due to their relatedness.

The Slovene treebanks closely adhere to the specification, while each of the Croatian treebanks implements slight adaptations of the tagset towards Croatian specifics. In *hr* PDT, the adaptation is governed by and documented in the Croatian Morphological Lexicon (Tadić and Fulgosi, 2003), and the modifications in *hr* SET were targeted to more closely match the ones for Slovene.[7]

### 2.3 Test Sets

Recent research by McDonald et al. (2013) has uncovered the downsides of experimenting with parsing using heterogenous dependency annotations, while at the same time providing possibly the first reliable results in cross-lingual parsing. They did so by creating the uniformly annotated Universal Dependency Treebanks collection based on Stanford Typed Dependencies (De Marneffe and Manning, 2008), which in turn also enabled measuring both labeled (LAS) and unlabeled (UAS) parsing accuracy.

Having four treebanks with three different annotation schemes, we seek to enable reliable experimentation through our test sets. Along with Croatian and Slovene, which are represented in the training sets, we introduce Serbian as a target-only language in the test data. Following the CoNLL shared tasks setup (Buchholz and Marsi, 2006; Nivre et al., 2007), our test sets have 200 sentences (approx. 5,000 tokens) per language, split 50:50 between newswire and Wikipedia text. Each test set is manually annotated for morphosyntax, following the MTE 4 guidelines for the respective languages, and checked by native speakers for validity. On top of that, all test sets are annotated with all three dependency schemes: PDT, SET and SSJ. This enables observing LAS in a heterogenous experimental environment, as we test each monolingual and cross-lingual parser on an anno-

[5] http://eng.slovenscina.eu/tehnologije/ucni-korpus

[6] http://nl.ijs.si/ME/V4/

[7] http://nlp.ffzg.hr/data/tagging/msd-hr.html

| Language | MSD tag | Attribute-value pairs |
|---|---|---|
| *hr* | `Vmn` | Category = **V**erb, Type = **m**ain, Vform = i**n**finitive |
| *sl* | `Vmen` | Category = **V**erb, Type = **m**ain, Aspect = p**e**rfective, VForm = i**n**finitive |
| *sr* | `Vmn----an-n---e` | Category = **V**erb, Type = **m**ain, VForm = i**n**finitive, Voice = **a**ctive, Negative = **n**o, Clitic = **n**o, Aspect = p**e**rfective |

Table 2: Illustration of the Multext East version 4 tagset for Croatian, Serbian and Slovene. The attributes are language-dependent, as well as their positions in the tag, which are also dependent on the part of speech, denoted by position zero in the tag.

tation layer matching its training set. In contrast, the MTE 4 tagsets are not adjusted, i.e., each test set only has a single language-specific MTE 4 annotation. We rely on their underlying similarities in feature representations to suffice for improved cross-lingual parsing performance.

## 3 Experiment Setup

This section describes the experiment settings. We list the general workflow of the experiment and then provide the details on the parser setup and the more advanced approaches used for target language adaptation of the models.

### 3.1 Workflow

The experiment consists of three work packages: (1) monolingual parsing, (2) direct cross-lingual parsing, and (3) cross-lingual parsing using synthetic training data from SMT. In the first one, we train dependency parsers on the four treebanks and test them on the corresponding languages, thus assessing the monolingual parsing performance. The second stage observes the effects of directly applying the parsers from the first stage across the languages. Finaly, in the third work package, we use four different approaches to automatic translation to create synthetic training data. We translate the Croatian treebanks to Slovene and vice versa, project the annotations using two different projection algorithms, and train and apply the adapted parsers across the languages. The details are included in the two following subsections.

Two general remarks apply to our experiment. First, we perform cross-lingual parsing, and not cross-annotation-scheme parsing. Thus, we do not compare the dependency parsing scores between the annotation schemes, but rather just between the in-scheme parsers. Second, we use Serbian as a test-set-only language. As there are no treebanks of Serbian, we cannot use it as a source language, and we leave SMT and annotation projection into Serbian for future work.

### 3.2 Dependency Parsing

In all experiments, we use the graph-based dependency parser by Bohnet (2010) with default settings. We base our parser choice on its state-of-the-art performance across various morphologically rich languages in the SPMLR 2013 shared task (Seddah et al., 2013). While newer contributions targeted at joint morphological and syntactic analysis (Bohnet and Kuhn, 2012; Bohnet et al., 2013) report slightly higher scores, we chose the former one for speed and robustness, and because we use gold standard POS/MSD annotations. The choice of gold standard preprocessing is motivated by previous research in parsing Croatian and Serbian (Agić et al., 2013), and by insight of Seddah et al. (2013), who report a predictable linear decrease in accuracy for automatic preprocessing. This decrease amounts to approximately 3 points LAS for Croatian and Serbian across various test cases in (Agić et al., 2013).

We observe effects of (de)lexicalization and of using full MSD tagset as opposed to only POS tags in all experiments. Namely, in all work packages, we compare parsers trained with {lexicalized, delexicalized} × {MSD, POS} features. In lexicalized parsers, we use word forms and features, while we exclude lemmas from all experiments – both previous research using MSTParser (McDonald et al., 2005) and our own test runs show no use for lemmas as features in dependency parsing. Delexicalized parsers are stripped of all lexical features, i.e., word forms are omitted from training and testing data. Full MSD parsers use both the POS information and the sub-POS features in the form of atomic attribute-value pairs, while POS-only parsers are stripped of the MSD features – they use just the POS information. The delexicalized POS scenario is thus very similar to the direct transfer by McDonald et al. (2013), since MTE 4 POS is virtually identical to Universal POS (Petrov et al., 2012).[8]

### 3.3 Treebank Translation and Annotation Projection

For machine translation, we closely adhere to the setup implemented by Tiedemann et al. (2014) in their treebank translation experiments. Namely, our translations are based on automatic word alignment and subsequent extraction of translation equivalents as common in phrase-based SMT. We perform word alignment by using GIZA++ (Och and Ney, 2003), while utilizing IBM model 4 for creating the Viterbi word alignments for parallel corpora. For the extraction of translation tables, we use the de facto standard SMT toolbox Moses (Koehn et al., 2007) with default settings. Phrase-based SMT models are tuned using minimum error rate training (Och, 2003). Our monolingual language modeling using KenLM tools[9] (Heafield, 2011) produces standard 5-gram language models using modified Kneser-Ney smoothing without pruning.

For building the translation models, we use the OpenSubtitles parallel resources from OPUS[10] (Tiedemann, 2009) for the Croatian-Slovene pair. Even if we expect this to be a rather noisy parallel resource, we justify the choice by (1) the fact that no other parallel corpora[11] of Croatian and Slovene exist, other than Orwell's *1984* from the Multext East project, which is too small for SMT training and falls into a very narrow domain, and (2) evidence from (Tiedemann et al., 2014) that the SMT-supported cross-lingual parsing approach is very robust to translation noise.

For translating Croatian treebanks into Slovene and vice versa, we implement and test four different methods of translation. They are coupled with approaches to annotation projection from the source side gold dependency trees to the target translations via the word alignment information available from SMT.

**LOOKUP:** The first approach to translation in our experiment is the dictionary lookup approach. We simply select the most reliable translations of single words in the source language into the target language by looking up the phrase translation tables extracted from the parallel corpus. This is very similar to what Agić et al. (2012) did for the Croatian-Slovene pair. However, their approach involved both translating and testing on the same small corpus (Orwell's novel), while here we extract the translations from full-blown SMT phrase tables on a much larger scale. The trees projection from source to target is trivial since the number and the ordering of words between them does not change. Thus, the dependencies are simply copied.

**CHAR:** By this acronym, we refer to an approach known as character-based statistical machine translation. It is shown to perform very well for closely related languages (Vilar et al., 2007; Tiedemann, 2012; Tiedemann and Nakov, 2013). The motivation for character-level translation is the ability of such models to better generalize the mapping between similar languages especially in cases of rich productive morphology and limited amounts of training data. With this, character-level models largely reduce the number of out-of-vocabulary words. In a nutshell, our character-based model performs word-to-word translation using character-level modeling. Similar to LOOKUP, this is also a word-to-word translation model, which also requires no adaptation of the source dependency trees – they are once again simply copied to target sentences.

**WORD:** Our third take on SMT is slightly more elaborate but still restricts the translation model to one-to-one word mappings. In particular, we extract all single word translation pairs from the phrase tables and apply the standard beam-search decoder implemented in Moses to translate the original treebanks to all target languages. Thus, we allow word reordering and use a language model while still keeping the projection of annotated data as simple as possible. The language model may influence not only the word order but also the lexical choice as we now allow multiple translation options in our phrase table. Also note that this approach may introduce additional non-projectivity in the projected trees. This system is the overall top-performer in (Tiedemann et al.,

[8] A mapping from Slovene MTE 4 to Universal POS is available at `https://code.google.com/p/universal-pos-tags/` as an example.

[9] `https://kheafield.com/code/kenlm/`

[10] `http://opus.lingfil.uu.se/`

[11] We note the Croatian-Slovene parallel corpus project described by Požgaj Hadži and Tadić (2000), but it appears that the project was not completed and the corpus itself is not publicly available.

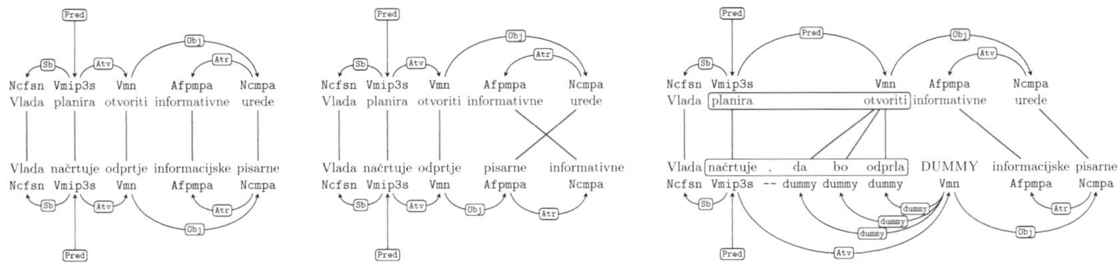


Figure 3: An illustration of the projections. Left side = CHAR, middle = WORD, right side = PHRASE. As illustrated, WORD might introduce reorderings, while PHRASE can enter dummy nodes and edges to the dependency trees. The sentence: *The government plans to open information offices.* See (Tiedemann et al., 2014; Tiedemann, 2014) for detailed insight into projection algorithms.

2014), where reordering played an important role in adapting the models to the target languages. We test whether it holds for related languages as well.

**PHRASE:** This model implements translation based on the entire phrase table using the standard approach to phrase-based SMT. We basically run the Moses decoder with default settings and the parameters and models trained on our parallel corpus. Here, we can have many-to-many word alignments, which require a more elaborate approach to the projection of the source side dependency annotations. It is important for the annotation transfer to keep track of the alignment between phrases and words of the input and output sentences. The Moses decoder provides both, phrase segmentation and word alignment. We use the annotation projection algorithm of Hwa et al. (2005). As illustrated in Figure 3, it resolves many-to-many alignments by introducing dummy nodes to the dependency trees. We use the implementation by Tiedemann (2014), which addresses certain issues with algorithm choices for ambiguous alignments which were left unaccounted for in the original work. Since this paper does not focus on the intricacies of annotation projection, but rather on applying it in an environment of related languages and rich MSD tagsets, we refer the reader to related work regarding the details.

We translate from Croatian to Slovene and vice versa using four different treebanks and these four different methods of translation and annotation projection. As we stated in the experiment overview, for each of these, we also experiment with (de)lexicalization and MSD vs. POS, and we test on all three languages. The three experimental batches – monolingual, direct and SMT-supported transfer – produce a large number of observations, all of which we assess in the following section.

## 4 Results and Discussion

We split our discussion of the parsing results into the following three subsections. We first observe the performance of monolingual parsers. Secondly, we measure the quality of these when applied directly on the other two languages. Finally, we look into the accuracy of parsers trained on SMT-generated artificial treebank data when applied across the test languages.

### 4.1 Monolingual Parsing

Accuracies of parsers trained and applied on training and testing data belonging to the same language – i.e., our monolingual parsers – are provided in the grayed out sections of Table 3.

Parsing Croatian using *hr* PDT yields a high score of 69.45 LAS, better than the former state of the art on this test set (Agić et al., 2013) simply due to applying a newer generation parser. This score is provided by a lexicalized model with the full MSD feature set. Replacing MSD with POS or delexicalizing this model results in a 3-point drop in LAS, while applying both replacements substantially decreases the score – by more than 11 points LAS. We observe virtually the same pattern for the other Croatian treebank, *hr* SET, where this latter drop is even more significant, at 14 points. Incidentally, 76.36 points LAS is also the new state of the art for *hr* SET parsing, owing to the recent enlargement of the treebank.

The Slovene parsers exhibit effectively the same behavior as the Croatian ones. The lexicalized MSD models of *sl* PDT and *sl* SSJ both record new state-of-the-art scores, although the latter one on a different test set than in previous research (Dobrovoljc et al., 2012). At over 92 points LAS, *sl* SSJ

| | | lexicalized | | | | | | delexicalized | | | | | |
|---|---|---|---|---|---|---|---|---|---|---|---|---|---|
| | | hr | | sl | | sr | | hr | | sl | | sr | |
| | | MSD | POS | MSD | POS | MSD | POS | MSD | POS | MSD | POS | MSD | POS |
| hr | PDT | 69.45 | 66.95 | 60.09 | 50.19 | 69.42 | 66.96 | 66.03 | 57.79 | 57.98 | 42.66 | 66.79 | 57.41 |
| | SET | 76.36 | 73.02 | 68.65 | 59.52 | 76.08 | 73.37 | 72.52 | 62.31 | 68.16 | 55.17 | 72.71 | 62.04 |
| sl | PDT | 51.19 | 47.99 | 76.46 | 73.33 | 52.46 | 49.64 | 49.58 | 42.59 | 71.96 | 62.99 | 50.41 | 44.11 |
| | SSJ | 78.50 | 74.18 | 92.38 | 88.93 | 78.94 | 75.96 | 75.23 | 66.23 | 87.19 | 77.92 | 75.25 | 67.47 |

Table 3: Monolingual and direct cross-lingual parsing accuracy, expressed by the labeled accuracy metric (LAS). Scores are split for lexicalized and delexicalized, full MSD and POS only parsers. Monolingual scores are in grey. Row indices represent source languages and treebanks.

expectedly shows to be the easiest to parse, most likely due to the relatively flat tree structure and its small label set.

We note the following general pattern of feature importance. Dropping MSD features seems to carry the most weight in all models, followed by lexicalization. Dropping MSD is compensated in part by lexical features paired with POS, while dropping both MSD and word forms severely degrades all models. At this point, it is very important to note that at 60-70 points LAS, these decreased scores closely resemble those of McDonald et al. (2013) for the six languages in the Universal Treebanks. This observation is taken further in the next subsection.

### 4.2 Direct Cross-lingual Parsing

The models used for monolingual parsing are here directly applied on all languages but the treebank source language, thus constituting a direct cross-lingual parsing scenario. Its scores are also given in Table 3, but now in the non-grey parts.

Croatian models are applied to Slovene and Serbian test sets. For *hr* PDT, the highest score is 60.09 LAS on Slovene and 69.42 LAS on Serbian, the latter noted as the state of the art for Serbian PDT parsing. Comparing the cross-lingual score to monolingual Slovene, the difference is substantial as expected and comparable to the drops observed by McDonald et al. (2013) in their experiments. Our ranking of feature significance established in the monolingual experiments holds here as well, or rather, the absolute differences are even more pronounced. Most notably, the difference between the lexicalized MSD model and the delexicalized POS model is 17 points LAS in favor of the former one on Slovene. *hr* SET appears to be more resilient to delexicalization and tagset reduction when applied on Slovene and Serbian, most likely due to the treebank's size, well-balanced dependency label set and closer conformance with the official MTE 4 guidelines. That said, the feature patterns still hold. Also, 76.08 LAS for Serbian is the new state of the art for SET parsing.

Slovene PDT is an outlier due to its small size, as its training set is just over 1,500 sentences. Still, the scores maintain the level of those in related research, and the feature rankings hold. Performance of parsing Croatian and Serbian using *sl* SSJ is high, arguably up to the level of usability in down-stream applications. These are the first recorded scores in parsing the two languages using SSJ, and they reach above 78 points LAS for both. Even if the scores are not comparable across the annotation schemes due to their differences, it still holds that the SSJ scores are the highest absolute parsing scores recorded in the experiment. This might hold significance in applications that require robust parsing for shallow syntax.

Generally, the best transfer scores are quite high in comparison with those on Universal Treebanks (McDonald et al., 2013; Tiedemann et al., 2014). This is surely due to the relatedness of the three languages. However, even for these arguably closely related languages, the performance of delexicalized models that rely only on POS features – averaging at around 55 points LAS – is virtually identical to that on more distant languages test-cased in related work. We see this as a very strong indicator of fundamental limitations of using linguistically impoverished shared feature representations in cross-lingual parsing.

### 4.3 Cross-lingual Parsing with Treebank Translation

Finally, we discuss what happens to parsing performance when we replace direct cross-lingual application of parsers with training models on translated treebanks. We take a treebank, Croatian or Slovene, and translate it into the other language.

| Target | Approach | PDT | SET | SSJ |
|---|---|---|---|---|
| *hr* | monolingual | 69.45 | 76.36 | – |
| | direct | 51.19 | – | 78.50 |
| | translated | 67.55 ♡ | 74.68 ◊ | 79.51 ♣ |
| *sl* | monolingual | 76.46 | – | 92.38 |
| | direct | 60.09 | 68.65 | – |
| | translated | 72.35 ♠ | 70.52 ♠ | 88.71 ♣ |
| *sr* | monolingual | – | – | – |
| | dircct | 69.42 | 76.08 | 78.94 |
| | translated | 68.11 ♣ | 74.31 ◊ | 79.81 ♡♣ |
| Legend: | ♠ CHAR ♡ LOOKUP ◊ PHRASE ♣ WORD | | | |

Table 4: Parsing score (LAS) summary for the top-performing systems with respect to language and approach to parser induction. All models are MSD + lexicalized.

We then train a parser on the translation and apply it on all three target test sets. We do this for all the treebanks, and in all variations regarding translation and projection methods, morphological features and lexicalization.

All scores for this evaluation stage are given in Table 5 for completeness. The table contains 192 different LAS scores, possibly constituting a tedious read. Thus, in Table 4 we provide a summary of information on the top-performing parsers from all three experimental stages, which includes treebank translation.

We can see that the best models based on translating the treebanks predominantly stem from word-to-word SMT, i.e., from WORD translation models that basically enrich the lexical feature space and perform word reordering, enabling straightforward copying of syntactic structures from translation sources to translation targets. Following them are the CHAR and LOOKUP models, expectedly leaving – although not too far behind – PHRASE behind given the similarities of the language pair. Since Croatian and Slovene are related languages, the differences between the models are not as substantial as in (Tiedemann et al., 2014), but WORD models still turn out to be the most robust ones, even if word reordering might not be so frequent in this language pair as in the data from (McDonald et al., 2013). Further, when comparing the best SMT-supported models to monolingual parsers, we see that the models with translation come really close to monolingual performance. In comparison with direct transfer, models trained on translated treebanks manage to outperform them in most cases, especially for the more distant language pairs. For example, the *sl* ↦ *hr* SSJ WORD model is 1 point LAS better on Croatian than the directly applied Slovene model, and the same holds for testing on Serbian with the same dataset. On the other side, directly applied models from Croatian SET outperform the translated ones for Serbian. For PDT, the translated models are substantially better between Croatian and Slovene since *sl* PDT is an outlier in terms of size and dataset selection, while direct transfer from Croatian seems to work better for Serbian than the translated models.

Reflecting on the summary in Table 4 more generally, by and large, we see high parsing accuracies. Averages across the formalisms reach well beyond 70 points LAS. We attribute this to the relatedness of the languages selected for this case study, as well as to the quality of the underlying language resources. From another viewpoint, the table clearly shows the prominence of lexical and especially rich morphosyntactic tagset features throughout the experiment. Across our monolingual, direct and SMT-supported parsing experiments, these features are represented in the best systems, and dropping them incurs significant decreases in accuracy.

## 5 Conclusions and Future Work

In this contribution, we addressed the topic of cross-lingual dependency parsing, i.e., applying dependency parsers from typically resource-rich source languages to under-resourced target languages. We used three Slavic languages – Croatian, Slovene and Serbian – as a test case for related languages in different stages of language resource development. As these are relatively free-word-order languages with rich morphology, we were able to test the cross-lingual parsers for performance when using training features drawing from large morphosyntactic tagsets – typically consisting of over 1,000 different tags – in contrast to impoverished common part-of-speech representations. We tested monolingual parsing, direct cross-lingual parsing and a very recent promising approach with artificial creation of training data via machine translation. In the experiments, we observed state-of-the-art results in dependency parsing for all three languages. We strongly argued and supported the case for using common rich representations of morphology in dependency parsing

| | | | *lexicalized* | | | | | | *delexicalized* | | | | | |
|---|---|---|---|---|---|---|---|---|---|---|---|---|---|---|
| | | | *hr* | | *sl* | | *sr* | | *hr* | | *sl* | | *sr* | |
| | | | *MSD* | *POS* | *MSD* | *POS* | *MSD* | *POS* | *MSD* | *POS* | *MSD* | *POS* | *MSD* | *POS* |
| CHAR | *hr* ↦ *sl* | PDT | 66.92 | 60.25 | 61.49 | 55.57 | 67.83 | 62.04 | 66.56 | 57.63 | 58.34 | 43.04 | 66.89 | 57.65 |
| | | SET | 73.65 | 64.64 | 70.52 | 66.11 | 72.95 | 64.44 | 72.98 | 62.98 | 69.03 | 54.81 | 72.74 | 62.73 |
| | *sl* ↦ *hr* | PDT | 51.96 | 48.14 | 72.35 | 63.71 | 53.11 | 49.47 | 49.58 | 42.59 | 71.96 | 62.99 | 50.41 | 44.11 |
| | | SSJ | 78.69 | 75.45 | 88.21 | 78.88 | 79.25 | 77.09 | 75.23 | 66.23 | 87.19 | 77.92 | 75.25 | 67.47 |
| LOOKUP | *hr* ↦ *sl* | PDT | 67.55 | 59.96 | 60.81 | 56.54 | 67.78 | 61.41 | 66.56 | 57.63 | 58.34 | 43.04 | 66.89 | 57.65 |
| | | SET | 73.58 | 64.98 | 69.93 | 68.09 | 73.70 | 64.25 | 72.52 | 62.72 | 68.47 | 55.27 | 72.71 | 62.73 |
| | *sl* ↦ *hr* | PDT | 51.74 | 49.15 | 72.02 | 63.08 | 53.49 | 51.33 | 49.58 | 42.59 | 71.96 | 62.99 | 50.41 | 44.11 |
| | | SSJ | 79.25 | 77.06 | 88.10 | 78.53 | 79.81 | 77.23 | 75.23 | 66.23 | 87.19 | 77.92 | 75.25 | 67.47 |
| WORD | *hr* ↦ *sl* | PDT | 67.33 | 59.24 | 61.80 | 57.14 | 68.11 | 61.13 | 65.84 | 57.12 | 58.17 | 42.99 | 67.12 | 57.70 |
| | | SET | 73.26 | 65.87 | 69.98 | 68.98 | 73.63 | 65.85 | 72.71 | 62.29 | 68.50 | 55.06 | 73.14 | 62.40 |
| | *sl* ↦ *hr* | PDT | 51.67 | 49.58 | 71.47 | 63.51 | 54.62 | 51.82 | 50.25 | 43.17 | 71.27 | 62.79 | 50.79 | 44.07 |
| | | SSJ | 79.51 | 76.89 | 88.71 | 79.69 | 79.81 | 78.03 | 75.95 | 67.19 | 86.92 | 77.28 | 75.89 | 68.18 |
| PHRASE | *hr* ↦ *sl* | PDT | 67.28 | 58.90 | 60.53 | 56.79 | 67.92 | 61.36 | 65.77 | 55.06 | 58.18 | 45.41 | 66.16 | 55.79 |
| | | SET | 74.68 | 65.29 | 69.42 | 68.55 | 74.31 | 65.17 | 73.36 | 60.77 | 68.16 | 58.42 | 72.15 | 61.55 |
| | *sl* ↦ *hr* | PDT | 49.92 | 46.82 | 68.18 | 58.18 | 52.15 | 49.42 | 47.73 | 41.08 | 68.51 | 55.29 | 48.93 | 42.59 |
| | | SSJ | 79.29 | 78.09 | 88.24 | 78.75 | 79.32 | 78.85 | 75.33 | 68.10 | 86.59 | 75.66 | 75.91 | 68.67 |

Table 5: Parsing scores (LAS) for cross-lingual parsers trained on translated treebanks. Scores are split for lexicalized and delexicalized, full MSD and POS only parsers, and with respect to the translation/projection approaches. Row indices represent source languages and treebanks, and indicate the direction of applying SMT (e.g., *hr* ↦ *sl* denotes a Croatian treebank translated to Slovene).

for morphologically rich languages. Through our multilayered test set annotation, we also facilitated a reliable cross-lingual evaluation in a heterogenous testing environment. We list our most important observations:

- Even for closely related languages, using only the basic POS features – which are virtually identical to the widely-used Universal POS of Petrov et al. (2012) – substantially decreases parsing accuracy up to the level comparable with results of McDonald et al. (2013) across the Universal Treebanks language groups.
- Adding MSD features heavily influences all the scores in a positive way. This has obvious implications for improving over McDonald et al. (2013) on the Universal Treebanks dataset.
- Other than that, we show that it is possible to cross-lingually parse Croatian, Serbian and Slovene using all three syntactic annotation schemes, and with high accuracy. A treebank for Serbian does not exist, but we accurately parse Serbian by using PDT, SET and SSJ-style annotations. We parse Croatian using SSJ (transferred from Slovene) and Slovene using SSJ (transferred from Croatian). This clearly indicates the possibilities of uniform downstream pipelining for any of the schemes.
- We show clear benefits of using the SMT approach for transferring SSJ parsers to Croatian and SET parsers to Slovene. We observe these benefits regardless of the low-quality, out-of-domain SMT training data (OpenSubs).

Given the current interest for cross-lingual dependency parsing in the natural language processing community, we will seek to further test our observations on shared morphological features by using other pairs of languages of varying relatedness, drawing from datasets such as Google Universal Treebanks (McDonald et al., 2013) or HamleDT (Zeman et al., 2012; Rosa et al., 2014). The goal of cross-lingual processing in general is to enable improved general access to under-resourced languages. With this in mind, seeing how we introduced a test case of Serbian as a language currently without a treebank, we hope to explore other options for performing cross-lingual experiments on actual under-resourced languages, rather than in an exclusive group of resource-rich placeholders, possibly by means of down-stream evaluation.

**Acknowledgments** The second author was supported by the Swedish Research Council (Vetenskapsrådet), project 2012-916. The fifth author is funded by the EU FP7 STREP project XLike.

## References


Anne Abeillé. 2003. *Treebanks: Building and Using Parsed Corpora*. Springer.

Željko Agić and Nikola Ljubešić. 2014. The SETimes.HR Linguistically Annotated Corpus of Croatian. In *Proc. LREC*, pages 1724–1727.

Željko Agić and Danijela Merkler. 2013. Three Syntactic Formalisms for Data-Driven Dependency Parsing of Croatian. *LNCS*, 8082:560–567.

Željko Agić, Danijela Merkler, and Daša Berović. 2012. Slovene-Croatian Treebank Transfer Using Bilingual Lexicon Improves Croatian Dependency Parsing. In *Proc. IS-LTC*, pages 5–9.

Željko Agić, Danijela Merkler, and Daša Berović. 2013. Parsing Croatian and Serbian by Using Croatian Dependency Treebanks. In *Proc. SPMRL*, pages 22–33.

Željko Agić, Daša Berović, Danijela Merkler, and Marko Tadić. 2014. Croatian Dependency Treebank 2.0: New Annotation Guidelines for Improved Parsing. In *Proc. LREC*, pages 2313–2319.

Emily Bender. 2011. On achieving and evaluating language-independence in nlp. *Linguistic Issues in Language Technology*, 6(3):1–26.

Emily Bender. 2013. *Linguistic Fundamentals for Natural Language Processing: 100 Essentials from Morphology and Syntax*. Morgan & Claypool Publishers.

Daša Berović, Željko Agić, and Marko Tadić. 2012. Croatian Dependency Treebank: Recent Development and Initial Experiments. In *Proc. LREC*, pages 1902–1906.

Alena Böhmová, Jan Hajič, Eva Hajičová, and Barbora Hladká. 2003. The Prague Dependency Treebank. In *Treebanks*, pages 103–127.

Bernd Bohnet and Jonas Kuhn. 2012. The Best of Both Worlds – A Graph-based Completion Model for Transition-based Parsers. In *Proc. EACL*, pages 77–87.

Bernd Bohnet, Joakim Nivre, Igor Boguslavsky, Richárd Farkas, Filip Ginter, and Jan Hajic. 2013. Joint Morphological and Syntactic Analysis for Richly Inflected Languages. *TACL*, 1:415–428.

Bernd Bohnet. 2010. Top Accuracy and Fast Dependency Parsing is not a Contradiction. In *Proc. COLING*, pages 89–97.

Sabine Buchholz and Erwin Marsi. 2006. CoNLL-X Shared Task on Multilingual Dependency Parsing. In *Proc. CoNLL*, pages 149–164.

Marie-Catherine De Marneffe and Christopher D Manning. 2008. The Stanford Typed Dependencies Representation. In *Proc. COLING*, pages 1–8.

Kaja Dobrovoljc, Simon Krek, and Jan Rupnik. 2012. Skladenjski razčlenjevalnik za slovenščino. In *Proc. IS-LTC*, pages 42–47.

Greg Durrett, Adam Pauls, and Dan Klein. 2012. Syntactic Transfer Using a Bilingual Lexicon. In *Proc. EMNLP-CoNLL*, pages 1–11.

Sašo Džeroski, Tomaž Erjavec, Nina Ledinek, Petr Pajas, Zdenek Žabokrtsky, and Andreja Žele. 2006. Towards a Slovene Dependency Treebank. In *Proc. LREC*, pages 1388–1391.

Tomaž Erjavec, Darja Fišer, Simon Krek, and Nina Ledinek. 2010. The JOS Linguistically Tagged Corpus of Slovene. In *Proc. LREC*, pages 1806–1809.

Tomaž Erjavec. 2012. MULTEXT-East: Morphosyntactic Resources for Central and Eastern European Languages. *Language Resources and Evaluation*, 46(1):131–142.

Kenneth Heafield. 2011. KenLM: Faster and Smaller Language Model Queries. In *Proc. WSMT*, pages 187–197.

Rebecca Hwa, Philip Resnik, Amy Weinberg, Clara Cabezas, and Okan Kolak. 2005. Bootstrapping Parsers via Syntactic Projection across Parallel Texts. *Natural Language Engineering*, 11(3):311–325.

Philipp Koehn, Hieu Hoang, Alexandra Birch, Chris Callison-Burch, Marcello Federico, Nicola Bertoldi, Brooke Cowan, Wade Shen, Christine Moran, Richard Zens, et al. 2007. Moses: Open Source Toolkit for Statistical Machine Translation. In *Proc. ACL*, pages 177–180.

Sandra Kübler, Ryan McDonald, and Joakim Nivre. 2009. *Dependency Parsing*. Morgan & Claypool Publishers.

Ryan McDonald, Fernando Pereira, Kiril Ribarov, and Jan Hajič. 2005. Non-projective Dependency Parsing Using Spanning Tree Algorithms. In *Proc. HLT-EMNLP*, pages 523–530.

Ryan McDonald, Slav Petrov, and Keith Hall. 2011. Multi-Source Transfer of Delexicalized Dependency Parsers. In *Proc. EMNLP*, pages 62–72.

Ryan McDonald, Joakim Nivre, Yvonne Quirmbach-Brundage, Yoav Goldberg, Dipanjan Das, Kuzman Ganchev, Keith Hall, Slav Petrov, Hao Zhang, Oscar Täckström, Claudia Bedini, Núria Bertomeu Castelló, and Jungmee Lee. 2013. Universal Dependency Annotation for Multilingual Parsing. In *Proc. ACL*, pages 92–97.

Joakim Nivre, Johan Hall, Sandra Kübler, Ryan McDonald, Jens Nilsson, Sebastian Riedel, and Deniz Yuret. 2007. The CoNLL 2007 Shared Task on Dependency Parsing. In *Proc. CoNLL*, pages 915–932.

Franz Josef Och and Hermann Ney. 2003. A Systematic Comparison of Various Statistical Alignment Models. *Computational Linguistics*, 29(1):19–51.

Franz Josef Och. 2003. Minimum Error Rate Training in Statistical Machine Translation. In *Proc. ACL*, pages 160–167.

Slav Petrov, Dipanjan Das, and Ryan McDonald. 2012. A Universal Part-of-Speech Tagset. In *Proc. LREC*, pages 2089–2096.

Vesna Požgaj Hadži and Marko Tadić. 2000. Croatian-Slovene Parallel Corpus. In *Proc. IS-LTC*.

Rudolf Rosa, Jan Mašek, David Mareček, Martin Popel, Daniel Zeman, and Zdeněk Žabokrtský. 2014. HamleDT 2.0: Thirty Dependency Treebanks Stanfordized. In *Proc. LREC*, pages 2334–2341.

Djamé Seddah, Reut Tsarfaty, Sandra Kübler, Marie Candito, Jinho D. Choi, Richárd Farkas, Jennifer Foster, Iakes Goenaga, Koldo Gojenola Galletebeitia, Yoav Goldberg, Spence Green, Nizar Habash, Marco Kuhlmann, Wolfgang Maier, Joakim Nivre, Adam Przepiórkowski, Ryan Roth, Wolfgang Seeker, Yannick Versley, Veronika Vincze, Marcin Woliński, Alina Wróblewska, and Eric Villemonte de la Clergerie. 2013. Overview of the SPMRL 2013 Shared Task: Cross-framework Evaluation of Parsing Morphologically Rich Languages. In *Proc. SPMRL*, pages 146–182.

Anders Søgaard. 2011. Data Point Selection for Cross-language Adaptation of Dependency Parsers. In *Proc. ACL*, pages 682–686.

Oscar Täckström, Ryan McDonald, and Jakob Uszkoreit. 2012. Cross-lingual Word Clusters for Direct Transfer of Linguistic Structure. In *Proc. NAACL*, pages 477–487.

Oscar Täckström, Ryan McDonald, and Joakim Nivre. 2013. Target Language Adaptation of Discriminative Transfer Parsers. In *Proc. NAACL*, pages 1061–1071.

Marko Tadić and Sanja Fulgosi. 2003. Building the Croatian Morphological Lexicon. In *Proc. BSNLP*, pages 41–46.

Marko Tadić and Tamás Váradi. 2012. Central and South-East European Resources in META-SHARE. *Proc. COLING*, pages 431–438.

Marko Tadić. 2007. Building the Croatian Dependency Treebank: The Initial Stages. *Suvremena lingvistika*, 63:85–92.

Jörg Tiedemann and Preslav Nakov. 2013. Analyzing the Use of Character-Level Translation with Sparse and Noisy Datasets. In *Proc. RANLP*, pages 676–684.

Jörg Tiedemann, Željko Agić, and Joakim Nivre. 2014. Treebank Translation for Cross-Lingual Parser Induction. In *Proc. CoNLL*, pages 130–140.

Jörg Tiedemann. 2009. News from OPUS: A Collection of Multilingual Parallel Corpora with Tools and Interfaces. In *Proc. RANLP*, volume 5, pages 237–248.

Jörg Tiedemann. 2012. Character-Based Pivot Translations for Under-Resourced Languages and Domains. In *Proc. EACL*, pages 141–151.

Jörg Tiedemann. 2014. Rediscovering Annotation Projection for Cross-Lingual Parser Induction. In *Proc. COLING*.

Erik F Tjong Kim Sang and Sabine Buchholz. 2000. Introduction to the CoNLL-2000 Shared Task: Chunking. In *Proc. CoNLL*, pages 127–132.

Hans Uszkoreit and Georg Rehm. 2012. *Language White Paper Series*. Springer.

David Vilar, Jan-Thorsten Peter, and Hermann Ney. 2007. Can We Translate Letters? In *Proc. WMT*, pages 33–39.

David Yarowsky, Grace Ngai, and Richard Wicentowski. 2001. Inducing Multilingual Text Analysis Tools via Robust Projection Across Aligned Corpora. In *Proc. HLT*, pages 1–8.

Daniel Zeman and Philip Resnik. 2008. Cross-Language Parser Adaptation between Related Languages. In *Proc. IJCNLP*, pages 35–42.

Daniel Zeman, David Marecek, Martin Popel, Loganathan Ramasamy, Jan Stepánek, Zdenek Zabokrtskỳ, and Jan Hajic. 2012. HamleDT: To Parse or Not to Parse? In *Proc. LREC*, pages 2735–2741.

# Language variety identification in Spanish tweets

**Wolfgang Maier**
Institute for Language and Information
University of Düsseldorf
Düsseldorf, Germany
maierw@hhu.de

**Carlos Gómez-Rodríguez**
Depto. de Computación
Universidade da Coruña
A Coruña, Spain
cgomezr@udc.es

## Abstract

We study the problem of *language variant identification*, approximated by the problem of labeling tweets from Spanish speaking countries by the country from which they were posted. While this task is closely related to "pure" language identification, it comes with additional complications. We build a balanced collection of tweets and apply techniques from language modeling. A simplified version of the task is also solved by human test subjects, who are outperformed by the automatic classification. Our best automatic system achieves an overall F-score of 67.7% on 5-class classification.

## 1 Introduction

Spanish (or *castellano*), a descendant of Latin, is currently the language with the second largest number of native speakers after Mandarin Chinese, namely around 414 million people (Lewis et al., 2014). Spanish has a large number of regional varieties across Spain and the Americas (Lipski, 1994).[1] They diverge in spoken language and vocabulary and also, albeit to a lesser extent, in syntax. Between different American varieties of Spanish, there are important differences; however, the largest differences can be found between American and European ("Peninsular") Spanish.

Language identification, the task of automatically identifying the natural language used in a given text segment, is a relatively well understood problem (see Section 2). To our knowledge, however, there is little previous work on the identification of the varieties of a single language, such as the regional varieties of Spanish. This task is especially challenging because the differences between variants are subtle, making it difficult to discern between them. This is evidenced by the fact that humans that are native speakers of the varieties are often unable to solve the problem, particularly when given short, noisy text segments (which are the focus of this work) where the amount of available information is limited.

In this paper, we approximate the problem of language variety identification by the problem of classifying status messages from the microblogging service Twitter ("tweets") from Spanish speaking countries by the country from which they were sent. With the tweet, the location of the device from which the tweet was sent can be recorded (depending on the Twitter users' permission) and can then be retrieved from the metadata of the tweet. The tweet location information does not always correlate with the actual language variety used in the tweet: it is conceivable, e.g., that migrants do not use the prevalent language variety of the country in which they live, but rather their native variety. Nevertheless, Twitter can give a realistic picture of actual language use in a certain region, which, additionally, is closer to spoken than to standard written language. Eventually and more importantly, Twitter data is available from almost all Spanish speaking countries.

We proceed as follows. We build a balanced collection of tweets sent by Twitter users from five countries, namely Argentina, Chile, Colombia, Mexico, and Spain. Applying different methods, we perform an automatic classification between all countries. In order to obtain a more detailed view of the difficulty of our task, we also investigate human performance. For this purpose, we build a smaller sample of tweets from Argentina, Chile and Spain and have them classified by both our system and three native human evaluators. The results show that automatic classification outperforms human annotators. The best variant of our system, using a meta-classifier with voting,

[1] We are aware that there are natively Spanish-speaking communities elsewhere, such as on the Philippines, but we do not consider them in this study.



*Language Technology for Closely Related Languages and Language Variants (LT4CloseLang)*, pages 25–35,
October 29, 2014, Doha, Qatar. 

reaches an overall F-score of 67.72 on the five-class problem. On the two-class problem, human classification is outperformed by a large margin.

The remainder of this paper is structured as follows. In the following section, we present related work. Section 3 presents our data collection. Sections 4 and 5 present our classification methodology and the experiments. Section 7 discusses the results, and Section 8 concludes the article.

## 2 Related Work

Research on language identification has seen a variety of methods. A well established technique is the use of character $n$-gram models. Cavnar and Trenkle (1994) build $n$-gram frequency "profiles" for several languages and classify text by matching it to the profiles. Dunning (1994) uses language modeling. This technique is general and not limited to language identification; it has also been successfully employed in other areas, e.g., in authorship attribution (Kešelj et al., 2003) and author native language identification (Gyawali et al., 2013). Other language identification systems use non-textual methods, exploiting optical properties of text such as stroke geometry (Muir and Thomas, 2000), or using compression methods which rely on the assumption that natural languages differ by their entropy, and consequently by the rate to which they can be compressed (Teahan, 2000; Benedetto et al., 2002). Two newer approaches are Brown (2013), who uses character $n$-grams, and Řehůřek and Kolkus (2009), who treat "noisy" web text and therefore consider the particular influence of single words in discriminating between languages.

Language identification is harder the shorter the text segments whose language is to be identified (Baldwin and Lui, 2010). Especially due to the rise of Twitter, this particular problem has recently received attention. Several solutions have been proposed. Vatanen et al. (2010) compare character $n$-gram language models with elaborate smoothing techniques to the approach of Cavnar and Trenkle and the Google Language ID API, on the basis of different versions of the Universal Declaration of Human Rights. Other researchers work on Twitter. Bergsma et al. (2012) use language identification to create language specific tweet collections, thereby facilitating more high-quality results with supervised techniques. Lui and Baldwin (2014) review a wide range of off-the-shelf tools for Twitter language identification, and achieve their best results with a voting over three individual systems, one of them being `langid.py` (Lui and Baldwin, 2012). Carter et al. (2013) exploit particular characteristics of Twitter (such as user profile data and relations between Twitter users) to improve language identification on this genre. Bush (2014) successfully uses LZW compression for Twitter language identification.

Within the field of natural language processing, the problem of language variant identification has only begun to be studied very recently. Zampieri et al. (2013) have addressed the task for Spanish newspaper texts, using character and word n-gram models as well as POS and morphological information. Very recently, the Discriminating between Similar Languages (DSL) Shared Task (Zampieri et al., 2014) proposed the problem of identifying between pairs of similar languages and language variants on sentences from newspaper corpora, one of the pairs being Peninsular vs. Argentine Spanish. However, all these approaches are tailored to the standard language found in news sources, very different from the colloquial, noisy language of tweets, which presents distinct challenges for NLP (Derczynski et al., 2013; Vilares et al., 2013). Lui and Cook (2013) evaluate various approaches to classify documents into Australian, British and Canadian English, including a corpus of tweets, but we are not aware of any previous work on variant identification in Spanish tweets.

A review of research on Spanish varieties from a linguistics point of view is beyond the scope of this article. Recommended further literature in this area is Lipski (1994), Quesada Pacheco (2002) and Alvar (1996b; 1996a).

## 3 Data Collection

We first built a collection of tweets using the Twitter streaming API,[2] requesting all tweets sent within the geographic areas given by the coordinates -120°, -55° and -29°, 30° (roughly delimiting Latin America), as well as -10°, 35° and 3°, 46° (roughly delimiting Spain). The download ran from July 2 to July 4, 2014. In a second step, we sorted the tweets according to the respective countries.

Twitter is not used to the same extent in all countries where Spanish is spoken. In the time

[2] `https://dev.twitter.com/docs/api/streaming`

it took to collect 2,400 tweets from Bolivia, we could collect over 700,000 tweets from Argentina.[3] To ensure homogeneous conditions for our experiments, our final tweet collection comprises exactly 100,000 tweets from each of the five countries from which most tweets were collected, that is, Argentina, Chile, Colombia, Mexico, and Spain.

At this stage, we do not perform any cleanup or normalization operations such as, e.g., deleting forwarded tweets ("re-tweets"), deleting tweets which are sent by robots, or tweets not written in Spanish (some tweets use code switching, or are entirely written in a different language, mostly in English or in regional and minority languages that coexist with Spanish in the focus countries). Our reasoning behind this is that the tweet production in a certain country captures the variant of Spanish that is spoken.

We mark the start and end of single tweets by <s> and </s>, respectively. We use 80% of the tweets of each language for training, and 10% for development and testing, respectively. The data is split in a round-robin fashion, i.e., every ninth tweet is put into the development set and every tenth tweet is put in the test set, all other tweets are put in the training set.

In order to help with the interpretation of classification results, we investigate the distribution of tweet lengths on the development set, as shown in Figure 1. We see that in all countries, tweets tend to be either short, or take advantage of all available characters. Lengths around 100 to 110 characters are the rarest. The clearest further trend is that the tweets from Colombia and, especially, Argentina tend to be shorter than the tweets from the other countries.

## 4 Automatic Tweet Classification

The classification task we envisage is similar to the task of language identification in short text segments. We explore three methods that have been used before for that task, namely character $n$-gram frequency profiles (Cavnar and Trenkle, 1994; Vatanen et al., 2010), character $n$-gram language models (Vatanen et al., 2010), as well as LZW compression (Bush, 2014). Furthermore, we explore the usability of syllable-based language models. For all four approaches, we train models for binary classification for each class, i.e., five models that decide for each tweet if it belongs to a single class. As final label, we take the output of the one of the five classifiers that has the highest score.

We finally use a meta-classifier on the basis of voting. All methods are tested on the development set. For evaluation, we compute precision, recall and $F_1$ overall as well as for single classes.

Note that we decided to rely on the tweet text only. An exploration of the benefit of, e.g., directly exploiting Twitter-specific information (such as user mentions or hash tags) is out of the scope of this paper.

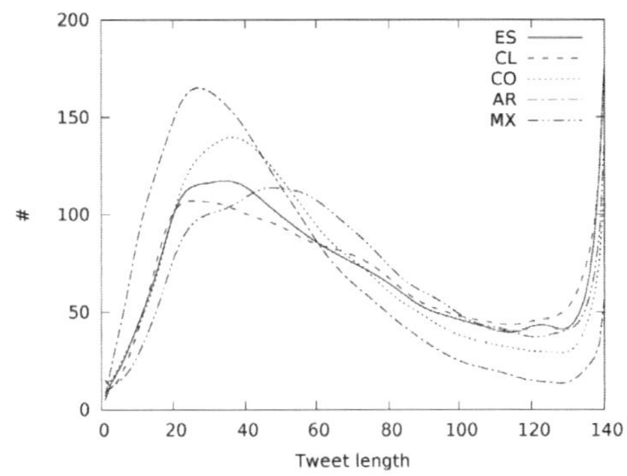


Figure 1: Tweet length distribution

| | 50 | 100 | 500 | 1k | 10k |
|---|---|---|---|---|---|
| AR | 31.68 | 29.72 | 43.93 | 31.77 | 18.42 |
| CO | 24.29 | 21.36 | 26.14 | 19.68 | 19.03 |
| MX | 31.86 | 28.97 | 32.58 | 30.28 | 22.27 |
| ES | 20.19 | 25.22 | 22.08 | 21.25 | 16.15 |
| CL | 22.95 | 29.74 | 35.67 | 26.01 | 16.69 |

Table 1: Results ($F_1$): $n$-gram frequency profiles (classes/profile sizes)

### 4.1 Character $n$-gram frequency profiles

We first investigate the $n$-gram frequency approach of Cavnar and Trenkle (1994). We use the well-known implementation `TextCat`.[4] The results for all classes with different profile sizes are shown in Table 1. Table 2 shows precision and recall for the best setting, a profile with a maximal size of 500 entries.

The results obtained with a profile size of 500

[3] We are aware that the Twitter API does not make all sent tweets available. However, we still assume that this huge difference reflects a variance in the number of Twitter users.

[4] As available from `http://odur.let.rug.nl/~vannoord/TextCat/`.

| class | precision | recall | $F_1$ |
|---|---|---|---|
| AR | 32.60 | 67.33 | 43.93 |
| CO | 31.66 | 22.26 | 26.14 |
| MX | 51.52 | 23.82 | 32.58 |
| ES | 32.83 | 16.63 | 22.08 |
| CL | 31.96 | 40.36 | 35.67 |
| *overall* | 34.08 | 34.08 | 34.08 |

Table 2: Results: $n$-gram frequency profile with 500 $n$-grams

| | AR | CO | MX | ES | CL |
|---|---|---|---|---|---|
| AR | 6,733 | 949 | 384 | 610 | 1,324 |
| CO | 4,207 | 2,226 | 720 | 803 | 2,044 |
| MX | 2,547 | 1,342 | 2,382 | 1,051 | 2,678 |
| ES | 3,781 | 1,361 | 649 | 1,663 | 2,546 |
| CL | 3,384 | 1,153 | 488 | 939 | 4,036 |

Table 3: Confusion matrix ($n$-gram freq. profiles, 500 $n$-grams)

entries for Colombia align with the results for Spain and Mexico in that the precision is higher than the recall. The results for Chile align with those for Argentina with the recall being higher than the precision. For Mexico and Argentina the differences between recall and precision are particularly large (28 and 35 points, respectively). The confusion matrix in Table 3 reveals that tweets from all classes are likely to be mislabeled as coming from Argentina, while, on the other hand, Mexican tweets are mislabeled most frequently as coming from other countries.

Overall, the $n$-gram frequency profiles are not very good at our task, achieving an maximal overall F-score of only 34.08 with a profile size of 500 entries. However, this performance is still well above the 20.00 F-score we would obtain with a random baseline. Larger profile sizes deteriorate results: with 10,000 entries, we only have an overall F-score of 18.23. As observed before (Vatanen et al., 2010), the weak performance can most likely be attributed to the shortness of the tweets and the resulting lack of frequent $n$-grams that hinders a successful profile matching. While Vatanen et al. alleviate this problem to some extent, they have more success with character-level $n$-gram language models, the approach which we explore next.

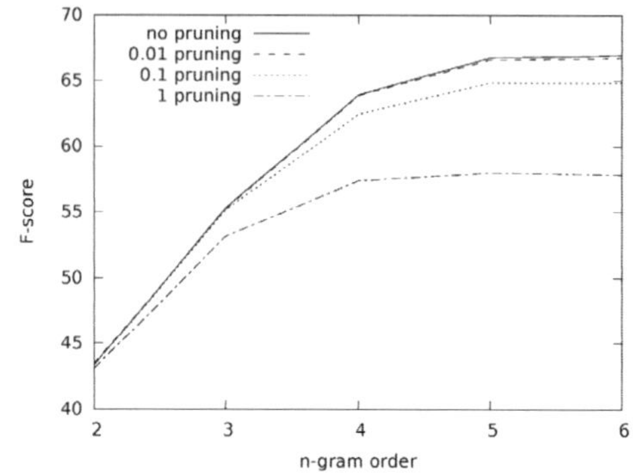


Figure 2: Character $n$-gram lm: Pruning vs. $n$-gram order

### 4.2 Character $n$-gram language models

We recur to $n$-gram language models as available in `variKN` (Siivola et al., 2007).[5] We run `variKN` with absolute discounting and the cross-product of four different pruning settings (no pruning, and thresholds 0.01, 0.1 and 1) and five different $n$-gram lengths (2 to 6).

Figure 2 contrasts the effect of different pruning settings with different $n$-gram lengths. While excessive pruning is detrimental to the result, slight pruning has barely any effect on the results, while reducing look-up time immensely. The order of the $n$-grams, however, does have an important influence. We confirm that also for this problem, we do not benefit from increasing it beyond $n = 6$, like Vatanen et al. (2010).

We now check if some countries are more difficult to identify than others and how they benefit from different $n$-gram orders. Figure 3 visualizes the corresponding results. Not all countries profit equally from longer $n$-grams. When comparing the 3- and 6-gram models without pruning, we see that the $F_1$ for Argentina is just 8 points higher, while the difference is more than 14 points for Mexico.

Table 4 shows all results including precision and recall for all classes, in the setting with 6-grams and no pruning. We can see that this approach works noticeably better than the frequency profiles, achieving an overall F-score of 66.96. The behavior of the classes is not uniform: Argentina shows the largest difference between precision and recall, and is furthermore the only class in which precision is higher than recall. Note also that in

[5] `https://github.com/vsiivola/variKN`

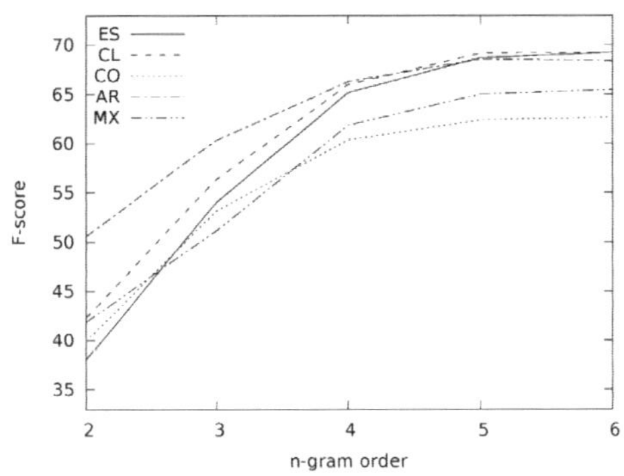


Figure 3: Character $n$-gram lm: Classes vs. $n$-gram order (no pruning)

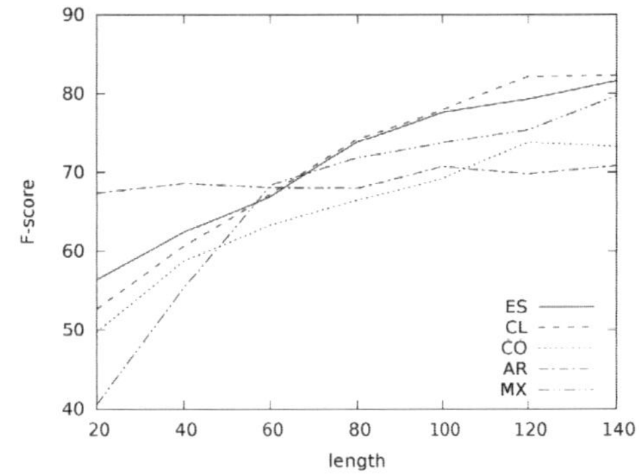


Figure 4: Character $n$-grams: Results ($F_1$) for tweet length intervals

| class | precision | recall | $F_1$ |
|---|---|---|---|
| AR | 70.67 | 66.22 | 68.37 |
| CO | 62.56 | 62.77 | 62.66 |
| MX | 65.23 | 65.74 | 65.48 |
| ES | 68.75 | 69.36 | 69.06 |
| CL | 67.81 | 70.73 | 69.24 |
| *overall* | 66.96 | 66.96 | 66.96 |

Table 4: Results: 6-grams without pruning

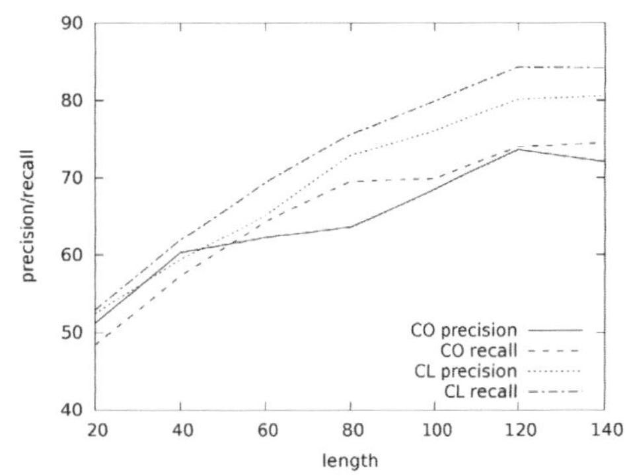


Figure 5: Character $n$-grams: Precision/recall for AR and CL

general, the differences between precision and recall are lower than for the $n$-gram frequency profile approach. The confusion matrix shown in Table 5 reveals that the Colombia class is the one with the highest confusion, particularly in combination with the Mexican class. This could indicate that those classes are more heterogeneous than the others, possibly showing more Twitter-specific noise, such as tweets consisting only of URLs, etc.

We finally investigate how tweet length influences classification performance in the 6-gram model. Figure 4 shows the F-scores for intervals of length 20 for all classes. The graph confirms that longer tweets are easier to classify. This correlates with findings from previous work. Over 82 points $F_1$ are achieved for tweets from Chile longer than 120 characters, while for those containing up to 20 characters, $F_1$ is almost 30 points lower. We investigate precision and recall separately. Figure 5 shows the corresponding curves for the best and worst performing classes, namely, CL and CO. For Chile, both precision and recall develop in parallel to the F-score (i.e., the longer the tweets, the higher the scores). For Colombia, the curves confirm that the low $F_1$ is rather due to a low precision than a low recall, particularly for tweets longer than 40 characters. This correlates with the counts in the confusion table (Tab. 5).

| | AR | CO | MX | ES | CL |
|---|---|---|---|---|---|
| AR | 6,622 | 1,036 | 702 | 740 | 900 |
| CO | 800 | 6,277 | 1,151 | 875 | 897 |
| MX | 509 | 1,237 | 6,574 | 847 | 833 |
| ES | 630 | 850 | 857 | 6,936 | 727 |
| CL | 809 | 634 | 794 | 690 | 7,073 |

Table 5: Confusion matrix (6-grams, no pruning)

### 4.3 Syllable $n$-gram language models

Since varieties of Spanish exhibit differences in vocabulary, we may think that models based on word $n$-grams can be more useful than character $n$-grams to discriminate between varieties. However, the larger diversity of word $n$-grams means that such models run into sparsity problems. An intermediate family of models can be built by us-

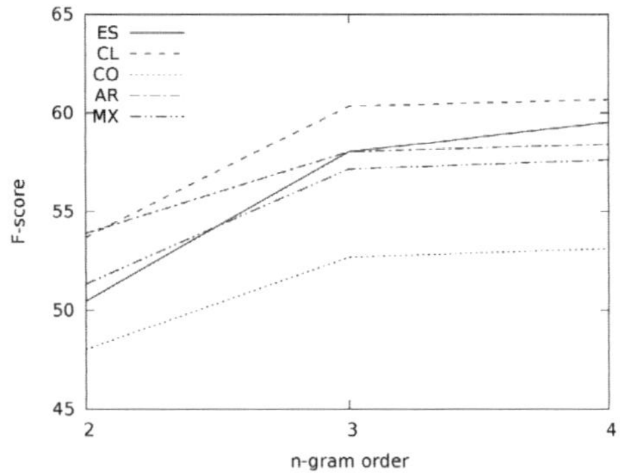


Figure 6: Syllable $n$-gram lm: pruning vs. $n$-gram order

ing syllable $n$-grams, taking advantage of the fact that Spanish variants do not differ in the criteria for syllabification of written words. Note that this property does not hold in general for the language identification problem, as different languages typically have different syllabification rules, which is a likely reason why syllable $n$-gram models have not been used for this problem.

To perform the splitting of Spanish words into syllables, we use the TIP syllabifier (Hernández-Figeroa et al., 2012), which applies an algorithm implementing the general syllabification rules described by the Royal Spanish Academy of Language and outlined in standard Spanish dictionaries and grammars. These rules are enough to correctly split the vast majority of Spanish words, excluding only a few corner cases related with word prefixes (Hernández-Figueroa et al., 2013). While accurate syllabification requires texts to be written correctly with accented characters, and this is often not the case in informal online environments (Vilares et al., 2014); we assume that this need not cause problems because the errors originated by unaccented words will follow a uniform pattern, producing a viable model for the purposes of classification.

We train $n$-gram language models with `variKN` as described in the last section, using absolute discounting. Due to the larger vocabulary size, we limit ourselves to 0.01 pruning, and to $n$-gram orders 2 to 4. Figure 6 shows the results ($F_1$) of all classes for the different $n$-gram orders, and Table 6 shows the results for all classes for the 4-gram language model.

As expected, shorter $n$-grams are more effective for syllable than for character language models.

| class | precision | recall | $F_1$ |
|---|---|---|---|
| AR | 55.94 | 61.11 | 58.41 |
| CO | 53.23 | 53.03 | 53.13 |
| MX | 59.10 | 56.17 | 57.60 |
| ES | 62.35 | 56.96 | 59.53 |
| CL | 59.31 | 62.12 | 60.68 |
| *overall* | 57.88 | 57.88 | 57.88 |

Table 6: Results ($F_1$): Syllable 4-gram lm

For the Chilean tweets, e.g., the F-score for the 2-gram language model is around 11 points higher than for the character 2-gram language model. Furthermore, the performance seems to converge earlier, given that the results change only slightly when raising the $n$-gram order from 3 to 4. The overall F-score for the 4-gram language model is around 6 points lower than for character 4-grams. However, the behavior of the classes is similar: again, Mexico and Colombia have slightly lower results than the other classes.

### 4.4 Compression

We eventually test the applicability of compression-based classification using the approach of Bush (2014). As mentioned earlier, the assumption behind compression-based strategies for text categorization is that different text categories have a different entropy. Classification is possible because the effectivity of compression algorithms depends on the entropy of the data to be compressed (less entropy $\approx$ more compression).

A simple classification algorithm is Lempel-Ziv-Welch (LZW) (Welch, 1984). It is based on a dictionary which maps sequences of symbols to unique indices. Compression is achieved by replacing sequences of input symbols with the respective dictionary indices. More precisely, compression works as follows. First, the dictionary is initialized with the inventory of symbols (i.e., with all possible 1-grams). Then, until the input is fully consumed, we repeat the following steps. We search the dictionary for the longest sequence of symbols $s$ that matches the current input, we output the dictionary entry for $s$, remove $s$ from the input and add $s$ followed by the next input symbol to the dictionary.

For our experiments, we use our own implementation of LZW. We first build LZW dictionaries by compressing our training sets as described

| | 1k | 8k | 25k | 50k |
|---|---|---|---|---|
| AR | 28.42 | 38.78 | 46.92 | 51.89 |
| CO | 19.81 | 28.27 | 32.81 | 36.05 |
| MX | 22.07 | 33.90 | 43.10 | 45.06 |
| ES | 22.08 | 29.48 | 35.15 | 38.61 |
| CL | 27.08 | 28.22 | 33.59 | 36.68 |

Table 7: Results ($F_1$): LZW without ties

| class | precision | recall | $F_1$ |
|---|---|---|---|
| AR | 70.96 | 68.36 | 69.64 |
| CO | 62.44 | 64.22 | 63.32 |
| MX | 66.37 | 65.67 | 66.02 |
| ES | 70.10 | 69.64 | 69.87 |
| CL | 68.97 | 70.72 | 69.83 |
| *overall* | 67.72 | 67.72 | 67.72 |

Table 8: Results: Voting

above, using different limits on dictionary lengths. As symbol inventory, we use bytes, not unicode symbols. Then we use these dictionaries to compress all tweets from all test sets, skipping the initialization stage. The country assigned to each tweet is the one whose dictionary yields the highest compression. We run LZW with different maximal dictionary sizes.

The problem with the evaluation of the results is that the compression produced many ties, i.e., the compression of a single tweet with dictionaries from different languages resulted in identical compression rates. On the concatenated dev sets (50k tweets, i.e., 10k per country) with a maximal dictionary size of 1k, 8k, 25k and 50k entries, we got 14.867, 20,166, 22,031, and 23,652 ties, respectively. In 3,515 (7%), 4,839 (10%), 5,455 (11%) and 6,102 (12%) cases, respectively, the correct result was hidden in a tie. If we replace the labels of all tied instances with a new label TIE, we obtain the F-scores shown in Table 7. While they are higher than the scores for $n$-gram frequency profiles, they still lie well below the results for both syllable and character language models.

While previous literature mentions an ideal size limit on the dictionary of 8k entries (Bush, 2014), we obtain better results the larger the dictionaries. Note that already with a dictionary of size 1000, even without including the ties, we are above the 20.00 F-score of a random baseline. The high rate of ties constitutes a major problem of this approach, and remains even if we would find improvements to the approach (one possibility could be to use unicode characters instead of bytes for dictionary initialization). It cannot easily be alleviated, because if the compression rate is taken as the score, particularly the scores for short tweets are likely to coincide.

### 4.5 Voting

*Voting* is a simple meta-classifying technique which takes the output of different classifiers and decides based on a predefined method on one of them, thereby combining their strengths and leveling out their weaknesses. It has been successfully used to improve language identification on Twitter data by Lui and Baldwin (2014).

We utilize the character 5-gram and 6-gram language models without pruning, as well as the syllable 3-gram and 4-gram models. We decide as follows. All instances for which the output of the 5-gram model coincides with the output of at least one of the syllable models are labeled with the output of the 5-gram model. For all other instances, the output of the 6-gram model is used. The corresponding results for all classes are shown in Table 8.

We obtain a slightly higher F-score than for the 6-gram character language model (0.8 points). In other words, even though the 6-gram language model leads to the highest overall results among individual models, in some instances it is outperformed by the lower-order character language model and by the syllable language models, which have a lower overall score.

## 5 Human Tweet Classification

In order to get a better idea of the difficulty of the task of classifying tweets by the country of their authors, we have tweets classified by humans.

Generally, speakers of Spanish have limited contact with speakers of other varieties, simply due to geographical separation of varieties. We therefore recur to a simplified version of our task, in which the test subjects only have to distinguish their own variety from one other variety, i.e., perform a binary classification. We randomly draw two times 150 tweets from the Argentinian test and 150 tweets from the Chilean and Spanish test sets, respectively. We then build shuffled concatenations of the first 150 Argentinian and the Chilean tweets, as well as of the remaining 150 Argentinian and the Spanish tweets. Then we let three

| data | subject | class | prec. | rec. | $F_1$ |
|---|---|---|---|---|---|
| AR-ES | AR | AR | 68.5 | 76.7 | 72.3 |
| | | ES | 73.5 | 64.7 | 68.8 |
| | ES | AR | 71.5 | 62.0 | 66.4 |
| | | ES | 66.5 | 75.3 | 70.6 |
| | $n$-gram | AR | **92.3** | **87.3** | **89.7** |
| | | ES | **88.0** | **92.7** | **90.3** |
| AR-CL | AR | AR | 61.0 | 77.3 | 68.2 |
| | | CL | 69.1 | 50.7 | 58.5 |
| | CL | AR | 70.0 | 70.0 | 70.0 |
| | | CL | 70.0 | 70.0 | 70.0 |
| | $n$-gram | AR | **93.4** | **84.7** | **88.8** |
| | | CL | **86.0** | **94.0** | **89.8** |

Table 9: Results: Human vs. automatic classification

| data | subject | class | prec. | rec. | $F_1$ |
|---|---|---|---|---|---|
| AR-ES | AR | AR | 71.8 | 80.0 | 75.7 |
| | | ES | 74.8 | 65.4 | 69.7 |
| | ES | AR | 74.6 | 62.9 | 68.2 |
| | | ES | 65.1 | 76.3 | 70.2 |
| | $n$-gram | AR | **93.2** | **88.6** | **90.8** |
| | | ES | **88.1** | **92.9** | **90.4** |
| AR-CL | AR | AR | 61.1 | 78.6 | 68.8 |
| | | CL | 68.8 | 48.5 | 56.9 |
| | CL | AR | 73.0 | 71.4 | 72.2 |
| | | CL | 71.2 | 72.8 | 72.0 |
| | $n$-gram | AR | **95.3** | **87.1** | **91.0** |
| | | CL | **87.8** | **95.6** | **91.5** |

Table 10: Results: Human vs. automatic classification (filtered)

natives classify them. The test subjects are not given any other training data samples or similar resources before the task, and they are instructed not to look up on the Internet any information within the tweet that might reveal the country of its author (such as hyperlinks, user mentions or hash tags).

Table 9 shows the results, together with the results on the same task of the character 6-gram model without pruning. Note that with 300 test instances out of 20,000, there is a sampling error of $\pm$ 4.7% (confidence interval 95%). The results confirm our intuition in the light of the good performance achieved by the $n$-gram approach in the 5-class case: when reducing the classification problem from five classes to two, human classification performance is much below the performance of automatic classification, by between 17 and 31 F-score points. In terms of error rate, the human annotators made between 3 and 4 times more classification errors than the automatic system. One can observe a tendency among the human test subjects that more errors come from labeling too many tweets as coming from their native country than vice versa (cf. the recall values).

In order to better understand the large result difference, we ask the test subjects for the strategies they used to label tweets. They stated that the easiest tweets where those specifying a location ("*Estoy en Madrid*"), or referencing local named entities (TV programs, public figures, etc.). In case of absence of such information, other clues were used that tend to occur in only one variety. They include the use of different words (such as *enfadado* (Spain) vs. *enojado* (America) ("angry")), a different distribution of the same word (such as the filler *pues*), and different inflection, such as the second person plural verb forms, which in American Spanish, albeit sometimes not in Chile, is replaced by the identical third person plural forms (for the verb *hacer* ("do"), the peninsular form would be *hacéis* instead of *hacen*), and the personal pronoun *vos* ("you"), which is rarely used in Chile, and not used in Spain. To sum up, the test subjects generally relied on lexical cues on the surface, and were therefore bound to miss non-obvious information captured by the character $n$-gram model.

Since the test subjects also stated that some tweets were impossible to assign to a country because they contained only URLs, emoticons, or similar, in Table 10 we show a reevaluation of a second version of the two shuffled concatenated samples in which we remove all tweets which contain only emoticons, URLs, or numbers; tweets which are entirely written in a language other than Spanish; and tweets which are only two or one words long (i.e., tweets with zero or one spaces). For the AR-ES data, we remove 23 Spanish and 10 Argentinian tweets, while for the AR-CL data, we remove 10 Argentinian and 14 Chilean tweets.

As for the human classification on the AR/ES data, the results for Spain do not change much. For Argentina, there is an increase in performance (2 to 3 points). On the AR/CL data, there is a slight improvement on all sets except for the Chilean data classified.

As for the automatic classification, the filtering gives better result on all data sets. However,

| | training | dev | test |
|---|---|---|---|
| AR | 57,546 (71.9%) | 7,174 | 7,196 |
| CO | 58,068 (72.6%) | 7,249 | 7,289 |
| MX | 48,527 (60.7%) | 6,117 | 6,061 |
| ES | 53,199 (66.5%) | 6,699 | 6,657 |
| CL | 56,865 (71.1%) | 6,998 | 7,071 |

Table 11: Data sizes (filtered by `langid.py`)

| class | precision | recall | $F_1$ |
|---|---|---|---|
| AR | 70.32 | 66.09 | 68.14 |
| CO | 63.76 | 62.22 | 62.98 |
| MX | 61.52 | 61.11 | 61.31 |
| ES | 69.13 | 69.20 | 69.17 |
| CL | 67.12 | 73.29 | 70.07 |
| *overall* | 66.45 | 66.45 | 66.45 |

Table 12: Results: Filtered by `langid.py`

the difference between the $F_1$ of the filtered and unfiltered data is larger on the AR/CL data set. This can be explained with the fact that among the tweets removed from the AR/ES data set, there were more longer tweets (not written in Spanish) than among the tweets removed from the CL/AR data set, the longer tweets being easier to identify. Note that the filtering of tweets does not cause much change in the difference between human and automatic classification.

## 6 Language Filtering

As mentioned before, our data has not been cleaned up or normalized. In particular, the data set contains tweets written in languages other than Spanish. We have reasoned that those can be seen as belonging to the "natural" language production of a country. However, in order to see what impact they have on our classification results, we perform an additional experiment on a version of the data were we only include the tweets that the state-of-the-art language identifier `langid.py` labels Spanish (Lui and Baldwin, 2012).[6] Table 11 shows the sizes of all data sets after filtering. Note that many of the excluded tweets are in fact written in Spanish, but are very noisy, due to orthography, Twitter hash tags, etc. The next most frequent labels across all tweets is English (9%). Note that in the data from Spain, 2% of the tweets are labeled as Catalan, 1.2% as Galician, and only 0.3% as Basque.

Table 12 finally shows the classification results for character 6-gram language models without pruning.

The changes in $F_1$ are minor, i.e., below one point, except for the Mexican tweets, which lose around 4 points. The previous experiments have already indicated that the Mexican data set is the most heterogeneous one which also resulted in the largest number of tweets being filtered out. In general, we see that the character $n$-gram method seems to be relatively stable with respect to a different number of non-Spanish tweets in the data. More insight could be obtained by performing experiments with advanced methods of tweet normalization, such as those of Han and Baldwin (2011). We leave this for future work.

[6] `https://github.com/saffsd/langid.py.`

## 7 Discussion

Human classification of language varieties was judged by our test subjects to be considerably more difficult that differentiating between languages. Additionally, the test subjects were only able to differentiate between two classes. While the automatic classification results lie below the results which one would expect for language identification, $n$-gram classification still achieves good performance.

Our experiments touch on the more general question of how a language variety is defined. In order to take advantage of the metadata provided by Twitter, we had to restrict the classification problem to identifying varieties associated with countries were tweets were sent. In reality, the boundaries between variants are often blurred, and there can also be variance within the same country (e.g., the Spanish spoken in the southern Spanish region of Andalusia is different from that of Asturias, even if they both share features common to Peninsular Spanish and larger differences with American Spanish). However, it would be difficult to obtain a reliable corpus with this kind of fine-grained distinctions.

It is also worth noting that not all the classification criteria used by the human test subjects were purely linguistic – for example, a subject could guess a tweet as being from Chile by recognizing a mention to a Chilean city, public figure or TV show. Note that this factor intuitively seems to benefit humans – who have a wealth of knowledge about entities, events and trending topics from their country – over the automatic system. In spite of this, automatic classification still vastly outperformed human classification, suggesting that the language models are capturing linguistic patterns that are not obvious to humans.

## 8 Conclusion

We have studied different approaches to the task of classifying tweets from Spanish-speaking countries according to the country from which they were sent. To the best of our knowledge, these are the first results for this problem. On the problem of assigning one of five classes (Argentina, Mexico, Chile, Colombia, Spain) to 10,000 tweets, the best performance, an overall F-score of 67.72, was obtained with a voting meta-classifier approach that recombines the results for four single classifiers, the 6-gram (66.96 $F_1$) and 5-gram (66.75 $F_1$) character-based language models, and the 4-gram (57.87 $F_1$) and 3-gram (57.24 $F_1$) syllable-based language models. For a simplified version of the problem that only required a decision between two classes (Argentina vs. Chile and Spain vs. Argentina), given a sample of 150 tweets from each class, human classification was outperformed by automatic classification by up to 31 points.

In future work, we want to investigate the effect of tweet normalization on our problem, and furthermore, how the techniques we have used can be applied to classify text from other social media sources, such as Facebook.

## Acknowledgements

The first author has been funded by Deutsche Forschungsgemeinschaft (DFG). The second author has been partially funded by Ministerio de Economía y Competitividad/FEDER (Grant TIN2010-18552-C03-02) and by Xunta de Galicia (Grant CN2012/008).

## References

Manuel Alvar, editor. 1996a. *Manual de dialectología hispánica. El español de América.* Ariel, Barcelona.

Manuel Alvar, editor. 1996b. *Manual de dialectología hispánica. El español de España.* Ariel, Barcelona.

Timothy Baldwin and Marco Lui. 2010. Language identification: The long and the short of the matter. In *Human Language Technologies: The 2010 Annual Conference of the North American Chapter of the Association for Computational Linguistics*, pages 229–237, Los Angeles, CA.

Dario Benedetto, Emanuele Caglioti, and Vittorio Loreto. 2002. Language trees and zipping. *Physical Review Letters*, 88(4).

Shane Bergsma, Paul McNamee, Mossaab Bagdouri, Clayton Fink, and Theresa Wilson. 2012. Language identification for creating language-specific twitter collections. In *Proceedings of the Second Workshop on Language in Social Media*, LSM '12, pages 65–74, Stroudsburg, PA, USA. Association for Computational Linguistics.

Ralph D. Brown. 2013. Selecting and weighting n-grams to identify 1100 languages. In Springer, editor, *Proceedings of the 16th International Conference on Text, Speech, and Dialogue*, volume 8082 of *LNCS*, pages 475–483, Pilsen, Czech Republic.

Brian O. Bush. 2014. Language identication of tweets using LZW compression. In *3rd Pacific Northwest Regional NLP Workshop: NW-NLP 2014*, Redmond, WA.

Simon Carter, Wouter Weerkamp, and Manos Tsagkias. 2013. Microblog language identification: overcoming the limitations of short, unedited and idiomatic text. *Language Resources and Evaluation*, 47(1):195–215.

William B. Cavnar and John M. Trenkle. 1994. N-gram-based text categorization. In *In Proceedings of SDAIR-94, 3rd Annual Symposium on Document Analysis and Information Retrieval*, pages 161–175, Las Vegas, NV.

Leon Derczynski, Alan Ritter, Sam Clark, and Kalina Bontcheva. 2013. Twitter part-of-speech tagging for all: Overcoming sparse and noisy data. In *Proceedings of the International Conference on Recent Advances in Natural Language Processing*, pages 198–206. Association for Computational Linguistics.

Ted Dunning. 1994. Statistical identification of language. Technical Report MCCS-94-273, Computing Research Lab, New Mexico State University.

Binod Gyawali, Gabriela Ramirez, and Thamar Solorio. 2013. Native language identification: a simple n-gram based approach. In *Proceedings of the Eighth Workshop on Innovative Use of NLP for Building Educational Applications*, pages 224–231, Atlanta, Georgia, June. Association for Computational Linguistics.

Bo Han and Timothy Baldwin. 2011. Lexical normalisation of short text messages: Makn sens a #twitter. In *Proceedings of the 49th Annual Meeting of the Association for Computational Linguistics: Human Language Technologies*, pages 368–378, Portland, Oregon, USA, June. Association for Computational Linguistics.

Zenón Hernández-Figeroa, Gustavo Rodríguez-Rodríguez, and Francisco J. Carreras-Riudavets. 2012. Separador de sílabas del español - silabeador TIP. Available at http://tip.dis.ulpgc.es.

Zenón Hernández-Figueroa, Francisco J. Carreras-Riudavets, and Gustavo Rodríguez-Rodríguez. 2013. Automatic syllabification for Spanish using lemmatization and derivation to solve the prefix's prominence issue. *Expert Syst. Appl.*, 40(17):7122–7131.

Vlado Kešelj, Fuchun Peng, Nick Cercone, and Calvin Thomas. 2003. N-gram-based author profiles for authorship attribution. In *Proceedings of PACLING*, pages 255–264.

M. Paul Lewis, Gary F. Simons, and Charles D. Fennig, editors. 2014. *Ethnologue: Languages of the World*. SIL International, Dallas, Texas, seventeenth edition edition. Online version: http://www.ethnologue.com.

John M. Lipski. 1994. *Latin American Spanish*. Longman, London.

Marco Lui and Timothy Baldwin. 2012. langid.py: An off-the-shelf language identification tool. In *Proceedings of the ACL 2012 System Demonstrations*, pages 25–30, Jeju Island, Korea, July. Association for Computational Linguistics.

Marco Lui and Timothy Baldwin. 2014. Accurate language identification of twitter messages. In *Proceedings of the 5th Workshop on Language Analysis for Social Media (LASM)*, pages 17–25, Gothenburg, Sweden.

Marco Lui and Paul Cook. 2013. Classifying english documents by national dialect. In *Proceedings of the Australasian Language Technology Association Workshop 2013 (ALTA 2013)*, pages 5–15, Brisbane, Australia, December.

Douglas W. Muir and Timothy R. Thomas. 2000. Automatic language identification by stroke geometry analysis, May 16. US Patent 6,064,767.

Miguel Ángel Quesada Pacheco. 2002. *El Español de América*. Editorial Tecnológica de Costa Rica, Cartago, 2a edition.

Vesa Siivola, Teemu Hirsimäki, and Sami Virpioja. 2007. On growing and pruning kneserney smoothed n-gram models. *IEEE Transactions on Speech, Audio and Language Processing*, 15(5):1617–1624.

William J. Teahan. 2000. Text classification and segmentation using minimum cross-entropy. In *Proceedings of RIAO'00*, pages 943–961.

Tommi Vatanen, Jaakko J. Vyrynen, and Sami Virpioja. 2010. Language identification of short text segments with n-gram models. In *Proceedings of the Seventh International Conference on Language Resources and Evaluation (LREC'10)*, Valletta, Malta. European Language Resources Association (ELRA).

David Vilares, Miguel A. Alonso, and Carlos Gómez-Rodríguez. 2013. Supervised polarity classification of spanish tweets based on linguistic knowledge. In *Proceedings of 13th ACM Symposium on Document Engineering (DocEng 2013)*, pages 169–172, Florence, Italy.

David Vilares, Miguel A. Alonso, and Carlos Gómez-Rodríguez. 2014. A syntactic approach for opinion mining on Spanish reviews. *Natural Language Engineering*, FirstView:1–25, 6.

Radim Řehůřek and Milan Kolkus. 2009. Language identification on the web: Extending the dictionary method. In *Proceedings of CICLing*, pages 357–368.

Terry A. Welch. 1984. A technique for high-performance data compression. *Computer*, 17(6):8–19, June.

Marcos Zampieri, Binyam Gebrekidan Gebre, and Sascha Diwersy. 2013. N-gram language models and pos distribution for the identification of spanish varieties. In *Proceedings of TALN2013*, pages 580–587.

Marcos Zampieri, Liling Tan, Nikola Ljubešić, and Jörg Tiedemann. 2014. A report on the dsl shared task 2014. In *Proceedings of the First Workshop on Applying NLP Tools to Similar Languages, Varieties and Dialects*, pages 58–67, Dublin, Ireland, August. Association for Computational Linguistics and Dublin City University.

# Exploiting Language Variants Via Grammar Parsing Having Morphologically Rich Information

**Qaiser Abbas**
Fachbereich Sprachwissenschaft
Universität Konstanz
78457 Konstanz, Germany
qaiser.abbas@uni-konstanz.de

**Abstract**

In this paper, the development and evaluation of the Urdu parser is presented along with the comparison of existing resources for the language variants Urdu/Hindi. This parser was given a linguistically rich grammar extracted from a treebank. This context free grammar with sufficient encoded information is comparable with the state of the art parsing requirements for morphologically rich and closely related language variants Urdu/Hindi. The extended parsing model and the linguistically rich grammar together provide us promising parsing results for both the language variants. The parser gives 87% of f-score, which outperforms the multi-path shift-reduce parser for Urdu and a simple Hindi dependency parser with 4.8% and 22% increase in recall, respectively.

## 1 Introduction

An Urdu invariant of Hindavi came into existence during the muslim rule from 1206 AD to 1858 AD (Khan, 2006). They used Persian/Urdu script for Urdu in contrast to the Devanagari script for Hindavi. The informal versions of the two language variants are quite similar, in fact so similar that they can really be called dialects of a same language. Loose examples would be how a Spanish speaker could comprehend Portuguese or Swedish speaker could comprehend Norwegian. However the formal version of the two languages will be much more different as Urdu vocabulary is influenced heavily from Persian, Arabic and Turkish whilst the emphasis in Hindi is on Sanskrit. Urdu became a literary language after existence of an increasing number of literature during the 18th and the 19th century (McLane, 1970). Urdu/Hindi is the national language of Pakistan and an official language in India. According to a report by the SIL Ethnologue (Lewis, 2013), Urdu/Hindi has 456.2 million speakers in the whole world.

Getting state of the art parsing results for morphologically rich languages (MRLs) is a challenge to date. According to Tsarfaty et al. (2010; 2013), without proper handling of morphological entities in the sentences, promising results for MRLs can not be achieved. Complex morphosyntactic interactions may impose constraints, which lead to explicit encoding of such information. The best broad coverage and robust parsers to date have grammars extracted from treebanks and the depth of information encoded in an annotation correlates with the parsing performance (Tsarfaty et al., 2013).

To fulfill the encoding of information in an annotation, a treebank for Urdu known as the URDU.KON-TB treebank with sufficient encoded information at morphological, POS, syntactic and functional level was constructed (Abbas, 2012). Its annotation was found reliable according to the Krippendorffs $\alpha$ values achieved in (Abbas, 2014) but its reliability or the suitability for machine learning (ML) can be evaluated with the development of an Urdu parser presented in Section 3. A context free grammar (CFG) is extracted from the URDU.KON-TB treebank computationally. The development procedure and the depth of encoded information in the grammar is presented in Section 2. The grammar is then given to an extended dynamic programming parsing model known as the Earley parsing algorithm (Earley, 1970). The extended parsing model for Urdu is then called as the Urdu parser and given in Section 3. This algorithm is language independent and is capable to parse the MRLs like the CKY (Cocke-Kasami-Younger) parsing algorithm as advocated in (Tsarfaty et al., 2013) and (Abbas et al., 2009). Issues faced during the parsing are discussed in Section 4. By applying a rich grammar along with the ex-



*Language Technology for Closely Related Languages and Language Variants (LT4CloseLang)*, pages 36–46,
October 29, 2014, Doha, Qatar. 

tended parsing model, promising results obtained are discussed in Section 5. Conclusions along with the future directions are presented in Section 6. Similarly, the related work of language variants is described in Section 1.1, which set a path towards the construction of the Urdu parser.

### 1.1 Related Work

In the Urdu ParGram project (Butt and King, 2007), the XLE[1] parser is in use. The encoding of LFG grammar in XLE interface is not a simple task. Such a grammar can be encoded only by those persons who have expertise in theoretical linguistics as well. The team of the ParGram project has made a tremendous effort in this regard. This project of Urdu LFG grammar development is still in progress and the parser evaluation results are not available yet. Similarly, the parser for evaluation of the NU-FAST treebank (Abbas et al., 2009) used a built in utility available in the inference engine of the Prolog to parse the Urdu sentences. This utility can only be used if you have a definite clause grammar (DCG) or probabilistic definite clause grammar (PDCG). In this work, a parser was not designed but a built-in prolog parser was used, due to which it was not considered to be the candidate for comparison.

A simple dependency parser for Hindi was developed by Bharati et al. (2009). The parser used a grammar oriented approach, which was designed on the basis of Paninian grammatical model (Begum et al., 2008; Bharati et al., 1995). The annotation scheme was designed on the basis of chunks, intra-chunks and karakas[2]. This scheme (Begum et al., 2008) of dependency structure (DS) is different from the annotation scheme (Abbas, 2012; Abbas, 2014) of phrase structure (PS) and the hyper dependency structure (HDS) of the URDU.KON-TB treebank along with the different data sets used. As compared to phrase/constituent structure, the dependency structure lacks in information at non-terminal nodes (Bharati et al., 2008) and often the information at POS level. This information can also be provided at dependency annotation but people are stick to the standard norms. The Hindi treebank is rich in functional information as compared to morphological, POS and syntactical information. Due to differences in the designs of the simple dependency parser for Hindi and the Urdu parser, only performance results are compared and presented in Section 5.

Ali and Hussain used the MaltParser with its default settings in Urdu dependency parser (Ali and Hussain, 2010). When somebody performs experiments with MaltParser with its default settings then such evaluation results are advised not to be compared according to MaltParser license.[3] The same exercise for parsing Hindi was performed in (Agrawal et al., 2013), but it was clearly mentioned in the work that MaltParser was used for error detection in the annotation of Hindi/Urdu treebank (HUTB).[4] Similarly, the Urdu sentences were parsed in (Bhat et al., 2012b) using the same MaltParser. The experiments were performed to identify the parsing issues of Urdu and a development of parser was not claimed. Moreover, these data-driven systems are highly criticized on a given set of annotated corpus because they are not able to observe all morphological variants of a word form from it (Tsarfaty et al., 2013).

A multi-path shift-reduce parsing algorithm was proposed in (Jiang et al., 2009) for Chinese. Later on, this algorithm was used for Urdu parsing by Mukhtar et al. (2012b). A probabilistic context free grammar (PCFG) developed in (Mukhtar et al., 2011) was given to the multi-path shift-reduce Urdu parsing model. A multi-path shift-reduce parser for Urdu has some limitations. It takes a POS tagged sentence as input and is not able to parse sentences without the POS tagging. The stack used has a fixed memory size, which is not reliable and it can overflow during the parsing of long sentences. A PCFG used in this parsing model is ambiguous (Mukhtar et al., 2012a). Both the fixed memory size and the ambiguous grammar can resist the parsing of long sentences,thats why the parser could not parse the sentences with length more than 10 words (Mukhtar et al., 2012b). In this work, the results were not evaluated properly by using some measure e.g. PARSEVAL. A number of 74 sentences having length not more than 10 words were parsed successfully from 100 sentences, which were then quoted as a 74% of accuracy. The raw corpus used in the development of this parser is partially the same as compared to the Urdu parser (Section 3). A comparative study made is detailed in Section 5.

[1] http://www2.parc.com/isl/groups/nltt/xle/

[2] Karakas are the syntactico-semantic relations between the verbs and other related constituents in a sentence (Bharati et al., 1996)

[3] http://www.maltparser.org/

[4] http://faculty.washington.edu/fxia/treebank/

| | | |
|---|---|---|
| V (Verb) | | |
| | . COP (Copula verb) | |
| | | . IMPERF (Imperfective copula verb) |
| | | . PERF (Perfective copula verb) |
| | | . ROOT (Root of copula verb) |
| | | . SUBTV (Subjunctive form of copula verb) |
| | | . PAST (Past tense of copula verb) |
| | | . PRES (Present tense of copula verb) |
| | . IMPERF (Imperfective verb) | |
| | | . REP (Repetition of Imperfective form of verb) |
| | . INF (Infinitive form verb) | |
| | . LIGHT (Light verb) | |
| | | . IMPERF (Imperfective form of light verb) |
| | | . INF (Infinitive form of light verb) |
| | | . PERF (Perfective form of light verb) |
| | | . PROG (Progressive form of light verb) |
| | | . ROOT (Root form of light verb) |
| | | . SUBTV (Subjunctive form of light verb) |
| | | . PAST (Past tense of light verb) |
| | | . PRES (Present tense of light verb) |
| | . LIGHTV (Light verb with verb) | |
| | | . IMPERF (Imperfective light verb with verb) |
| | | . INF (Infinitive light verb with verb) |
| | | . PERF (Perfective light verb with verb) |
| | | . ROOT (Root light verb with verb) |
| | | . SUBTV (Subjunctive light verb with verb) |
| | . MOD (Modal verb) | |
| | | . IMPERF (Imperfective modal verb) |
| | | . PERF (Perfective modal verb) |
| | | . SUBTV (Subjunctive modal verb) |
| | . PERF (Perfective form of verb) | |
| | | . REP (Repetition of perfective form of verb) |
| | . ROOT (Root form of verb) | |
| | | . REP (Repetition of root form of verb) |
| | . SUBTV (Subjunctive form of verb) | |
| | . PAST (Past tense of verb) | |
| | . PRES (Present tense of verb) | |

Figure 1: A verb V example from the URDU.KON-TB treebank

## 2 Setup

The URDU.KON-TB treebank having phrase structure (PS) and the hyper dependency structure (HDS) annotation with rich encoded information (Abbas, 2012; Abbas, 2014) is used for the training of the Urdu parser discussed in Section 3. The treebank has a semi-semantic POS (SSP) tag set, a semi-semantic syntactic (SSS) tag set and a functional (F) tag set. The morphological information in the labeling of the parsers lexicon can be explained by discussing the POS tag set of the URDU.KON-TB treebank.

The SSP tag set hierarchy has 22 main tag categories which are divided into sub-categories based on morphology and semantics. In Figure 1, an example of only a verb V is given. A dot '.' symbol is used for the representation of morphology and semantics at POS level. In Figure 1, the hierarchy of tag labels for verb V is divided into three levels of depth. The first level contains only one label to distinguish a verb V from other POS labels. The second level contains 11 subcategories of V to represent different morphological or functional forms e.g. V.COP (V as a copula verb (Abbas and Raza, 2014)), V.IMPERF (V has an imperfective form (Butt and Rizvi, 2010; Butt and Ramchand, 2001)), V.INF (V has an infinitive form (Butt, 1993; Abbas and Nabi Khan, 2009)), etc. The third level contains further 25 subcategories to represent the morphological information in depth e.g. V.COP.IMPERF (copula verb has an imperfective form), V.COP.PERF (copula verb has a perfective form), V.COP.ROOT (copula verb has a ROOT form), V.COP.PAST (copula verb has a past tense), V.LIGHT.PAST (light verb has a past tense (Butt and Rizvi, 2010; Butt, 2003)), etc. These types of combinations are also possible in case of an auxiliary verb as described in (Abbas, 2014). This short discussion is about the idea of morphological and functional information encoded at POS level. This lexical information can be passed up to the syntactical level because the lexical items have some relationship with other lexical items in a sentence. The detail of syntactic (SSS) and functional (F) tag sets can be seen in (Abbas, 2012).

A stack based extraction Algorithm 1 was designed to extract a context free grammar (CFG) from the URDU.KON-TB treebank. The CFG obtained is then given to the Urdu parser (Section 3) for sentence parsing.

## 3 Urdu Parser

The URDU.KON-TB treebank is a manually annotated set of 1400 parsed sentences, which were then recorded in a text file on a computer in the form of 1400 bracketed sentences. Initial twenty bracketed-sentences from each hundred were separated in another text file, whose total 280 sentences were then used for the development of a test suite. The test suite was further divided into two halves representing test data and held out data resulting in 140 sentences in each half.

The held out data was used in the development of the Urdu parser, while the test data was used for the evaluation of results after the completion of the Urdu parser. From the first residual text file with 1120 bracketed sentences, a context free grammar (CFG) was extracted using a stack based extraction module given in Algorithm 1. The CFG was then processed by the Urdu parser to produce a grammar database with unique productions. During this process, production type (TYPE) labeling as lexical (L) and non-lexical (NL) at the end of each production was done. The productions having only the lexical items at their right hand side (RHS) were labelled as L and the productions containing non-lexical items on their RHS only were labelled as NL. The purpose of this labeling is to provide an already processed mechanism, through which the Urdu parser can identify a production type L or NL speedily without checking it thoroughly.

**Algorithm 1** A CFG extraction algorithm

```
Input: A input and an empty output file
(Sentence, Top, Counter) ← 0
Read: InputString
while InputString ≠ Input.EOF() do                    ▷ Loop until end of file
    if InputString = $ then
        Print: ++Sentence
        Read: InputString                              ▷ Read a string from an input file
        Write: \n \n                                   ▷ Writing two newlines in output file
        (Stack[0], StrArray[0]) ← ∅                    ▷ Initializing stack and array
        (Top, Counter) ← 0                             ▷ Initializing stack and array variables
    end if
    if InputString ≠ ")" then
        Stack[Top] ← InputString; Top++
    else                                               ▷ When ')' comes
        Top−−
        while Stack[Top] ≠ "(" do
            StrArray[Counter] = Stack[Top]
            Stack[Top] = ∅; Counter++; Top−−
        end while
        Counter−−
        Stack[Top] = StrArray[Counter]
        Top++ and Check = Counter
        while Counter ≥ 0 do
            if Counter = Check then
                Write: StrArray[Counter] →; StrArray[Counter] = ∅
            else
                Write: StrArray[Counter] + ""; StrArray[Counter] = ∅
            end if
            Counter−−
        end while
        Write: \n; Counter = 0                         ▷ In output file
    end if
    Read: InputString                                  ▷ Read a string from an input file
end while
Output: An output file having complete CFG productions for each sentence
```

Without handling the issues discussed in Section 4, the Earley's algorithm simply was not able to provide the state of the art evaluation results for Urdu. These issues caused the parsing discontinuities, due to which extensions are made on the basic algorithm. The extended version of the Urdu parser is depicted in Algorithm 2. The grammar database of the Urdu parser has three fields in the form of a left hand side (LHS), a RHS and a TYPE. After taking a sentence as input, variables are initialized along with a starting value of the chart as `ROOT @ S`. In place of a dot symbol '•' used in the Earley algorithm, here an '@' symbol is used because the dot symbol is extensively used in the hierarchal annotation of the URDU.KON-TB treebank, from which the grammar productions are extracted. The working of the algorithm is similar to the Earley's algorithm except the modifications in the `PREDICTOR()`, `SCANNER()` and a `COMPLETER()` presented in Sections 4.1, 4.2 and 4.7, respectively. Besides these some additional functions are introduced like an `EDITOR()` for an automatic editing of discontinuous parses, a `BUILDER()` for building the parse trees and a `BACKPOINTER()` for calculating the back-pointers.

**Algorithm 2** Urdu Parser

```
function URDU-PARSER(grammar)
    Input: Sentence                                    ▷ reading a sentence
    (id, fi, fj, fid) ← 0
    chart[0].add("id", "ROOT @ S", "0,0", " ", "Seed")
    for i ← 0 to LENGTH(sentence[]) do
        scannerFlag ← false, id ← 1
        Print: chart[i] → (StateId, Rule, @Position, BackPointer, Operation)
        for j ← 0 to ChartSize[i] do                   ▷ Loop for chart entries
            currentRule ← chart[i].getRule(j).split(" ")
            (tempString, index) ←(string-after-@, @Position) in currentRule
            if tempString = " " then
                call COMPLETER()                       ▷ calling completer procedure
            else
                rs ← All grammar rules with LHS = tempString
                if rs.next() ≠ false then              ▷ checking rs is not empty
                    call PREDICTOR()                   ▷ calling predictor procedure
                else
                    call SCANNER()
                end if
            end if
            if scannerFlag=false & j+1=chartSize[i] & i ≠LENGTH(sentence[]) then
                call EDITOR()
            end if
        end for
    end for
    call BUILDER()
end function
```

During processing of `COMPLETER()`, `PREDICTOR()` and `SCANNER()`, some sort of parsing discontinuities can happen. To check these types of phenomena, an `EDITOR()` will come into an action and it will remove all the faulty states and the charts causing discontinuity up to a right choice of parsing as discussed in Section 4.6. At the end of external loop, the generated parsed-solutions have been stored in the form of the charts with entries, but not in the form of parsed trees. To represent parsed solutions in the form of bracketed parsed trees, a `BUILDER()` function will be executed, which will construct the parsed trees of solutions by manipulating the back-pointers calculated in the `COMPLETER()` function. The `BUILDER()` is able to display all parsed solutions of a given sentence as discussed in Section 4.4 and then the Algorithm 2 for the Urdu parser is exited with the complete generation of charts and bracketed parsed trees. The algorithms called by the Urdu parser are discussed briefly in Section 4 along with their issues.

## 4 Issues Analysis and Their Evaluation Through Extensions

### 4.1 Eliminating L Type Useless Predictions

Earley's Predictor() adds useless productions in charts which causes the Urdu parser to end up with a discontinuous parse for a given sentence. Suppose, the current token to be parsed in an input sentence is a proper noun خان 'Khan' and there is a NL type production NP → @ N.PROP N.PROP residing in the current chart of the parser, where N.PROP is the tag for proper noun. The '@' symbol before a non-terminal on the RHS of the production is the case of predictor and the non-extended `PREDICTOR()` adds all the available L type productions of N.PROP into the chart from the grammar, even they are not required. Only the relevant production N.PROP → @ خان has to be added in the chart. This addition of irrelevant/useless productions is also true for other lexical items e.g. adjectives, personal pronouns, case markers, etc. These useless additions cause the wastage of time and increase the chance of misleading direction towards a discontinuous parse. To resolve this issue, the `PREDICTOR()` of the existing Earley's Algorithm is modified in the Urdu parser as follows.

When the main parsing Algorithm 2 calls the extended `PREDICTOR()` then it checks the type of production either as NL or L in contrast of the Earley algorithm. The handling of NL type productions is same but in dealing of L type of productions, the `PREDICTOR()` is introduced with another condition, which enforces the predictor to add only the relevant productions into the respective charts. It matches the token at the RHS of the predicted-production with the current token in an input sentence. This condition eliminates the limited possibility of misleading direction towards the discontinuous state. The wastage-time factor is reduced to $O(n)$ after the removal of irrelevant matching, where $n$ is the number of tokens in an input sentence.

### 4.2 Irrelevant POS Selection

In the Earley's parsing algorithm, the `Scanner()` only matches the RHS of the L type production with the current token in a given sentence and causes a selection of L type production with the wrong POS. For example, the verb ہے 'is' has different tags in the grammar. It can act as an auxiliary in a sentence with present tense e.g. VAUX.PRES → ہے. It can behave as a copula verb e.g. V.COP.PRES → ہے and it can also act as a main verb e.g. V.PRES → ہے. This concept of having more than one tag is true for other lexical items. So, if this L type production VAUX.PRES → @ ہے is existed in a current chart as right candidate then the `Scanner()` of the Earley algorithm can select other available productions from the grammar due to a check on the RHS only. This can cause the wrong solution or a discontinuous state during the parsing. To remove this issue, the `Scanner()` is extended in the same way as was done with the `PREDICTOR()` in Section 4.1. At this level, this solution solves the issue described below, but it is completed in Section 4.6.

When the `SCANNER()` is called, it extracts a relevant L type production from the grammar after matching the LHS and the RHS completely. It adds only the true L type production in a new chart after checking three additional conditions. At first, it checks that the chart number is not exceeding the length of a sentence. At second, it checks that the token in the current processing L type production is equal to the current token in a given sentence. After that if the `scannerFlag` is false, then the new entry of the matched L type production is added into the new chart. During this process, the `scannerFlag` is set to a true value along with a record of some variables `fi`, `fj`, and `fid`, which will be used in the `EDITOR()` discussed in Section 4.6. By introducing this modification, the possibility of wrong selection of the production from the grammar is abandoned. An issue related to this problem is still remained, which is addressed and resolved in Section 4.6.

### 4.3 Back-Pointers Calculation

Earley parsing algorithm is a generator or a recognizer and hence can not produce the parse trees or the bracketed trees. To produce the parse trees or the bracketed trees, an unimplemented idea of back-pointers by Earley (1968) is implemented and presented in Algorithm 3. To understand the calculation of the back pointers, a sentence given in example 1 is parsed from the Urdu parser. The charts generated through the Urdu parser are depicted in Figure 2. Only the relevant states are displayed as can be inferred from the non-sequential values of the STATEID column. The column DOT-POSITION is basically the position of '@' in productions.

**Algorithm 3** Back Pointer

```
function BACKPOINTER(previousRule, dummy@Position, i, chartSize, chart)
    backPointer ← ""
    tempIndex ← previousRule.indexOf("@")
    tempIndex ← tempIndex-1                              ▷ subtracting index
    NT ← previousRule.get(tempIndex)
    k ← dummy@Position[0]
    for l ← i to k step -1 do                ▷ loop for backward backpointers
        if tempIndex > 0 then
            for m ← 0 to chartSize[l]-1 do
                pString ← chart[l].getRule(m).split(" ")
                cRule.add(pString[])         ▷ store pString in cRule
                tIndex ← cRule.indexOf("@")
                if (NT = cRule[0]) & (tIndex+1 = SIZE(cRule)) then
                    backPointer ← (l + "-" + chart[l].getStateId(m) +" "+backPointer)
                    dummy@P = chart[l].get@Position(m).split(",")   ▷ getting '@' position
                    l ← dummy@P[0]           ▷ updating loop counter l
                    l ← l + 1
                    tempIndex ← tempIndex-1
                    NT ← previousRule[tempIndex]
                    break
                else
                    cRule.clear()
                end if
            end for
        else
            break
        end if
    end for
end function
```

**Algorithm 4** Builder

```
function BUILDER(Sentence[], chartSize[], chart[])
    num=0, chartN = LENGTH(Sentence[])
    for count ← chartSize[LENGTH(Sentence[]]-1 to 0 step -1 do
        dummystr ←"S" and rule ← chart[chartN].getRule(count).split(" ")
        if rule[0] = dummystr then
            num = num + 1
            bp.add(chartN+"-"+chart[chartN].getStateId(count))
        end if
    end for
    tree[] ← new BTree[num]
    for i ← 0 to SIZE(bp)-1 do
        tree[i].build(bp.get(i), chart)      ▷ building tree with pointers
    end for
    for i ←0 to SIZE(bp)-1 do
        tree[i].prepare(chart)
    end for
    for i ←0 to SIZE(bp)-1 do                ▷ loop for displaying all parsed trees
        bracketedSentenceLength ← tree[i].getSize() and left ← 0
        if bracketedSentenceLength > 0 then
            Print : Bracketed Parse Tree "+(i+1)+" of "+SIZE(bp)+"
            for j ←0 to bracketedSentenceLength-1 do
                if tree[i].getString(j) = "(" then
                    left = left + 1 and Print : newline
                    for tab ←0 to left-1 do
                        Print : eight spaces
                    end for
                    Print : tree[i].getString(j)
                else if tree[i].getString(j) = ")" then
                    left = left − 1 and Print : tree[i].getString(j)
                else
                    Print : space+tree[i].getString(j)+space
                end if
            end for
        end if
    end for
end function
```

(1) ان کا ذکر بھی یہاں ضروری ہے

| | | | | |
|---|---|---|---|---|
| *un* | *kA* | *zikr* | *bHI* | *yahAN* |
| their/P.PERS | of/CM | reference/N | also/PT.INTF | here/ADV.SPT |
| *zarUrI* | *hE* | | | |
| essential/ADJ.MNR | is/V.COP.PRES | | | |

'Their reference is also essential here'

The `COMPLETER()` calls the Algorithm 3 of `BACKPOINTER()` to calculate the values of the back-pointers. For example, during the processing of a production KP.POSS P.PERS @ CM at `STATEID` 3 in chart 1 of Figure 2, a processed non-terminal P.PERS before the '@' in the RHS of the production is located in the chart 1 at $0^{th}$ position. The located "1-0" value of the `backPointer` is then displayed by the `COMPLETER()` in the same state of the chart. The rest of the back pointers are calculated in the same way. These back-pointers are further used in building the bracketed parse trees discussed in Sections 4.4 and 4.7.

## 4.4 Building Bracketed Parse Trees

The possible bracketed parse trees are evaluated and displayed by the `BUILDER()` function displayed in Algorithm 4. Both the `BUILDER()` and the `BACKPOINTER()` contribute to shift our Algorithm 2 from a generator to a parser in contrast of the Earley's algorithm. After displaying chart entries in Figure 2 for a sentence given in example 1, the Urdu parser calls the `BUILDER()`. At first, it locates all the solution productions from the last chart and stores their back-pointers in a list e.g. "8-1" value for the solution production ROOT S @ in the last chart of Figure 2. A user defined method `build()` is called then. This method builds an unformatted intermediate bracketed parse tree with the interlinked back-pointers from the chart states and reveals the leaf nodes only as ( 8-1 ( 4-1 ( 2-2 ( 1-0 ان ) ( 2-0 کا ) ) ( 3-0 ذکر ) ( 4-0 بھی ) ) ( 5-1 ( 5-0 یہاں ) ) ( 6-1 ( 6-0 ضروری ) ) ( 7-1 ( 7-0 ہے ) ) ( 8-0 . ) ). This intermediate parse tree can be understood well by looking at the given back-pointers in the respective chart states.

Another user defined method `prepare()` prepares the intermediate parse tree into a complete unformatted parse tree as ( S ( NP.NOM-SUB ( KP.POSS ( P.PERS ان ) ( CM کا ) ) ( N ذکر ) ( PT.INTF بھی ) ) ( ADVP-SPT-MODF ( ADV.SPT یہاں ) ) ( ADJP-MNR-

| STATEID | RULE | DOT-POSITON | BACK-POINTER | OPERATION |
|---|---|---|---|---|
| | **CHART(0)** | | | |
| 0 | ROOT @ S | 0,0 | | Seed |
| 2 | S @ NP.NOM-SUB ADVP-SPT-MODF ADJP-MNR-PLINK VCMAIN M.S | 0,0 | | Predictor |
| 52 | NP.NOM-SUB @ KP.POSS N PT.INTF | 0,0 | | Predictor |
| 113 | KP.POSS @ P.PERS CM | 0,0 | | Predictor |
| 148 | P.PERS @ ان | 0,0 | | Predictor |
| | **CHART(1)=ان** | | | |
| STATEID | RULE | DOT-POSITON | BACK-POINTER | OPERATION |
| 0 | P.PERS ان @ | 0,1 | | Scanner |
| 3 | KP.POSS P.PERS @ CM | 0,1 | 1-0 | Completer |
| 4 | CM @ کا | 1,1 | | Predictor |
| | **CHART(2)=کا** | | | |
| STATEID | RULE | DOT-POSITON | BACK-POINTER | OPERATION |
| 0 | CM کا @ | 1,2 | | Scanner |
| 2 | KP.POSS P.PERS CM @ | 0,2 | 1-0 2-0 | Completer |
| 9 | NP.NOM-SUB KP.POSS @ N PT.INTF | 0,2 | 2-2 | Completer |
| 22 | N @ ذکر | 2,2 | | Predictor |
| | **CHART(3)=ذکر** | | | |
| STATEID | RULE | DOT-POSITON | BACK-POINTER | OPERATION |
| 0 | N ذکر @ | 2,3 | | Scanner |
| 1 | NP.NOM-SUB KP.POSS N @ PT.INTF | 0,3 | 2-2 3-0 | Completer |
| 12 | PT.INTF @ بھی | 3,3 | | Predictor |
| | **CHART(4)=بھی** | | | |
| STATEID | RULE | DOT-POSITON | BACK-POINTER | OPERATION |
| 0 | PT.INTF بھی @ | 3,4 | | Scanner |
| 1 | NP.NOM-SUB KP.POSS N PT.INTF @ | 0,4 | 2-2 3-0 4-0 | Completer |
| 2 | S NP.NOM-SUB @ ADVP-SPT-MODF ADJP-MNR-PLINK VCMAIN M.S | 0,4 | 4-1 | Completer |
| 17 | ADVP-SPT-MODF @ ADV.SPT | 4,4 | | Predictor |
| 74 | ADV.SPT @ یہاں | 4,4 | | Predictor |
| | **CHART(5)=یہاں** | | | |
| STATEID | RULE | DOT-POSITON | BACK-POINTER | OPERATION |
| 0 | ADV.SPT یہاں @ | 4,5 | | Scanner |
| 1 | ADVP-SPT-MODF ADV.SPT @ | 4,5 | 5-0 | Completer |
| 2 | S NP.NOM-SUB ADVP-SPT-MODF @ ADJP-MNR-PLINK VCMAIN M.S | 0,5 | 4-1 5-1 | Completer |
| 3 | ADJP-MNR-PLINK @ ADJ.MNR | 5,5 | | Predictor |
| 4 | ADJ.MNR @ ضروری | 5,5 | | Predictor |
| | **CHART(6)=ضروری** | | | |
| STATEID | RULE | DOT-POSITON | BACK-POINTER | OPERATION |
| 0 | ADJ.MNR ضروری @ | 5,6 | | Scanner |
| 1 | ADJP-MNR-PLINK ADJ.MNR @ | 5,6 | 6-0 | Completer |
| 2 | S NP.NOM-SUB ADVP-SPT-MODF ADJP-MNR-PLINK @ VCMAIN M.S | 0,6 | 4-1 5-1 6-1 | Completer |
| 12 | VCMAIN @ V.COP.PRES | 6,6 | | Predictor |
| 42 | V.COP.PRES @ ہے | 6,6 | | Predictor |
| | **CHART(7)=ہے** | | | |
| STATEID | RULE | DOT-POSITON | BACK-POINTER | OPERATION |
| 0 | V.COP.PRES ہے @ | 6,7 | | Scanner |
| 1 | VCMAIN V.COP.PRES @ | 6,7 | 7-0 | Completer |
| 2 | S NP.NOM-SUB ADVP-SPT-MODF ADJP-MNR-PLINK VCMAIN @ M.S | 0,7 | 4-1 5-1 6-1 7-1 | Completer |
| 3 | M.S @ - | 7,7 | | Predictor |
| | **CHART(8)=-** | | | |
| STATEID | RULE | DOT-POSITON | BACK-POINTER | OPERATION |
| 0 | M.S - @ | 7,8 | | Scanner |
| 1 | S NP.NOM-SUB ADVP-SPT-MODF ADJP-MNR-PLINK VCMAIN M.S @ | 0,8 | 4-1 5-1 6-1 7-1 8-0 | Completer |
| 2 | ROOT S @ | 0,8 | 8-1 | Completer |

Figure 2: A back-pointer calculation example of the Urdu parser

PLINK ( ADJ.MNR ضروری ) ) ( VCMAIN ( V.COP.PRES ہے ) ) ( M.S . ) ) . This `prepare()` method only replaces the back-pointers with the LHS of the relevant productions. Finally, the bracketed parse tree is displayed in a formatted way as depicted in Figure 3.

**Bracketed Parse Tree 1 of 1**

```
( S
    ( NP.NOM-SUB
        ( KP.POSS
            ( P.PERS ان )
            ( CM کا ))
        ( N ذکر )
        ( PT.INTF بھی ))
    ( ADVP-SPT-MODF
        ( ADV.SPT یہاں ))
    ( ADJP-MNR-PLINK
        ( ADJ.MNR ضروری ))
    ( VCMAIN
        ( V.COP.PRES ہے ))
    ( M.S - ))
```

Figure 3: An output of the `BUILDER()` method

### 4.5 Empty Productions

Empty productions are divided into two categories. The first one is related to diacritic productions and the second one is related to non-diacritic productions. It can cause the discontinuity during the parsing because the lexical item may or may not present for both the categories in a given sentence. Only the first category of diacritic productions is discussed here to provide an idea about the issues related to empty productions.

In modern Urdu, the diacritics may or may not appear in the text e.g. آبِ حَیات *AbE h2ayAt* 'The water of life' and تقرِیباً *taqrIban* 'almost'. The first example is related to compound words and the second one is an independent word. The *zErE-Iz3Afat* (a diacritic for addition) under the last letter بِ *b* of the first word in the first example is still in use in the modern Urdu writing. Similar is the case of *tanwin* (a diacritic for final post-nasalization) on the last letter اً *a* in the second example. There are also other diacritics in use as well e.g. *zEr, zabar, pEsh, taSdId*, etc.

In the grammar of the Urdu parser, a DIA tag is used to represent the diacritics e.g. DIA → *, where '*' represents the absence of a diacritic or an empty production. During parsing, a compound word may or may not appear with a diacritic e.g.شہرِمکہ *Sehr makkah* 'The city of

Makkah'. This example has two words شہر *Sehr* 'city' and the مکہ *makkah* 'Makkah', but the diacritic is absent between the two words. In such cases, its presence is by default understood by the native speakers. The production extracted from the grammar to handle this compound word is the NP-SPT → @ N.SPT DIA N.PROP.SPT. After processing of the first word *Sehr*/N.SPT by the `SCANNER()`, the production becomes NP-SPT → N.SPT @ DIA N.PROP.SPT. Now, the `PREDICTOR()` deals this DIA empty production implicitly by moving the '@' ahead and adds the updated production NP-SPT → N.SPT DIA @ N.PROP.SPT in the same chart. Similarly, the second word *makkah*/N.PROP.SPT is processed by the `SCANNER()` and the production final state becomes like this NP-SPT → N.SPT DIA N.PROP.SPT @. The problem with this solution adopted from (Aycock and Horspool, 2002) is that it performs the transaction silently with the compound words and also with the non-compound words at such positions where it is not needed. For example, If this is the case as discussed then the solution is perfect, but in the case of the non compound words, if two independent words گھر *gHar* 'The house' and مکہ *makkah* 'Makkah' appear in the same position like compound words e.g. گھر مکہ میں ہے *gHar makkah mEN hE* 'The house is in Makkah', then this solution can not identify the context and it applies the transaction in the same way due to the same POS tagging of *gHar* and the *Sehr*. This solution causes frequent discontinuity during the parsing and its property of self decision at the irrelevant places makes the things more worse.

Due to high frequency of the DIA productions in the grammar, the proposed solution (Aycock and Horspool, 2002) was implemented in the `PREDICTOR()` but the results found were not promising. So, an explicit method to represent the absent value has been chosen, through which an asterisk '*' is usually typed in a given sentence to represent the absence of the diacritics, arguments, lexical items, etc. At present, due to this explicit approach, the Urdu parser is jelling with the grammar without any issue related to empty productions.

### 4.6 Lexical Dynamic Behavior

The issue is related to a class of words which has the following attributes like the homonym, homograph, homophone, heteronym and the polysemes. A strict definition is considered to these attributes, that means at least the words have the same spelling. The case of homonym words in a strict sense is discussed here and the same concept is applicable on other attributes as well.

For example, the word کی *kI* is a homonym in Urdu. It can behave in two ways e.g. a possessive case marker and a verb. Being a possessive case marker, it contains a possessive meaning 'of' in 2. On the other hand, it contains a meaning of 'did' in 3. In the grammar, this word has different POS tags as a case marker (CM), a perfective verb (V.PERF) and a perfective light verb (V.LIGHT.PERF). Suppose the word 'kI' actually comes as a V.PERF at the end of a given sentence. For its processing, the `Scanner()` can pick up the wrong choice with the CM and the V.LIGHT.PERF, if these choices are available in the current chart at earlier positions as compared to the right choice. Due to this wrong selection, the relevant productions of a verb will not be completed in the next chart and the parser will go into the discontinuous state. To address this issue, the `Scanner()` of the Earley algorithm is modified, which records the failed state in variables $fi, fj$ and $fid$. These failed states are then utilized by the `EDITOR()` in Algorithm 5, which is called by the Urdu parser to heal this discontinuous state. The failed chart and the states are deleted first. After skipping the wrong choice e.g. the CM → کی in a chart, the next choice from available homonyms is selected and tried to parse. In this way, the next choice V.PERF → کی is located and the $i_{th}$ and $j_{th}$ loop variables of the Urdu parser are set to that choice for further processing. Continuing in this way, the parser finally gets a direction towards the optimal solution.

**Algorithm 5** Editor

```
function EDITOR(i, id, fi, fj, fid, chart, chartSize)
    Drop and re-initialize chart[i + 1]
    for z ← i to fi+1 step -1 do
        Drop and re-initialize chart[z]
    end for
    rule ← chart[fi].getRule(fj).split(" ")   ▷ splitting rule with space
    for z ← 0 to chartSize[fi]-1 do
        temprule ← chart[fi].getRule(z).split(" ")
        if temprule[2] = rule[2] then
            if !(temprule[0] = rule[0]) then
                j ← z − 1, i ← fi, id ← z
                break
            end if
        end if
    end for
end function
```

(2) جولیا کی کتاب

*jUlIA=kI* *kitAb*
Julia.Fem.Sg=Poss book.Fem.Sg
'The book of Julia'

(3) اس نے ایک بات کی ہے

*us=nE* *Ek* *bAt* *kI* *hE*
he.Sg=Erg a talk.Fem.Sg do.Perf.Sg be.Pres.Sg
'He did a talk'

### 4.7 Subordinate Clause Limitations

Basically, the issue is related to conjuncted sub-sentences or the subordinate clause, when the number of conjuncted sub-sentences becomes greater than one. The issue does not appear often and it is related to the NL type productions, specially the conjuncted sub-sentences denoted by SBAR as below. A sentence of 23 tokens with two conjuncted sub-sentences highlighted with the SBAR is an evidence of this issue. During the processing of a production for the sentence marker M.S → - @ in the last (23rd) chart, the order of the complete productions should be as follows. The '@' at the end represents the complete status of the productions.

M.S → - @
SBAR → C.SBORD NP.NOM-SUB **SBAR** ADVP-MNR-MODF NP.NOM-MNR-OBJ VCMAIN M.S @
S → KP-INST-MODF KP.DAT-SUB NP.NOM-OBJ VCMAIN **SBAR** @

But, unfortunately, the parser went into a discontinuous state during the processing of the last chart with the following productions.

M.S → - @
SBAR → C.SBORD NP.NOM-SUB SBAR ADVP-MNR-MODF NP.NOM-MNR-OBJ VCMAIN M.S @
SBAR → C.SBORD NP.NOM-SUB SBAR @ ADVP-MNR-MODF NP.NOM-MNR-OBJ VCMAIN M.S
ADVP-MNR-MODF → @ ADV.MNR

Up to completion of the first SBAR → ... @ production, the parser performed well. Then `Completer()` went back to search another production which contained an incomplete non-terminal SBAR having '@' before it e.g. @ SBAR. The `Completer()` made a fault there in chart 12 in the presence of wrong choices at higher precedence. It found an incomplete SBAR production. After moving the '@' forward, it added the updated production in the last chart as can be seen in the given productions. Afterwards, the `PREDICTOR()` became activated by seeing the '@' before the ADVP-MNR-MODF and the parser went into a wrong direction. To resolve this issue, it is needed to allow the Earley's `Completer()` to go back further until a successful parse. The description of the extended `Completer()` is as follows.

When the Urdu parser called the `COMPLETER()`, it first sets the `completerCheck` flag to false, which will be used to back track a right choice among the NL type productions. After calculating the back-pointers, the updated production entry is then added and printed by setting the `completerCheck` to true. If the `completerCheck` is found to be true and the chart number is less than the length of a sentence then a solution has been found and there is no need to go back. However, if the `completerCheck` is found to be true and the chart number is greater or equal to the length of a sentence then the `COMPLETER()` is allowed to back track by setting its flag to its default value.

## 5 Results

The division of training and test data is discussed in Section 3. To make the test data more valuable and reliable for results, the beginning ten sentences from each hundred of 1400 sentences of the URDU.KON-TB treebank were selected. The test data so contained 140 sentences in all. In test data, the minimum, average and the maximum length is found to be 5, 13.73 and 46 words per sentence. All items which can exists in a normal text are considered e.g. punctuation, null elements, diacritics, headings, regard titles, Hadees (the statements of prophets), antecedents and anaphors within a sentence, and others except the unknown words, which will be dealt in future. The PARSEVAL measures are used to evaluate the results. The PARSEVAL measures are calculated in two ways which are depicted in Table 1.

At first, the values as per columns headings in Table 1 are calculated on the basis of constituents for each individual sentence. Then these values are stored in a text file with these headings. The values existed in each column of the text file are summed up and then divided by the total number of 140 values in each column. The results thus obtained are recorded in a row A-1 of Table 1 on average basis. Similarly, all the values in the Length, Matched, Gold and the Test columns are summed up individually from that text file and their sums are recorded as can be seen in row T-2 of the table. Their respective results for the Precision, Recall, F-score and the Crossing Brackets are calculated

| | Sentences | Length | Matched | Gold | Test | Precision | Recall | F-score | Crossing |
|---|---|---|---|---|---|---|---|---|---|
| A-1 | 140 | 13.73 | 17 | 22 | 18 | 0.952 | 0.811 | 0.848 | 2 |
| T-2 | 140 | 1922 | 2449 | 3107 | 2531 | 0.968 | 0.788 | 0.869 | 329 |

Table 1: Evaluation results of the Urdu parser

from these sums, which is a standard method of calculation.

The Urdu parser outperforms the simple Hindi dependency parser by Bharati et al. (2009) with an additional recall of 22%. In (Bharati et al., 2009), only precision and recall percentages are given. Thats why only the precision and recall percentages of labeled attachment (LA) are compared. For chunks, intra-chunks and karakas, the precision percentages of LA (LA-P) achieved by the simple Hindi dependency parser are 82.3%, 71.2% and 74.1%, respectively. The average of these LA-P percentages is 75.9%, which is 20.9% less precision than the Urdu parser in row T-2. Similarly, Hindi dependency parser achieved LA recalls in case of chunks, intra-chunks and karakas as 65.4%, 58.2% and 46.7% respectively. The average of these percentages is calculated as 56.8%, which is now the final LA recall percentage of the Hindi dependency parser. For comparison, the recall percentage of the Urdu parser used is mentioned in row T-2 as 78.8%. The values obtained for the language variant parsers concludes that the Urdu parser outperforms the simple Hindi dependency parser with 22% increase in recall.

Multi-path shift-reduce parser (Mukhtar et al., 2012b) for Urdu parsed 74 sentences successfully out of 100 and it was then reported as a 74% of accuracy. This evaluation is very weak because the successful parsed sentences were not compared with the gold standard. Recall is a value obtained through dividing the Matched constituents with the constituents available in the Gold data. As recall percentage in our case is 78.8%, so we can say that the Urdu parser beats the multi-path shift-reduce parser with a 4.8% increase in recall. On the other hand, from the first 100 sentences of the test data, the Urdu parser provides 89 sentences with parsed solutions. Comparatively, the Urdu parser has 15% more accuracy than the Multi-path shift-reduce parser, but the parsed solutions were not compared with the Gold data. So, by considering the safe side, we can repeat our argument that the Urdu parser beats the multi-path shift-reduce parser with a 4.8% increase in recall.

## 6 Conclusion

The extended Urdu parser with rich encoded information in the form of a grammar is a state of the art parsing candidate for morphologically rich language variant Urdu. After removal of issues, the output of the parser is so directed, speedy and refined in a sense that no extra or the irrelevant L type productions can be introduced by the Urdu parser. It is really hard now that the Urdu parser will select a wrong choice of production. If it happens then the Urdu parser has a tendency to correct itself automatically. These all features enables the Urdu parser comparable or better than the state of the art in the domain of both the language variants. Urdu parser can help the linguists analyze the Urdu sentences computationally and can be useful in Urdu language processing and machine learning domains. By using this parser, the limited size of the URDU.KON-TB treebank can also be increased. This can be done after getting the partial parsed trees of unknown sentences. These partial parsed trees can be corrected and then imported into the URDU.KON-TB treebank.

## Acknowledgment

I would like to express my sincere gratitude to my Supervisor Prof. Dr. Miriam Butt for her motivation, enthusiasm, and immense knowledge. Her guidance helped me in all the time of this work.

## References

Qaiser Abbas and A Nabi Khan. 2009. Lexical Functional Grammar For Urdu Modal Verbs. In *Emerging Technologies, 2009. ICET 2009. International Conference on*, pages 7–12. IEEE.

Qaiser Abbas and Ghulam Raza. 2014. A Computational Classification Of Urdu Dynamic Copula Verb. *International Journal of Computer Applications*, 85(10):1–12, January.

Qaiser Abbas, Nayyara Karamat, and Sadia Niazi. 2009. Development Of Tree-Bank Based Probabilistic Grammar For Urdu Language. *International Journal of Electrical & Computer Science*, 9(09):231–235.

Qaiser Abbas. 2012. Building A Hierarchical Annotated Corpus Of Urdu: The URDU.KON-TB

Treebank. *Lecture Notes in Computer Science*, 7181(1):66–79.

Qaiser Abbas. 2014. Semi-Semantic Part Of Speech Annotation And Evaluation. In *Proceedings of 8th ACL Linguistic Annotation Workshop*, pages 75–81, Dublin, Ireland. Association for Computational Linguistics.

Bhasha Agrawal, Rahul Agarwal, Samar Husain, and Dipti M Sharma. 2013. An Automatic Approach To Treebank Error Detection Using A Dependency Parser. In *Computational Linguistics and Intelligent Text Processing*, pages 294–303. Springer.

Wajid Ali and Sarmad Hussain. 2010. Urdu Dependency Parser: A Data-Driven Approach. In *Proceedings of Conference on Language and Technology (CLT10)*.

John Aycock and R Nigel Horspool. 2002. Practical Earley Parsing. *The Computer Journal*, 45(6):620–630.

Rafiya Begum, Samar Husain, Arun Dhwaj, Dipti Misra Sharma, Lakshmi Bai, and Rajeev Sangal. 2008. Dependency Annotation Scheme For Indian Languages. In *IJCNLP*, pages 721–726.

Akshar Bharati, Vineet Chaitanya, Rajeev Sangal, and KV Ramakrishnamacharyulu. 1995. *Natural Language Processing: A Paninian Perspective*. Prentice-Hall of India New Delhi.

Akshar Bharati, Medhavi Bhatia, Vineet Chaitanya, and Rajeev Sangal. 1996. Paninian Grammar Framework Applied To English. Technical report, Technical Report TRCS-96-238, CSE, IIT Kanpur.

Akshar Bharati, Samar Husain, Dipti Misra Sharma, and Rajeev Sangal. 2008. A Two-Stage Constraint Based Dependency Parser For Free Word Order Languages. In *Proceedings of the COLIPS International Conference on Asian Language Processing 2008 (IALP)*.

Akshar Bharati, Mridul Gupta, Vineet Yadav, Karthik Gali, and Dipti Misra Sharma. 2009. Simple Parser For Indian Languages In A Dependency Framework. In *Proceedings of the Third Linguistic Annotation Workshop*, pages 162–165. Association for Computational Linguistics.

Riyaz Ahmad Bhat, Sambhav Jain, and Dipti Misra Sharma. 2012b. Experiments On Dependency Parsing Of Urdu. In *In Proceedings of The 11th International Workshop on Treebanks and Linguistic Theories (TLT11)*.

Miriam Butt and Tracy Holloway King. 2007. Urdu In A Parallel Grammar Development Environment. *Language Resources and Evaluation*, 41(2):191–207.

Miriam Butt and Gillian Ramchand. 2001. Complex Aspectual Structure In Hindi/Urdu. *M. Liakata, B. Jensen, & D. Maillat, Eds*, pages 1–30.

Miriam Butt and Jafar Rizvi. 2010. Tense And Aspect In Urdu. *Layers of Aspect. Stanford: CSLI Publications*.

Miriam Butt. 1993. Hindi-Urdu Infinitives As NPs. *South Asian Language Review: Special Issue on Studies in Hindi-Urdu*, 3(1):51–72.

Miriam Butt. 2003. The Light Verb Jungle. In *Workshop on Multi-Verb Constructions*.

Jay Clark Earley. 1968. *An Efficient Context-Free Parsing Algorithm*. Ph.D. thesis, Carnegie Mellon University, Pittsburgh, PA, USA. AAI6907901.

Jay Earley. 1970. An Efficient Context-Free Parsing Algorithm. *Communications of the ACM*, 13(2):94–102.

Wenbin Jiang, Hao Xiong, and Qun Liu. 2009. Mutipath Shift-Reduce Parsing With Online Training. *CIPS-ParsEval-2009 shared task*.

Abdul Jamil Khan. 2006. *Urdu/Hindi: An Artificial Divide: African Heritage, Mesopotamian Roots, Indian Culture & Britiah Colonialism*. Algora Pub.

Gary F. Simons & Charles D. Fennig Lewis, M. Paul. 2013. *Ethnologue: Languages Of The World, 17th Edition*. Dallas: SIL International.

John R McLane. 1970. *The Political Awakening In India*. Prentice Hall.

Neelam Mukhtar, Mohammad Abid Khan, and Fatima Tuz Zuhra. 2011. Probabilistic Context Free Grammar For Urdu. *Linguistic and Literature Review*, 1(1):86–94.

Neelam Mukhtar, Mohammad Abid Khan, and Fatima Tuz Zuhra. 2012a. Algorithm For Developing Urdu Probabilistic Parser. *International journal of Electrical and Computer Sciences*, 12(3):57–66.

Neelam Mukhtar, Mohammad Abid Khan, Fatima Tuz Zuhra, and Nadia Chiragh. 2012b. Implementation Of Urdu Probabilistic Parser. *International Journal of Computational Linguistics (IJCL)*, 3(1):12–20.

Reut Tsarfaty, Djamé Seddah, Yoav Goldberg, Sandra Kuebler, Marie Candito, Jennifer Foster, Yannick Versley, Ines Rehbein, and Lamia Tounsi. 2010. Statistical Parsing Of Morphologically Rich Languages (SPMRL): What, How And Whither. In *Proceedings of the NAACL HLT 2010 First Workshop on Statistical Parsing of Morphologically-Rich Languages*, pages 1–12. Association for Computational Linguistics.

Reut Tsarfaty, Djamé Seddah, Sandra Kübler, and Joakim Nivre. 2013. Parsing Morphologically Rich Languages: Introduction To The Special Issue. *Computational Linguistics*, 39(1):15–22.

# Adapting Predicate Frames for Urdu PropBanking

**Riyaz Ahmad Bhat♣, Naman Jain♣, Dipti Misra Sharma♣, Ashwini Vaidya♠, Martha Palmer♠, James Babani♠ and Tafseer Ahmed♢**
LTRC, IIIT-H, Hyderabad, India♣
University of Colorado, Boulder, CO 80309 USA♠
DHA Suffa University, Karachi, Pakistan♢
{riyaz.bhat, naman.jain}@research.iiit.ac.in, dipti@iiit.ac.in,
{vaidyaa, mpalmer, james.babani}@colorado.edu, tafseer@dsu.edu.pk

## Abstract

Hindi and Urdu are two standardized registers of what has been called the Hindustani language, which belongs to the Indo-Aryan language family. Although, both the varieties share a common grammar, they differ significantly in their vocabulary to an extent where both become mutually incomprehensible (Masica, 1993). Hindi draws its vocabulary from Sanskrit while Urdu draws its vocabulary from Persian, Arabic and even Turkish. In this paper, we present our efforts to adopt frames of nominal and verbal predicates that Urdu shares with either Hindi or Arabic for Urdu PropBanking. We discuss the feasibility of porting such frames from either of the sources (Arabic or Hindi) and also present a simple and reasonably accurate method to automatically identify the origin of Urdu words which is a necessary step in the process of porting such frames.

## 1 Introduction

Hindi and Urdu, spoken primarily in northern India and Pakistan, are socially and even officially considered two different language varieties. However, such a division between the two is not established linguistically. They are two standardized registers of what has been called the Hindustani language, which belongs to the Indo-Aryan language family. Masica (1993) explains that, while they are different languages officially, they are not even different dialects or sub-dialects in a linguistic sense; rather, they are different literary styles based on the same linguistically defined sub-dialect. He further explains that at the colloquial level, Hindi and Urdu are nearly identical, both in terms of core vocabulary and grammar. However, at formal and literary levels, vocabulary differences begin to loom much larger (Hindi drawing its higher lexicon from Sanskrit and Urdu from Persian and Arabic) to the point where the two styles/languages become mutually unintelligible. In written form, not only the vocabulary but the way Urdu and Hindi are written makes one believe that they are two separate languages. They are written in separate orthographies, Hindi being written in Devanagari, and Urdu in a modified Persio-Arabic script. Given such (apparent) divergences between the two varieties, two parallel treebanks are being built under *The Hindi-Urdu treebanking Project* (Bhatt et al., 2009; Xia et al., 2009). Both the treebanks follow a multi-layered and multi-representational framework which features Dependency, PropBank and Phrase Structure annotations. Among the two treebanks the Hindi treebank is ahead of the Urdu treebank across all layers. In the case of PropBanking, the Hindi treebank has made considerable progress while Urdu PropBanking has just started.

The creation of predicate frames is the first step in PropBanking, which is followed by the actual annotation of verb instances in corpora. In this paper, we look at the possibility of porting related frames from Arabic and Hindi PropBanks for Urdu PropBanking. Given that Urdu shares its vocabulary with Arabic, Hindi and Persian, we look at verbal and nominal predicates that Urdu shares with these languages and try to port and adapt their frames from the respective PropBanks instead of creating them afresh. This implies that identification of the source of Urdu predicates becomes a necessary step in this process. Thus, in order to port the relevant frames, we need to first identify the source of Urdu predicates and then extract their frames from the related PropBanks. To state briefly, we present the following as contributions of this paper:

- Automatic identification of origin or source of Urdu vocabulary.



*Language Technology for Closely Related Languages and Language Variants (LT4CloseLang)*, pages 47–55,
October 29, 2014, Doha, Qatar. 

- Porting and adapting nominal and verbal predicate frames from the PropBanks of related languages.

The rest of the paper is organised as follows: In the next Section we discuss the Hindi-Urdu treebanking project with the focus on PropBanking. In Section 3, we discuss our efforts to automatically identify the source of Urdu vocabulary and in Section 4, we discuss the process of adapting and porting Arabic and Hindi frames for Urdu PropBanking. Finally we conclude with some future directions in Section 5.

## 2 A multi-layered, multi-representational treebank

Compared to other existing treebanks, Hindi/Urdu Treebanks (HTB/UTB) are unusual in that they are multi-layered. They contain three layers of annotation: dependency structure (DS) for annotation of modified-modifier relations, PropBank-style annotation (PropBank) for predicate-argument structure, and an independently motivated phrase-structure (PS). Each layer has its own framework, annotation scheme, and detailed annotation guidelines. Due to lack of space and relevance to our work, we only look at PropBanking with reference to Hindi PropBank, here.

### 2.1 PropBank Annotation

The first PropBank, the English PropBank (Kingsbury and Palmer, 2002), originated as a one-million word subset of the Wall Street Journal (WSJ) portion of Penn Treebank II (an English phrase structure treebank). The verbs in the PropBank are annotated with predicate-argument structures and provide semantic role labels for each syntactic argument of a verb. Although these were deliberately chosen to be generic and theory-neutral (e.g., ARG0, ARG1), they are intended to consistently annotate the same semantic role across syntactic variations. For example, in both the sentences *John broke the window* and *The window broke*, *'the window'* is annotated as ARG1 and as bearing the role of '*Patient*'. This reflects the fact that this argument bears the same semantic role in both the cases, even though it is realized as the structural subject in one sentence and as the object in the other. This is the primary difference between PropBank's approach to semantic role labels and the Paninian approach to karaka labels, which it otherwise resembles closely. PropBank's ARG0 and ARG1 can be thought of as similar to Dowty's prototypical '*Agent*' and '*Patient*' (Dowty, 1991). PropBank provides, for each sense of each annotated verb, its "roleset", i.e., the possible arguments of the predicate, their labels and all possible syntactic realizations. The primary goal of PropBank is to supply consistent, simple, general purpose labeling of semantic roles for a large quantity of coherent text that can provide training data for supervised machine learning algorithms, in the same way that the Penn Treebank supported the training of statistical syntactic parsers.

#### 2.1.1 Hindi PropBank

The Hindi PropBank project has differed significantly from other PropBank projects in that the semantic role labels are annotated on dependency trees rather than on phrase structure trees. However, it is similar in that semantic roles are defined on a verb-by-verb basis and the description at the verb-specific level is fine-grained; e.g., a verb like '*hit*' will have '*hitter*' and '*hittee*'. These verb-specific roles are then grouped into broader categories using numbered arguments (ARG). Each verb can also have a set of modifiers not specific to the verb (ARGM). In Table 1, PropBank-style semantic roles are listed for the simple verb *de* 'to give'. In the table, the numbered arguments correspond to the giver, thing given and recipient. Frame file definitions are created manually and include role information as well as a unique roleset ID (e.g. de.01 in Table 1), which is assigned to every sense of a verb. In addition, for Hindi the frame file also includes the transitive and causative forms of the verb (if any). Thus, the frame file for *de* 'give' will include *dilvaa* 'cause to give'.

| de.01 | *to give* |
|---|---|
| `Arg0` | the giver |
| `Arg1` | thing given |
| `Arg2` | recipient |

Table 1: A Frame File

The annotation process for the PropBank takes place in two stages: the creation of frame files for individual verb types, and the annotation of predicate argument structures for each verb instance. The annotation for each predicate in the corpus is carried out based on its frame file definitions.

The PropBank makes use of two annotation tools viz. Jubilee (Choi et al., 2010b) and Cornerstone (Choi et al., 2010a) for PropBank instance annotation and PropBank frame file creation respectively. For annotation of the Hindi and Urdu PropBank, the Jubilee annotation tool had to be modified to display dependency trees and also to provide additional labels for the annotation of empty arguments.

## 3 Identifying the source of Urdu Vocabulary

Predicting the source of a word is similar to language identification where the task is to identify the language a given document is written in. However, language identification at word level is more challenging than a typical document level language identification problem. The number of features available at document level is much higher than at word level. The available features for word level identification are word morphology, syllable structure and phonemic (letter) inventory of the language(s).

In the case of Urdu, the problem is even more complex as the borrowed words don't necessarily carry the inflections of their source language and don't retain their identity as such (they undergo phonetic changes as well). For example, $khabar$ 'news' which is an Arabic word declines as per the morphological paradigm of feminine nominals in Hindi and Urdu as shown in Table (2). However, despite such challenges, if we look at the character histogram in Figure (1), we can still identify the source of a sufficiently large portion of Urdu vocabulary just by using letter-based heuristics. For example neither Arabic nor Persian has aspirated consonants like bʱ, pʰ *Aspirated Bilabial Plosives*; tʃʰ, dʒʱ *Aspirated Alveolar Fricatives*; ɖʱ *Aspirated Retroflex Plosive*; gʱ, kʰ *Aspirated Velar Plosives* etc. while Hindi does. Similarly, the following sounds occur only in Arabic and Persian: ʒ *Fricative Postalveolar*; θ, ð *Fricative Dental*; ħ *Fricative Pharyngeal*; χ *Fricative Uvular* etc. Using these heuristics we could identify 2,682 types as Indic, and 3,968 as either Persian or Arabic out of 12,223 unique types in the Urdu treebank (Bhat and Sharma, 2012).

| | **Singular** | **Plural** |
|---|---|---|
| **Direct** | *khabar* | *khabarain* |
| **Oblique** | *khabar* | *khabaron* |

Table 2: Morphological Paradigm of $khabar$

This explains the efficiency of n-gram based approaches to either document level or word level language identification tasks as reported in the recent literature on the problem (Dunning, 1994; Elfardy and Diab, 2012; King and Abney, 2013; Nguyen and Dogruoz, 2014; Lui et al., 2014).

In order to predict the source of an Urdu word, we frame two classification tasks: (1) binary classification into Indic and Persio-Arabic and, (2) tri-class classification into Arabic, Indic and Persian. Both the problems are modeled using smoothed n-gram based language models.

### 3.1 N-gram Language Models

Given a word $w$ to classify into one of $k$ classes $c_1$, $c_2$, ... , $c_k$, we will choose the class with the maximum conditional probability:

$$\begin{aligned} \mathbf{c}^* &= \arg\max_{c_i} \; p(c_i|w) \\ &= \arg\max_{c_i} \; p(w|c_i) * p(c_i) \end{aligned} \tag{1}$$

The prior distribution $p(c)$ of a class is estimated from the respective training sets shown in Table (3). Each training set is used to train a separate letter-based language model to estimate the probability of word $w$. The language model $p(w)$ is implemented as an n-gram model using the IRSTLM-Toolkit (Federico et al., 2008) with Kneser-Ney smoothing. The language model is defined as:

$$p(w) = \prod_{i=1}^{n} p(l_i|l_{i-k}^{i-1}) \tag{2}$$

where, $l$ is a letter and $k$ is a parameter indicating the amount of context used (e.g., $k = 4$ means 5-gram model).

### 3.2 Etymological Data

In order to prepare training and testing data marked with etymological information for our classification experiments, we used the *Online*

[1]http://www.langsci.ucl.ac.uk/ipa/IPA_chart_%28C%292005.pdf

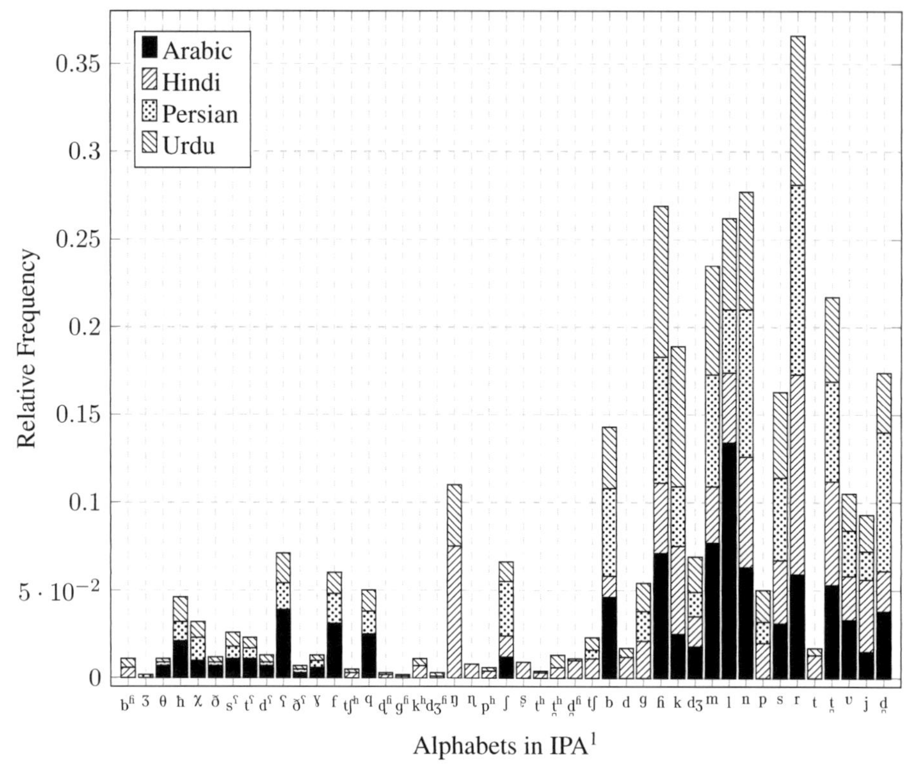


Figure 1: *Relative Distribution of Arabic, Hindi, Persian and Urdu Alphabets (Consonants only)*

*Urdu Dictionary*[2] (henceforth OUD). OUD has been prepared under the supervision of the e-government Directorate of Pakistan[3]. Apart from basic definition and meaning, it provides etymological information for more than 120K Urdu words. Since the dictionary is freely[4] available and requires no expertise for extraction of word etymology which is usually the case with manual annotation, we could mark the etymological information on a reasonably sized word list in a limited time frame. The statistics are provided in Table (3). We use **Indic** as a cover term for all the words that are either from Sanskrit, Prakrit, Hindi or local languages.

| Language | Data Size | Average Token Length |
|---|---|---|
| Arabic | 6,524 | 6.8 |
| Indic | 3,002 | 5.5 |
| Persian | 4,613 | 6.5 |

Table 3: Statistics of Etymological Data

[2]http://182.180.102.251:8081/oud/default.aspx

[3]www.e-government.gov.pk

[4]We are not aware of an offline version of OUD.

### 3.3 Experiments

We carried out a number of experiments in order to explore the effect of data size and the order of n-gram models on the classification performance. By varying the size of training data, we wanted to identify the lower bound on the training size with respect to the classification performance. We varied the training size per training iteration by 1% for n-grams in the order 1-5 for both the classification problems. For each n-gram order 100 experiments were carried out, i.e overall 800 experiments for binary and tri-class classification. The impact of training size on the classification performance is shown in Figures (2) and (3) for binary and tri-class classification respectively. As expected, at every iteration the additional data points introduced into the training data increased the performance of the model. With a mere 3% of the training data, we could reach a reasonable accuracy of 0.85 in terms of F-score for binary classification and for tri-class classification we reached the same accuracy with 6% of the data.

Similarly, we tried different order n-gram models to quantify the effect of character context on the classification performance. As with the increase in data size, increasing the n-gram order profoundly improved the results. In both the classification tasks, unigram based models converge faster than the higher order n-gram based models. The obvious reason for it is the small, finite set of characters that a language operates with ($\sim$ 37 in Arabic, $\sim$ 39 in Persian and $\sim$ 48 in Hindi). A small set of words (unique in our case) is probably enough to capture at least a single instance of each character. As no new n-gram is introduced with subsequent additions of new tokens in the training data, the accuracy stabilizes. However, the accuracy with higher order n-grams kept on increasing with an increase in the data size, though it was marginal after 5-grams. The abrupt increase after 8,000 training instances is probably due to the addition of an unknown bigram sequence(s) to the training data. In particular, the Recall of Persio-Arabic increased by 2.2%.

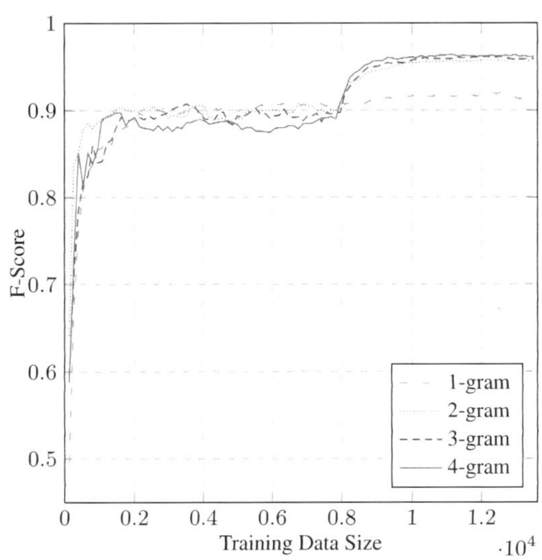


Figure 2: *Learning Curves for Binary Classification of Urdu Vocabulary*

### 3.4 Results

We performed 10-fold cross validation over all the instances of the etymological data for both the binary and tri-class classification tasks. We split the data into training and testing sets with a ratio of 80:20 using the stratified sampling. Stratified sampling distributes the samples of each class in training and testing sets with the same percentage as in the complete set. For all the 10-folds, the order of

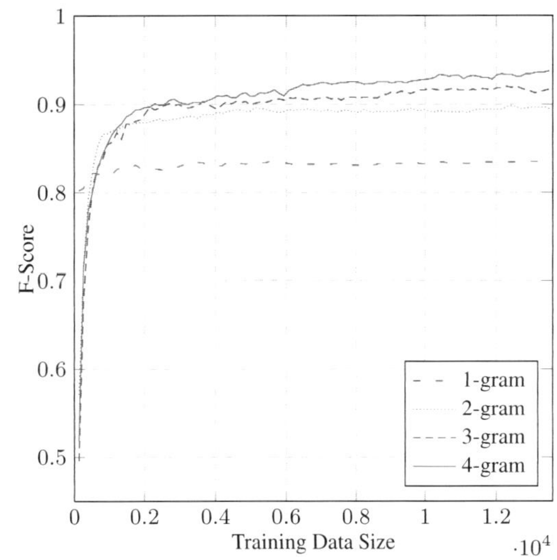


Figure 3: *Learning Curves for Tri-class Classification of Urdu Vocabulary*

n-gram was varied again from 1-5. Tables (4) and (5) show the consolidated results for these tasks with a frequency based baseline to evaluate the classification performance. In both the tasks, we achieved highest accuracy with language models trained with 5-gram letter sequence context. The best results in terms of F-score are 0.96 and 0.93 for binary and tri-class classification respectively.

| **Type** | **Precision** (P) | **Recall** (R) | **F1-Score** (F) |
|---|---|---|---|
| **Baseline** | 0.40 | 0.50 | 0.40 |
| **1-gram** | 0.89 | 0.89 | 0.89 |
| **2-gram** | 0.95 | 0.95 | 0.95 |
| **3-gram** | 0.96 | 0.96 | 0.96 |
| **4-gram** | 0.96 | 0.96 | 0.96 |
| **5-gram** | 0.96 | 0.96 | 0.96 |

Table 4: Results of 10-fold Cross Validation on Binary Classification

Although, we have achieved quite reasonable accuracies in both the tasks, a closer look at the confusion matrices shown in Tables (6) and (7) show that we can still improve the accuracies by balancing the size of data across classes. In binary classification our model is more biased towards Persio-Arabic as the data is highly imbalanced. Our binary classifier misclassifies 0.86% of Indic tokens as Persio-Arabic since the prior probability of the latter is much higher than that of the former. While in the case of tri-class classification, using

| Type | Precision (P) | Recall (R) | F1-Score (F) |
|---|---|---|---|
| **Baseline** | 0.15 | 0.33 | 0.21 |
| **1-gram** | 0.83 | 0.83 | 0.83 |
| **2-gram** | 0.89 | 0.89 | 0.89 |
| **3-gram** | 0.91 | 0.91 | 0.91 |
| **4-gram** | 0.93 | 0.93 | 0.93 |
| **5-gram** | 0.93 | 0.93 | 0.93 |

Table 5: Results of 10-fold Cross Validation on Tri-Class Classification

higher order n-gram models can resolve the prominent confusion between Arabic and Persian. Since both Arabic and Persian share almost the same phonetic inventory, working with lower order n-gram models doesn't seem ideal.

| Class | Indic | Persio-Arabic |
|---|---|---|
| Indic | 235 | 60 |
| Persio-Arabic | 15 | 1,057 |

Table 6: Confusion Matrix of Binary Classification

| Class | Arabic | Indic | Persian |
|---|---|---|---|
| Arabic | 605 | 5 | 26 |
| Indic | 11 | 268 | 18 |
| Persian | 22 | 9 | 415 |

Table 7: Confusion Matrix of Tri-class Classification

## 4 Adapting Frames from Arabic and Hindi PropBanks

As discussed in Section 2.1.1, the creation of predicate frames precedes the actual annotation of verb instances in a given corpus. In this section, we describe our approach towards the first stage of Urdu PropBanking by adapting related predicate frames from Arabic and Hindi PropBanks (Palmer et al., 2008; Vaidya et al., 2011). Since a PropBank is not available for Persian, we could only adapt those predicate frames which are shared with Arabic and Hindi.

Although, Urdu shares or borrows most of its literary vocabulary from Arabic and Persian, it retains its simple verb (as opposed to compound or complex verbs) inventory from Indo-Aryan ancestry. Verbs from Arabic and Persian are borrowed less frequently, although there are examples such as '$khariid$' $buy$, '$farma$' $say$ etc.[5] This overlap in the verb inventory between Hindi and Urdu might explain the fact that they share the same grammar.

The fact that Urdu shares its lexicon with these languages, prompted us towards exploring the possibility of using their resources for Urdu PropBanking. We are in the process of adapting frames for those Urdu predicates that are shared with either Arabic or Hindi.

Urdu frame file creation must be carried out for both simple verbs and complex predicates. Since Urdu differs very little in simple verb inventory from Hindi, this simplifies the development process as the frames could be ported easily. However, this is not the case with nominal predicates. In Urdu, many nominal predicates are borrowed from Arabic or Persian as shown in Table (8). Given that a PropBank for Persian is not available, the task of creating the frames for nominal predicates in Urdu would have been fairly daunting in the paucity of the Arabic PropBank, as well.

| | Simple Verbs | | Nominal Predicates | |
|---|---|---|---|---|
| **Language** | **Total** | **Unique** | **Total** | **Unique** |
| **Arabic** | 12 | 1 | 6,780 | 765 |
| **Hindi** | 7,332 | 441 | 1,203 | 258 |
| **Persian** | 69 | 3 | 2,276 | 352 |
| **Total** | 7,413 | 445 | 10,259 | 1,375 |

Table 8: Urdu Treebank Predicate Statistics

### 4.1 Simple Verbs

The simple verb inventory of Urdu and Hindi is almost similar, so the main task was to locate and extract the relevant frames from Hindi frame files. Fortunately, with the exception of $farmaa$ '$say$', all the other simple verbs which Urdu borrows from Persian or Arabic (cf. Table (8)) were also borrowed by Hindi. Therefore, the Hindi simple verb frame files sufficed for porting frames for Urdu simple verbs.

There were no significant differences found between the Urdu and Hindi rolesets, which describe either semantic variants of the same verb or its causative forms. Further, in order to name the frame files with their corresponding Urdu lemmas, we used Konstanz's Urdu transliteration scheme

[5]Borrowed verbs often do not function as simple verbs rather they are used like nominals in complex predicate constructions such as **mehsoos** in '*mehsoos karnaa*' *to feel*.

(Malik et al., 2010) to convert a given lemma into its romanized form. Since the Hindi frame files use the WX transliteration scheme[6], which is not appropriate for Urdu due to lack of coverage for Persio-Arabic phonemes or sounds like $\mathbf{d}^{\text{ʕ}}$ *'pharyngealized voiced alveolar stop'*. The frame files also contain example sentences for each predicate, in order to make the PropBank annotation task easier. While adapting the frame files from Hindi to Urdu, simply transliterating such examples for Urdu predicates was not always an option, because sentences consisting of words with Sanskrit origin may not be understood by Urdu speakers. Hence, all the examples in the ported frames have been replaced with Urdu sentences by an Urdu expert.

In general we find that the Urdu verbs are quite similar to Hindi verbs, and this simplified our task of adapting the frames for simple verbs. The nouns, however, show more variation. Since a large proportion (up to 50%) of Urdu predicates are expressed using verb-noun complex predicates, nominal predicates play a crucial role in our annotation process and must be accounted for.

### 4.2 Complex Predicates

In the Urdu treebank, there are 17,672 predicates, of which more than half have been identified as noun-verb complex predicates (NVC) at the dependency level. Typically, a noun-verb complex predicate *chorii* 'theft' *karnaa* 'to do' has two components: a noun *chorii* and a light verb *karnaa* giving us the meaning 'steal'. The verbal component in NVCs has reduced predicating power (although it is inflected for person, number, and gender agreement as well as tense, aspect and mood) and its nominal complement is considered the true predicate. In our annotation of NVCs, we follow a procedure common to all PropBanks, where we create frame files for the nominal or the 'true' predicate (Hwang et al., 2010). An example of a frame file for a noun such as *chorii* is described in Table (9).

The creation of a frame file for the set of true predicates that occur in an NVC is important from the point of view of linguistic annotation. Given the large number of NVCs, a semi-automatic method has been proposed for creating Hindi nominal frame files, which saves the manual effort required for creating frames for nearly

[6]http://en.wikipedia.org/wiki/WX_notation

| **Frame file for *chorii*-n(oun)** | |
|---|---|
| *chorii*.01: theft-n | light verb: *kar*'do; to steal' |
| `Arg0` | person who steals |
| `Arg1` | thing stolen |
| *chorii*.02 : theft-n | light verb: *ho* 'be/become; to get stolen' |
| `Arg1` | thing stolen |

Table 9: Frame file for predicate noun *chorii* 'theft' with two frequently occurring light verbs *ho* and *kar*. If other light verbs are found to occur, they are added as additional rolesets as chorii.03, chorii.04 and so on.

3,015 unique Hindi noun and light verb combinations (Vaidya et al., 2013).

For Urdu, the process of nominal frame file creation is preceded by the identification of the etymological origin for each nominal. If that nominal has an Indic or Arabic origin, relevant frames from Arabic or Hindi PropBanks were adapted for Urdu. On the other hand, if the Urdu nominal originates from Persian, then frame creation will be done either manually or using other available Persian language resources, in the future.

In Table (8), there are around 258 nominal predicates that are common in Hindi and Urdu, so we directly ported their frames from Hindi PropBank with minor changes as was done for simple verb frames. Out of 765 nominal predicates shared with Arabic, 308 nominal predicate frames have been ported to Urdu. 98 of these nominal predicate frames were already present in the Arabic PropBank and were ported as such. However, for the remaining 667 unique predicates, frames are being created manually by Arabic PropBanking experts and will be ported to Urdu once they become available.

Porting of Arabic frames to Urdu is not that trivial. We observed that while Urdu borrows vocabulary from Arabic it does not borrow all the senses for some words. In such cases, the rolesets that are irrelevant to Urdu have to be discarded manually. The example sentences for all the frames ported from Arabic PropBank have to be sourced from either the web or manually created by an Urdu expert, as was the case with Hindi simple verbs.

## 5 Conclusion

In this paper we have exploited the overlap between the lexicon of Urdu, Arabic and Hindi for the creation of predicate frames for Urdu Prop-

Banking. We presented a simple and accurate classifier for the identification of source or origin of Urdu vocabulary which is a necessary step in the overall process of extraction of predicate frames from the related PropBanks. In the case of simple verbs that occur in the Urdu treebank, we have extracted all the frames from the Hindi PropBank and adapted them for Urdu PropBanking. Similarly for complex predicates, frames for Urdu treebank nominal predicates are extracted from Hindi as well as from Arabic PropBanks. Since a PropBank is not available for Persian, the creation of frames for shared predicates with Persian is a prospect for future work. We plan to create these frames either manually or semi-automatically, using the available Persian Dependency treebanks (Rasooli et al., 2011; Rasooli et al., 2013).

## Acknowledgments

We would like to thank Himani Chaudhry for her valuable comments that helped to improve the quality of this paper.

The work reported in this paper is supported by the NSF grant (Award Number: CNS 0751202; CFDA Number: 47.070)[7].

## References

Riyaz Ahmad Bhat and Dipti Misra Sharma. 2012. A dependency treebank of urdu and its evaluation. In *Proceedings of the Sixth Linguistic Annotation Workshop*, pages 157–165. Association for Computational Linguistics.

Rajesh Bhatt, Bhuvana Narasimhan, Martha Palmer, Owen Rambow, Dipti Misra Sharma, and Fei Xia. 2009. A multi-representational and multi-layered treebank for hindi/urdu. In *Proceedings of the Third Linguistic Annotation Workshop*, pages 186–189. Association for Computational Linguistics.

Jinho D Choi, Claire Bonial, and Martha Palmer. 2010a. Propbank frameset annotation guidelines using a dedicated editor, cornerstone. In *LREC*.

Jinho D Choi, Claire Bonial, and Martha Palmer. 2010b. Propbank instance annotation guidelines using a dedicated editor, jubilee. In *LREC*.

David Dowty. 1991. Thematic proto-roles and argument selection. *Language*, 67(3):547–619.

[7]Any opinions, findings, and conclusions or recommendations expressed in this material are those of the author(s) and do not necessarily reflect the views of the National Science Foundation.

Ted Dunning. 1994. *Statistical identification of language*. Computing Research Laboratory, New Mexico State University.

Heba Elfardy and Mona T Diab. 2012. Token level identification of linguistic code switching. In *COLING (Posters)*, pages 287–296.

Marcello Federico, Nicola Bertoldi, and Mauro Cettolo. 2008. Irstlm: an open source toolkit for handling large scale language models. In *Interspeech*, pages 1618–1621.

Jena D Hwang, Archna Bhatia, Clare Bonial, Aous Mansouri, Ashwini Vaidya, Nianwen Xue, and Martha Palmer. 2010. Propbank annotation of multilingual light verb constructions. In *Proceedings of the Fourth Linguistic Annotation Workshop*, pages 82–90. Association for Computational Linguistics.

Ben King and Steven P Abney. 2013. Labeling the languages of words in mixed-language documents using weakly supervised methods. In *HLT-NAACL*, pages 1110–1119.

Paul Kingsbury and Martha Palmer. 2002. From treebank to propbank. In *LREC*. Citeseer.

Marco Lui, Jey Han Lau, and Timothy Baldwin. 2014. Automatic detection and language identification of multilingual documents. *Transactions of the Association for Computational Linguistics*, 2:27–40.

Muhammad Kamran Malik, Tafseer Ahmed, Sebastian Sulger, Tina Bögel, Atif Gulzar, Ghulam Raza, Sarmad Hussain, and Miriam Butt. 2010. Transliterating urdu for a broad-coverage urdu/hindi lfg grammar. In *LREC*.

Colin P Masica. 1993. *The Indo-Aryan Languages*. Cambridge University Press.

Dong Nguyen and A Seza Dogruoz. 2014. Word level language identification in online multilingual communication. In *Proceedings of the 2013 Conference on Empirical Methods in Natural Language Processing*.

Martha Palmer, Olga Babko-Malaya, Ann Bies, Mona T Diab, Mohamed Maamouri, Aous Mansouri, and Wajdi Zaghouani. 2008. A pilot arabic propbank. In *LREC*.

Mohammad Sadegh Rasooli, Amirsaeid Moloodi, Manouchehr Kouhestani, and Behrouz Minaei-Bidgoli. 2011. A syntactic valency lexicon for persian verbs: The first steps towards persian dependency treebank. In *5th Language & Technology Conference (LTC): Human Language Technologies as a Challenge for Computer Science and Linguistics*, pages 227–231.

Mohammad Sadegh Rasooli, Manouchehr Kouhestani, and Amirsaeid Moloodi. 2013. Development of a persian syntactic dependency treebank. In *Proceedings of the 2013 Conference of the North American Chapter of the Association for Computational*

*Linguistics: Human Language Technologies*, pages 306–314.

Ashwini Vaidya, Jinho D Choi, Martha Palmer, and Bhuvana Narasimhan. 2011. Analysis of the hindi proposition bank using dependency structure. In *Proceedings of the 5th Linguistic Annotation Workshop*, pages 21–29. Association for Computational Linguistics.

Ashwini Vaidya, Martha Palmer, and Bhuvana Narasimhan. 2013. Semantic roles for nominal predicates: Building a lexical resource. *NAACL HLT 2013*, 13:126.

Fei Xia, Owen Rambow, Rajesh Bhatt, Martha Palmer, and Dipti Misra Sharma. 2009. Towards a multi-representational treebank. In *The 7th International Workshop on Treebanks and Linguistic Theories. Groningen, Netherlands*.

# Measuring Language Closeness by Modeling Regularity

**Javad Nouri** and **Roman Yangarber**
Department of Computer Science
University of Helsinki, Finland
first.last@cs.helsinki.fi

## Abstract

This paper addresses the problems of measuring similarity between languages—where the term *language* covers any of the senses denoted by *language*, *dialect* or *linguistic variety*, as defined by any theory. We argue that to devise an effective way to measure the similarity between languages one should build a probabilistic model that tries to capture as much regular correspondence between the languages as possible. This approach yields two benefits. First, given a set of language data, for any two models, this gives a way of objectively determining which model is better, i.e., which model is more likely to be accurate and informative. Second, given a model, for any two languages we can determine, in a principled way, how close they are. The better models will be better at judging similarity. We present experiments on data from three language families to support these ideas. In particular, our results demonstrate the arbitrary nature of terms such as *language* vs. *dialect*, when applied to related languages.

## 1 Introduction

In the context of building and applying NLP tools to similar languages, language varieties, or dialects,[1] we are interested in principled ways of capturing the notion of language *closeness*.

Starting from scratch to develop resources and tools for languages that are close to each other is expensive; the hope is that the cost can be reduced by making use of pre-existing resources and tools for related languages, which are richer in resources.

In the context of this workshop, we assume that we deal with some method, "Method X," that is applied to two (or more) related languages. For example, Method X may involve adapting/porting a linguistic resource from one language to another; or may be trying to translate between the languages; etc. We also assume that the success of Method X directly depends in some way on how similar—or close—the languages are: that is, the similarity between the languages is expected to be a good predictor of how successful the application of the method will be. Thus, in such a setting, it is worthwhile to devote some effort to devising good ways of measuring similarity between languages. This is the main position of this paper.

We survey some of the approaches to measuring inter-language similarity in Section 2. We assume that we are dealing with languages that are *related* genetically (i.e., etymologically). Related languages may be (dis)similar on many levels; in this paper, we focus on similarity on the lexical level. This is admittedly a potential limitation, since, e.g., for Method X, similarity on the level of syntactic structure may be more relevant than similarity on the lexical level. However, as is done in other work, we use lexical similarity as a "general" indicator of relatedness between the languages.[2]

Most of the surveyed methods begin with *alignment* at the level of individual phonetic segments (phones), which is seen as an essential phase in the process of evaluating similarity. Alignment procedures are applied to the input data, which are sets of words which are judged to be similar (cognate)—drawn from the related languages.

Once an alignment is obtained using some method, the natural question arises: how effective is the particular output alignment?

Once the data is aligned (and, hopefully, aligned

[1] We use the term *language* to mean any of: *language*, *dialect*, or *linguistic variety*, according to any definition.

[2] This is a well-studied subject in linguistics, with general consensus that the lexical level has stronger resistance to change than other levels.



*Language Technology for Closely Related Languages and Language Variants (LT4CloseLang)*, pages 56–65,
October 29, 2014, Doha, Qatar. ©2014 Association for Computational Linguistics

well), it becomes possible to devise measures for computing *distances* between the aligned words. One of the simplest of such measures is the Levenshtein edit distance (LED), which is a crude count of edit operations needed to transform one word into one another. Averaging across LEDs between individual word pairs gives an estimate of the distance between the languages. The question then arises: how accurate is the obtained distance?

LED has obvious limitations. LED charges an edit operation for substituting similar as well as dissimilar phones—regardless of how regular (and hence, probable) a given substitution is. Conversely, LED charges nothing for substituting a phone $x$ in language A for the same phone in language B, even if $x$ in A *regularly* (e.g., always!) corresponds to $y$ in B. More sophisticated variants of LED are then proposed, which try to take into account some aspects of the natural alignment setting (such as assigning different weights to different edit operations, e.g., by saying that it is cheaper to transform $t$ into $d$ than $t$ into $w$).

Thus, in pursuit of effective similarity measures, we are faced with a sequence of steps: procedures for aligning data produce alignments; from the individual word-level alignments we derive distance measures; averaging distances across all words we obtain similarity measures between languages; we then require methods for comparing and *validating* the resulting language distance measures. At various phases, these steps involve *subjectivity*—typically in the form of gold standards. We discuss the kinds of subjectivity encountered with this approach in detail in Section 2.1.

As an alternative approach, we advocate viewing closeness between languages in terms of *regularity* in the data: if two languages are very close, it means that either the differences between them are very few, or—if they are many—then they are very regular.[3] As the number of differences grows and their nature becomes less regular, the languages grow more distant. The goal then is to build probabilistic models that capture regularity in the data; to do this, we need to devise algorithms to discover as much regularity as possible.

This approach yields several advantages. First, a model assigns a probability to observed data. This has deep implications for this task, since it allows us to quantify uncertainty in a principled fashion, rather than commit to ad-hoc decisions and prior assumptions. We will show that probabilistic modeling requires us to make fewer subjective judgements. Second, the probabilities that the models assign to data allow us to build natural distance measures. A pair of languages whose data have a higher probability under a given model are closer than a pair with a lower probability, in a well-defined sense. This also allows us to define distance between individual word pairs. The smarter the model—i.e., the more regularity it captures in the data—the more we will be able to trust in the distance measures based on the model. Third—and equally important for this problem setting—this offers a principled way of comparing methods: if model X assigns higher probability to real data than model Y, then model X is better, and can be trusted more. The key point here is that we can then compare models without any "ground truth" or gold-standard, pre-annotated data.

One way to see this is by using the model to predict *unobserved* data. We can withhold one word pair $(w_A, w_B)$ from languages A and B before building the model (so the model does not see the true correspondence); once the model is built, show it $w_A$, and ask what is the corresponding word in B. Theoretically, this is simple: the best guess for $\hat{w}_B$ is simply the one that maximizes the probability of the pair $p_M(w_A, \hat{w}_B)$ under the model, over *all* possible strings $\hat{w}_B$ in B.[4] Measuring the distance between $w_B$ and $\hat{w}_B$ tells how good $M$ is at predicting unseen data. Now, if model $M_1$ consistently predicts better than $M_2$, it is very difficult to argue that $M_1$ is in any sense the worse model; and it is able to predict better only because it has succeeded in learning more about the data and the regularities in it.

Thus we can compare different models for measuring linguistic similarity. And this can be done in a principled fashion—if the distances are based on probabilistic models.

The paper is organized as follows. We continue with a discussion of related work. In Section 3 we present one particular approach to modeling, based on information-theoretic principles. In Section 4 we show some applications of these models to several linguistic data sets, from three different language families. We conclude with plans for fu-

[3]In the former case, the differences form a short list; in the latter, the *rules* describing the differences form a short list.

[4]In practice, this can be done efficiently, using heuristics to constrain the search over all strings $\hat{w}_B$ in B.

ture work, in Section 5.

## 2 Related work

In this section we survey related work on similarity measures between languages, and contrast the principles on which this work relies against the principles which we advocate.

### 2.1 Subjectivity

Typically, alignment-based approaches use several kinds of inputs that have a subjective nature.

One such input is the data itself, which is to be aligned. For a pair of closely related dialects, deciding which words to align may appear "self-evident." However, as we take dialects/languages that are progressively more distant, such judgements become progressively less self-evident; therefore, in all cases, we should keep in mind that the input data itself is a source of subjectivity in measuring similarity based on data that is comprised of lists of related words.

Another source of subjectivity in some of the related work is *gold-standard* alignments, which accompany the input data. Again, for very close languages, the "correct" alignment may appear to be obvious. However, we must recognize that this necessarily involves subjective judgements from the creators of the gold-standard alignment.

Further, many alignment methods pre-suppose one-to-one correspondence between phones. On one hand, this is due to limitations of the methods themselves (there exist methods for aligning phones in other than one-to-one fashion); on another hand, it violates accepted linguistic understanding that phones do not need to correspond in a one-to-one fashion among close languages. Another potential source of subjectivity comes in the form of prior assumptions or restrictions on permissible alignments.[5] Another common assumption is insistence on consonant-to-consonant and vowel-to-vowel alignments. More relaxed assumptions may come in the form of prior probabilities of phone alignments. Although these may appear "natural" in some sense, it is important to keep in mind that they are *ad hoc*, and reflect a subjective judgement which may not be correct.

After alignment and computation of language distance, the question arises: which of the distance measures is more accurate? Again, one way to answer this question is to resort to gold standards. For example, this can be done via phylogenetic clustering; if method A says language $l_1$ is closer to $l_2$ than to $l_3$, and method B says the opposite (that $l_1$ is closer to $l_3$), and if we "know" the latter to be true—from a gold standard—then we can prefer method B. Further, if we have a gold-standard tree for the group of languages, we can apply tree-distance measures[6] to check how the trees generated by a given method differ from the gold-standard. The method that deviates least from the gold standard is then considered best.

### 2.2 Levenshtein-based algorithms

The Levenshtein algorithm is a dynamic programming approach for aligning a word pair $(A, B)$ using a least expensive set of insertion, deletion and substitution operations required for transforming $A$ into $B$. While the original Levenshtein edit distance is based on these three operations without any restrictions, later algorithms adapt this method by additional edit operations or restrictions.

Wieling et al. (2009) compare several alignment algorithms applied to dialect pronunciation data. These algorithms include several adaptations of the Levenshtein algorithm and the Pair Hidden Markov Model. They evaluate the algorithms by comparing the resulting pairwise alignments to alignments generated from a set of manually corrected multiple alignments. Standard Levenshtein edit distance is used for comparing the output of each algorithm to the gold standard alignment, to determine which algorithm is preferred.

All alignment algorithms based on Levenshtein distance evaluated by Wieling et al. (2009) restrict aligning vowels with consonants.

VC-sensitive Levenshtein algorithm: uses the standard Levenshtein algorithm, prohibits aligning vowels with consonants, and assigns unit cost for all edit operations. The only sense in which it captures *regularities* is the assumption that the same symbol in two languages represents same sound, which results in assigning a cost of 0 to aligning a symbol to itself. It also prevents the algorithm from finding vowel-to-consonant correspondences (found in some languages), such as *u–v*, *u–l*, etc.

Levenshtein algorithm with Swap: adds an edit operation to enable the algorithm to capture phenomena such as metathesis, via a *transposition*:

[5] One-to-one alignment is actually one such restriction.

[6] Tree-distance measures are developed in the context of work on phylogenetic trees in biological/genetic applications.

aligning $ab$ in $A$ to $ba$ in $B$ costs a single edit operation. This algorithm also forbids aligning vowels to consonants, except in a swap.

Levenshtein algorithm with generated segment distances based on phonetic features: The above algorithms assign unit cost for all edit operations, regardless of how the segments are related. Heeringa (2004) uses a variant where the distances are obtained from differences between phonetic features of the segment pairs. The authors observe that this is subjective because one could choose from different possible feature sets.

Levenshtein algorithm with generated segment distances based on acoustic features: To avoid subjectivity of feature selection, Heeringa (2004) experiments with assigning different costs to different segment pairs based on how phonetically close they are; segment distances are calculated by comparing *spectrograms* of recorded pronunciations. These algorithms do not attempt to discover regularity in data, since they only consider the word pair at a time, using no information about the rest of the data.

Levenshtein algorithm with distances based on PMI: Wieling et al. (2009) use Point-wise Mutual Information (PMI) as the basis for segment distances. They assign different costs to segments, and use the entire dataset for each alignment. PMI for outcomes $x$ and $y$ of random variables $X$ and $Y$ is defined as:

$$pmi(x, y) = \log_2 \frac{p(x, y)}{p(x)p(y)} \quad (1)$$

PMI is calculated using estimated probabilities of the events. Since greater PMI shows higher tendency of $x$ and $y$ to co-occur, it is reversed and normalized to obtain a dissimilarity measure to be used as segment distance. Details about this method are in (Wieling and Nerbonne, 2011).

### 2.3 Other distance measures

Ellison and Kirby (2006) present a distance measure based on comparing intra-language lexica only, arguing that there is no well-founded common language-independent phonetic space to be used for comparing word forms across languages. Instead, they focus on inferring the distances by comparing how meanings in language $A$ are likely to be confused for each other, and comparing it to the confusion probabilities in language $B$.

Given a lexicon containing mappings from a set of meanings $M$ to a set of forms $F$, confusion probability $P(m_1|m_2; L)$ for each pair of meanings $(m_1, m_2)$ in $L$ is the probability of confusing $m_1$ for $m_2$. This probability is formulated based on an adaptation of *neighborhood activation model*, and depends on the edit distance between the corresponding forms in the lexicon. Following this approach, they construct a confusion probability matrix for each language, which can be viewed as a probability distribution. Inter-language distances are then calculated as the distance between the corresponding distributions, using symmetric Kullback-Liebler distance and Rao distance . The inferred distances are used to construct a phylogenetic tree of the Indo-European languages. The approach is evaluated by comparing the resulting taxonomy to a gold-standard tree, which is reported to be a good fit.

As with other presented methods, although this method can be seen as measuring distances between languages, there remain two problems. First, they do not reflect the genetic differences and similarities—and regularities—between the languages in a transparent, easily interpretable way. Second, they offer no direct way to compare competing approaches, except indirectly, and using (subjective) gold-standards.

## 3 Methods for measuring language closeness

We now discuss an approach which follows the proposal outlined in Section 1, and allows us to build probabilistic models for measuring closeness between languages. Other approaches that rely on probabilistic modeling would serve equally well. A comprehensive survey of methods for measuring language closeness may be found in (Wieling and Nerbonne, 2015). Work that is probabilistically oriented, similarly to our proposed approaches, includes (Bouchard-Côté et al., 2007; Kondrak, 2004) and others. We next review two types of models (some of which are described elsewhere), which are based on information-theoretic principles. We discuss how these models suit the proposed approach, in the next section.

### 3.1 1-1 symbol model

We begin with our "basic" model, described in (Wettig and Yangarber, 2011; Wettig et al., 2011), which makes several simplifying assumptions—which the subsequent, more advanced models relax (Wettig et al., 2012; Wettig et al., 2013).[7] The basic model is based on alignment, similarly to much of the related work mentioned above: for every word pair in our data set—the "corpus"—it builds a complete alignment for all symbols (Wettig et al., 2011). The basic model considers *pairwise* alignments only, i.e., two languages at a time; we call them the *source* and the *target* languages. Later models relax this restriction by using N-dimensional alignment, with $N > 2$ languages aligned simultaneously. The basic model allows only *1-1* symbol alignments: one source symbol[8] may correspond to one target symbol—or to the empty symbol $\epsilon$ (which we mark as "**.**"). More advanced models align substrings of more than one symbol to each other. The basic model also ignores *context*, whereas in reality symbol correspondences are heavily conditioned on their context. Finally, the basic model treats the symbols as *atoms*, whereas more advanced models treat the symbols as vectors of distinctive features.

We distinguish between the raw, *observed* data and *complete* data—i.e., complete with the alignment; the *hidden* data is where the insertions and deletions occur. For example, if we ask what is the "correct" alignment between Finnish *vuosi* and Khanty *al* (cognate words from these two Uralic languages, both meaning "year"):

$$\begin{array}{cccccc} v & u & o & . & s & i \\ | & | & | & | & | & | \\ . & a & . & l & . & . \end{array} \qquad \begin{array}{ccccc} v & u & o & s & i \\ | & | & | & | & | \\ . & . & a & l & . \end{array}$$

are two possible alignments, among many others. From among all alignments, we seek the *best* alignment: one that is *globally* optimal, i.e., one that is consistent with as many regular sound correspondences as possible. This leads to a chicken-and-egg problem: on one hand, if we had the best alignment for the data, we could simply read off a set of rules, by observing which source symbol corresponds frequently to which target symbol. On the other hand, if we had a complete set of rules, we could construct the best alignment, by using dynamic programming (*à la* one of the above mentioned methods, since the costs of all possible edit operations are determined by the rules). Since at the start we have neither, the rules and the alignment are bootstrapped in tandem.

Following the Minimum Description Length (MDL) principle, the best alignment is the one that can be *encoded* (i.e., written down) in the shortest space. That is, we aim to code the complete data—for all word pairs in the given language pair—as compactly as possible. To find the optimal alignment, we need A. an objective function—a way to measure the quality of any given alignment—and B. a search algorithm, to sift through all possible alignments for one that optimizes the objective.

We can use various methods to code the complete data. Essentially, they all amount to measuring how many bits it costs to "transmit" the complete set of alignment "events", where each alignment event $e$ is a pair of aligned symbols $(\sigma : \tau)$

$$e = (\sigma : \tau) \in \Sigma \cup \{.,\#\} \times T \cup \{.,\#\}$$

drawn from the source alphabet $\Sigma$ and the target alphabet $T$, respectively.[9] One possible coding scheme is "prequential" coding, or the Bayesian marginal likelihood, see, e.g., (Kontkanen et al., 1996), used in (Wettig et al., 2011); another is normalized maximum likelihood (NML) code, (Rissanen, 1996), used in (Wettig et al., 2012).

Prequential coding gives the total code length

$$\begin{aligned} L_{base}(D) = &- \sum_{e \in E} \log c(e)! \\ &+ \log \left[ \sum_{e \in E} c(e) + K - 1 \right]! - \log(K-1)! \end{aligned} \quad (2)$$

for data $D$. Here, $c(e)$ denotes the event count, and $K$ is the total number of event types.

To find the optimal alignments, the algorithm starts with aligning word pairs randomly, and then iteratively searching for the best alignment given rest of the data for each word pair at a time. To do this, we first exclude the current alignment from our *complete* data. The best alignment in the re-aligning process is found using a *Dynamic Programming* matrix, with source word symbols in the rows and target word symbols as the columns. Each possible alignment of the word pair corresponds to a path from top-left cell of the matrix to the bottom-right cell. Each cell $V(\sigma_i, \tau_j)$ holds the cost of aligning sub-string $\sigma_1..\sigma_i$ with $\tau_1..\tau_j$, and is computed as:

$$V(\sigma_i, \tau_j) = \min \begin{cases} V(\sigma_i, \tau_{j-1}) & +L(. : \tau_j) \\ V(\sigma_{i-1}, \tau_j) & +L(\sigma_i : .) \\ V(\sigma_{i-1}, \tau_{j-1}) & +L(\sigma_i : \tau_j) \end{cases} \quad (3)$$

[7]The models can be downloaded from *etymon.cs.helsinki.fi*

[8]In this paper, we equate *symbols* with *sounds*: we assume our data to be given in *phonetic* transcription.

[9]Note, that the alphabets need not be the same, or even have any symbols in common. We add a special end-of-word symbol, always aligned to itself: $(\# : \#)$. Empty alignments $(. : .)$ are not allowed.

where $L(e)$ is the cost of coding event $e$. The cost of aligning the full word pair, is then found in the bottom-right cell, and the corresponding path is chosen as the new alignment, which is registered back into the complete data.

We should mention that due to vulnerability of the algorithm to local optima, we use simulated annealing with (50) random restarts.

### 3.2 Context model

Context model is described in detail in (Wettig et al., 2013). We use a modified version of this model to achieve faster run-time.

One limitation of the basic model described above is that it uses no information about the context of the sounds, thus ignoring the fact that linguistic sound change is regular and highly depends on context. The 1-1 model also treats symbols of the words as $atoms$, ignoring how two sounds are phonetically close. The context model, addresses both of these issues.

Each sound is represented as a vector of distinctive phonetic features. Since we are using MDL as the basis of the model here, we need to code (i.e., transmit) the data. This can be done by coding one feature at a time on each level.

To code a feature $F$ on a level $L$, we construct a decision tree. First, we collect all instances of the sounds in the data of the corresponding level that have the current feature, and then build a count matrix based on how many instances take each value. Here is an example of such a matrix for feature *V* (vertical articulation of a vowel).

| V | Close | Mid-close | Mid-open | Open |
|---|---|---|---|---|
| | 10 | 25 | 33 | 24 |

This shows that there are 10 *close* vowels, 25 *mid-close* vowels, etc.

This serves as the root node of the tree. The tree can then query features of the sounds in the current context by choosing from a set of candidate contexts. Each candidate is a triplet $(L, P, F)$, representing *Level*, *Position*, and *Feature* respectively.

$L$ can be either source or target, since we are dealing with a pair of language varieties at a time. $P$ is the position of the sound that is being queried relative to current sound, and $F$ is the feature being queried. Examples of a *Position* are *previous vowel*, *previous position*, *itself*, etc. The tree expands depending on the possible responses to the query, resulting in child nodes with their own count matrix. The idea here is to make the matrices in the child nodes as sparse as possible in order to code them with fewer bits.

This process continues until the tree cannot be expanded any more. Finally the data in each leaf node is coded using *prequential* coding as before with the same cost explained in Equation 2.

Code length for the complete data consists of cost of encoding the trees and the cost of encoding the data given the trees. The search algorithm remains the same as the 1-1 algorithm, but uses the constructed trees to calculate the cost of events.

This method spends much time rebuilding the trees on each iteration; its run-time is very high. In the modified version used in this paper, the trees are not allowed to expand initially, when the model has just started and everything is random due to simulated annealing. Once the simulated annealing phase is complete, the trees are expanded fully normally. Our experiments show that this results in trees that are equally good as the original ones.

### 3.3 Normalized Compression Distance

The cost of coding the data for a language pair under a model reflects the amount of regularity the model discovered, and thus is a means of measuring the distance between these languages. However the cost also depends on the size of the data for the language pair; thus, a way of normalizing the cost is needed to make them comparable across language pairs. We use "*Normalized Compression Distance*" (NCD), described in (Cilibrasi and Vitanyi, 2005) to achieve this.

Given a model that can compress a language pair $(a, b)$ with cost $C(a, b)$, NCD of $(a, b)$ is:

$$NCD(a,b) = \frac{C(a,b) - \min\big(C(a), C(b)\big)}{\max\big(C(a), C(b)\big)} \tag{4}$$

Since $NCD$ of different pairs are comparable under the same model, it can be used as a distance measure between language varieties.

### 3.4 Prediction of unobserved data

The models mentioned above are also able to predict unobserved data as described in Section 1 (Wettig et al., 2013).

For the basic 1-1 model, since no information about the context is used, prediction simply means looking for the most probable symbol in target language for each symbol of $w_A$. For the context model, a more sophisticated dynamic-programming heuristic is needed to predict the unseen word, (Hiltunen, 2012). The predicted word

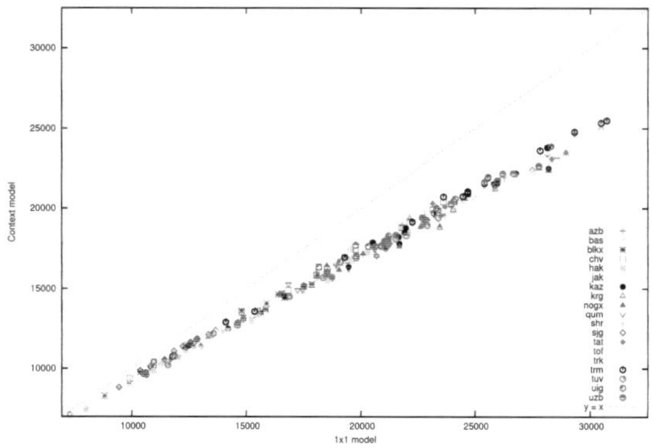


Figure 1: Model comparison: MDL costs.

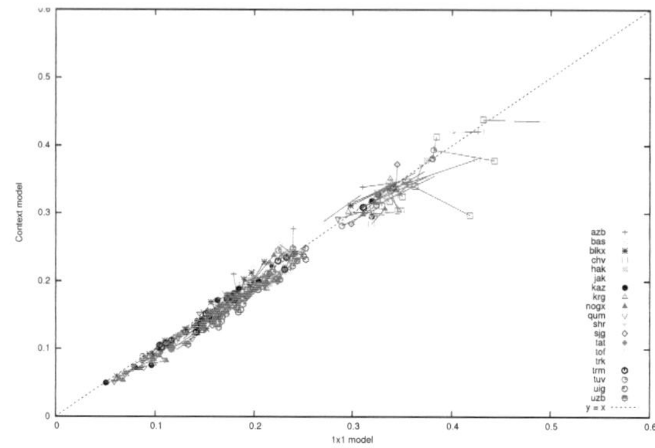


Figure 2: Model comparison: NFED.

$\hat{w}_B$ is then compared to the real corresponding word $w_B$ to measure how well the model performed on the task.

Feature-wise Levenshtein edit distance is used for this comparison. The edit distances for all word pairs are normalized, resulting in *Normalized Feature-wise Edit Distance* (*NFED*) which can serve as a measure of model quality.

## 4 Experiments

To illustrate the principles discussed above, we experiment with the two principal model types described above—the baseline 1-1 model and the context-sensitive model, using data from three different language families.

### 4.1 Data

We use data from the StarLing data bases, (Starostin, 2005), for the Turkic and Uralic language families, and for the Slavic branch of the Indo-European family. For dozens of language families, StarLing has rich data sets (going beyond Swadesh-style lists, as in some other lexical data collections built for judging language and dialect distances). The databases are under constant development, and have different quality. Some datasets, (most notably the IE data) are drawn from multiple sources, which use different notation, transcription, etc., and are not yet unified. The data we chose for use is particularly clean.

For the Turkic family, StarLing at present contains 2017 cognate sets; we use 19 (of the total 27) languages, which have a substantial amount of attested word-forms in the data collection.

### 4.2 Model comparison

We first demonstrate how the "best" model can be chosen from among several models, in a principled way. This is feasible if we work with probabilistic models—models that assign probabilities to the observed data. If the model is also able to perform prediction (of unseen data), then we can measure the model's predictive power and select the best model using predictive power as the criterion. We will show that in the case of the two probabilistic models presented above, these two criteria yield the same result.

We ran the baseline 1-1 model and the context model against the entire Turkic dataset, i.e., the $19 \times 18$ language pairs,[10] (with 50 restarts for each pair, a total of 17100 runs). For each language pair, we select the best out of 50 runs for each model, according to the cost it assigns to this language pair. Figure 1 shows the costs obtained by the best run: each point denotes a language pair; X-coordinate is the cost according to the 1-1 model, Y-coordinate is the cost of the context model. The Figure shows that all $19 \times 18$ points lie below the diagonal (x=y), i.e., for every language pair, the context model finds a code with lower cost—as is expected, since the context model is "smarter," uses more information from the data, and hence finds more regularity in it.

Next, for each language pair, we take the run that found the lowest cost, and use it to impute unseen data, as explained in Section 3—yielding NFED, the distance from the imputed string to the

[10]Turkic languages in tables and figures are: azb:Azerbaijani, bas:Bashkir, blk:Balkar, chv:Chuvash, hak:Khakas, jak:Yakut, kaz:Kazakh, krg:Kyrgyz, nog:Nogaj, qum:Qumyk, shr:Shor, sjg:Sary Uyghur, tat:Tatar, tof:Tofalar, trk:Turkish, trm:Turkmen, tuv:Tuva, uig:Uyghur, uzb:Uzbek.

| | ru | ukr | cz | slk | pl | usrb | lsrb | bulg | scr |
|---|---|---|---|---|---|---|---|---|---|
| **ru** | 0 | .41 | .41 | .39 | .41 | .51 | .53 | .48 | .40 |
| **ukr** | .41 | 0 | .48 | .46 | .51 | .49 | .50 | .48 | .47 |
| **cz** | .40 | .48 | 0 | **.29** | .38 | .45 | .52 | .50 | .39 |
| **slk** | .38 | .45 | **.29** | 0 | .38 | .41 | .44 | .45 | .38 |
| **pl** | .43 | .51 | .39 | .41 | 0 | .48 | .50 | .52 | .45 |
| **usrb** | .50 | .48 | .44 | .40 | .46 | 0 | **.29** | .49 | .48 |
| **lsrb** | .52 | .51 | .49 | .44 | .47 | **.30** | 0 | .52 | .50 |
| **bulg** | .46 | .47 | .48 | .45 | .51 | .47 | .49 | 0 | .41 |
| **scr** | .40 | .47 | .38 | .38 | .43 | .49 | .51 | .44 | 0 |

Table 1: NCDs for 9 Slavic languages, StarLing database: context model

| Language pair | | NCD |
|---|---|---|
| kom_s | kom_p | .18 |
| kom_p | kom_s | .19 |
| udm_s | udm_g | .20 |
| udm_g | udm_s | .21 |
| mar_b | mar_kb | .28 |
| mar_kb | mar_b | .28 |
| mrd_m | mrd_e | .29 |
| mrd_e | mrd_m | .29 |
| est | fin | .32 |
| fin | est | .32 |
| man_p | man_so | .34 |
| khn_v | khn_dn | .35 |
| khn_dn | khn_v | .36 |
| man_so | man_p | .36 |
| saa_n | saa_l | .37 |
| saa_l | saa_n | .37 |

Table 2: Comparison of Uralic dialect/language pairs, sorted by NCD: context model.

actual, correct string in the target language. This again yields $19 \times 18$ points, shown in Figure 2; this time the X and Y values lie between 0 and 1, since NFED is normalized. (In the figure, the points are linked with line segments as follows: for any pair (a,b) the point (a,b) is joined by a line to the point (b,a). This is done for easier identification, since the point (a,b) displays the legend symbol for only language a.) Overall, many more points lie below the diagonal, (approximately 10% of the points are above). The context model performs better, and it would therefore be a safer/wiser choice, if we wish to measure language closeness; which agrees with the result obtained using raw compression costs.

The key point here is that this comparison method can accommodate *any* probabilistic model: for any new candidate model we check—over the same datasets—what probability values does the model assign to each data point. Probabilities and (compression) costs are interchangeable: information theory tells us that for a data set D and model M, the probability P of data D under model M and the cost (code length) L of D under M are related by: $L_M(D) = -\log P_M(D)$. If the new model assigns higher probability (or lower cost) to observed data, it is preferable—*obviating the need for gold-standards*, or subjective judgements.

### 4.3 Language closeness

We next explore various datasets using the context model—the better model we have available.

**Uralic:** We begin with Uralic data from StarLing.[11] The Uralic database contains data from more than one variant of many languages: we extracted data for the top two dialects—in terms of counts of available word-forms—for Komi, Udmurt, Mari, Mordva, Mansi, Khanty and Saami. Table 2 shows the normalized compression distances for each of the pairs; the NCD costs for Finnish and Estonian are given for comparison.

It is striking that the pairs that score below Finnish/Estonian are all "true" dialects, whereas those that score above are not. E.g., the Mansi variants Pelym and Sosva, (Honti, 1998), and Demjanka and Vakh Khanty, (Abondolo, 1998), are mutually unintelligible. The same is true for North and Lule Saami.

**Turkic:** We compute NCDs for the Turkic languages under the context model. Some of the Turkic languages are known to form a much tighter dialect continuum, (Johanson, 1998), which is evident from the NCDs in Table 3. E.g., Tofa is most-closely related to the Tuvan language and forms a dialect continuum with it, (Johanson, 1998). Turkish and Azerbaijani closely resemble each other and are mutually intelligible. In the table we highlight language pairs with NCD $\leq 0.30$.

**Slavic:** We analyzed data from StarLing for 9 Slavic languages.[12] The NCDs are shown in Table 1. Of all pairs, the normalized compression costs for (cz, slk) and (lsrb, usrb) fall below the .30 mark, and indeed these pairs have high mutual intelligibility, unlike all other pairs.

When the data from Table 1 are fed into the NeighborJoining algorithm, (Saitou and Nei, 1987), it draws the phylogeny in Figure 3, which clearly separates the languages into the 3 accepted branches of Slavic: East (ru, ukr), South

[11] We use data from the Finno-Ugric sub-family. The language codes are: est:Estonian, fin:Finnish, khn:Khanty, kom:Komi, man:Mansi, mar:Mari, mrd:Mordva, saa:Saami, udm:Udmurt.

[12] The Slavic languages from StarLing: bulg:Bulgarian, cz:Czech, pl:Polish, ru:Russian, slk:Slovak, scr:Serbo-Croatian, ukr:Ukrainian, lsrb/usrb:Lower and Upper Sorbian.

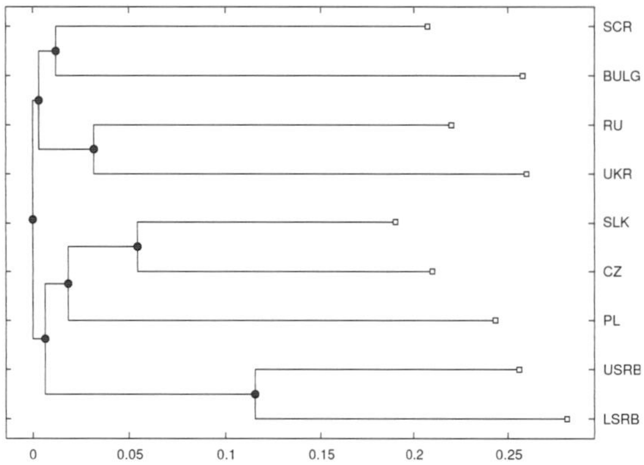


Figure 3: NeighborJoining tree for Slavic languages in Table 1.

(scr, bulg) and West (pl, cz, slk, u/lsrb). The phylogeny also supports later separation (relative time depth $> 0.05$) of the pairs with higher mutual intelligibility—Upper/Lower Sorbian, and Czech/Slovak.[13]

## 5 Conclusions and future work

We have presented a case for using probabilistic modeling when we need reliable quantitative measures of language closeness. Such needs arise, for example, when one attempts to develop methods whose success directly depends on how close the languages in question are. We attempt to demonstrate two main points. One is that using probabilistic models provides a principled and natural way of comparing models—to determine which candidate model we can trust more when measuring how close the languages are. It also lets us compare models without having to build gold-standard datasets; this is important, since gold-standards are subjective, not always reliable, and expensive to produce. We are really interested in regularity, and the proof of the model's quality is in its ability to assign high probability to observed and unobserved data.

The second main point of the paper is showing how probabilistic models can be employed to measure language closeness. Our best-performing model seems to provide reasonable judgements of closeness when applied to languages/linguistic variants from very different language families. For all of Uralic, Turkic and Slavic data, those that fell below the $0.30$ mark on the NCD axis are known to have higher mutual intelligibility, while those that are above the mark have lower or no mutual intelligibility. Of course, we do not claim that $0.30$ is a magic number; for a different model the line of demarcation may fall elsewhere entirely. However, it shows that the model (which we selected on the basis of its superiority according to our selection criteria) is quite *consistent* in predicting the degree of mutual intelligibility, overall.

Incidentally, these experiments demonstrate, in a principled fashion, the well-known arbitrary nature of the terms language vs. dialect—this distinction is simply not supported by real linguistic data. More importantly, probabilistic methods require us to make fewer subjective judgements, with no *ad hoc* priors or gold-standards, which in many cases are difficult to obtain and justify—and rather rely on the observed data as the ultimate and sufficient truth.

[13]We should note that the NCDs produce excellent phylogenies also for the Turkic and Uralic data; not included here due to space constraints.

## Acknowledgments

This research was supported in part by: the FinUgRevita Project of the Academy of Finland, and by the National Centre of Excellence "Algorithmic Data Analysis (ALGODAN)" of the Academy of Finland.

## References

Daniel Abondolo. 1998. Khanty. In Daniel Abondolo, editor, *The Uralic Languages*, pages 358–386. Routledge.

Alexandre Bouchard-Côté, Percy Liang, Thomas Griffiths, and Dan Klein. 2007. A probabilistic approach to diachronic phonology. In *Proceedings of the Joint Conference on Empirical Methods in Natural Language Processing and Computational Natural Language Learning (EMNLP-CoNLL:2007)*, pages 887–896, Prague, Czech Republic.

Rudi Cilibrasi and Paul M.B. Vitanyi. 2005. Clustering by compression. *IEEE Transactions on Information Theory*, 51(4):1523–1545.

T. Mark Ellison and Simon Kirby. 2006. Measuring language divergence by intra-lexical comparison. In *Proceedings of the 21st International Conference on Computational Linguistics and the 44th Annual Meeting of the Association for Computational Linguistics (COLING/ACL-2006)*, pages 273–280, Sydney, Australia.

Wilbert Heeringa. 2004. *Measuring Dialect Pronunciation Differences using Levenshtein Distance*. Ph.D. thesis, Rijksuniversiteit Groningen.

| | azb | bas | blk | chv | hak | jak | kaz | krg | nog | qum | shr | sjg | tat | tof | trk | trm | tuv | uig | uzb |
|---|---|---|---|---|---|---|---|---|---|---|---|---|---|---|---|---|---|---|---|
| **azb** | 0 | .40 | .35 | .60 | .48 | .59 | .38 | .39 | .35 | .34 | .43 | .41 | .38 | .45 | **.27** | .33 | .46 | .40 | .37 |
| **bas** | .39 | 0 | **.28** | .58 | .45 | .59 | **.27** | .31 | **.24** | **.26** | .40 | .41 | **.21** | .46 | .39 | .38 | .45 | .36 | .34 |
| **blk** | .35 | **.30** | 0 | .57 | .42 | .57 | **.26** | **.28** | **.22** | **.19** | .36 | .40 | **.27** | .42 | .34 | .36 | .42 | .35 | **.30** |
| **chv** | .59 | .59 | .56 | 0 | .62 | .67 | .56 | .58 | .55 | .53 | .60 | .57 | .56 | .60 | .56 | .60 | .62 | .61 | .58 |
| **hak** | .47 | .44 | .41 | .63 | 0 | .58 | .41 | .40 | .37 | .40 | **.27** | .43 | .43 | .39 | .46 | .50 | .40 | .46 | .46 |
| **jak** | .57 | .57 | .57 | .70 | .58 | 0 | .56 | .57 | .55 | .54 | .55 | .54 | .57 | .51 | .58 | .57 | .56 | .58 | .57 |
| **kaz** | .38 | **.28** | **.27** | .57 | .42 | .57 | 0 | **.24** | **.16** | **.24** | .38 | .39 | **.29** | .44 | .37 | .39 | .41 | .36 | .33 |
| **krg** | .38 | .31 | **.27** | .60 | .40 | .57 | **.23** | 0 | **.21** | **.26** | .35 | .40 | .32 | .41 | .36 | .39 | .40 | .35 | .33 |
| **nog** | .35 | **.25** | **.22** | .57 | .39 | .55 | **.15** | **.22** | 0 | **.19** | .36 | .38 | **.26** | .43 | .33 | .35 | .41 | .35 | .31 |
| **qum** | .34 | **.27** | **.19** | .57 | .41 | .55 | **.23** | **.26** | **.19** | 0 | .35 | .37 | **.26** | .41 | .33 | .35 | .41 | .33 | .31 |
| **shr** | .43 | .40 | .36 | .63 | **.28** | .55 | .38 | .36 | .35 | .34 | 0 | .40 | .40 | .36 | .43 | .44 | .38 | .42 | .42 |
| **sjg** | .43 | .42 | .41 | .58 | .45 | .55 | .40 | .41 | .39 | .38 | .40 | 0 | .42 | .44 | .43 | .43 | .43 | .41 | .41 |
| **tat** | .36 | **.22** | **.27** | .60 | .44 | .59 | **.28** | .32 | **.26** | **.26** | .40 | .41 | 0 | .45 | .38 | .38 | .45 | .36 | .33 |
| **tof** | .47 | .45 | .42 | .61 | .39 | .50 | .42 | .42 | .42 | .41 | .36 | .42 | .45 | 0 | .48 | .46 | **.24** | .44 | .43 |
| **trk** | **.28** | .40 | .35 | .58 | .48 | .59 | .37 | .36 | .33 | .34 | .43 | .42 | .39 | .47 | 0 | .34 | .46 | .40 | .38 |
| **trm** | .32 | .40 | .36 | .62 | .51 | .59 | .39 | .40 | .36 | .35 | .44 | .43 | .39 | .46 | .34 | 0 | .49 | .41 | .36 |
| **tuv** | .46 | .46 | .41 | .63 | .40 | .56 | .41 | .40 | .41 | .41 | .38 | .42 | .45 | **.23** | .45 | .48 | 0 | .45 | .46 |
| **uig** | .40 | .39 | .34 | .60 | .49 | .58 | .36 | .36 | .36 | .33 | .43 | .40 | .38 | .45 | .41 | .42 | .46 | 0 | .33 |
| **uzb** | .37 | .36 | .31 | .60 | .48 | .58 | .34 | .34 | .32 | .32 | .43 | .41 | .34 | .44 | .38 | .36 | .47 | .33 | 0 |

Table 3: Normalized compression distances for 19 Turkic languages (StarLing database): context model


Suvi Hiltunen. 2012. Minimum description length modeling of etymological data. Master's thesis, University of Helsinki.

László Honti. 1998. Ob' Ugrian. In Daniel Abondolo, editor, *The Uralic Languages*, pages 327–357. Routledge.

Lars Johanson. 1998. The history of Turkic. In Lars Johanson & Éva Ágnes Csató, editor, *The Turkic Languages*, pages 81–125. London, New York: Routledge. Classification of Turkic languages (at Turkiclanguages.com).

Grzegorz Kondrak. 2004. Combining evidence in cognate identification. In *Proceedings of the Seventeenth Canadian Conference on Artificial Intelligence (Canadian AI 2004)*, pages 44–59, London, Ontario. Lecture Notes in Computer Science 3060, Springer-Verlag.

Petri Kontkanen, Petri Myllymäki, and Henry Tirri. 1996. Constructing Bayesian finite mixture models by the EM algorithm. Technical Report NC-TR-97-003, ESPRIT NeuroCOLT: Working Group on Neural and Computational Learning.

Jorma Rissanen. 1996. Fisher information and stochastic complexity. *IEEE Transactions on Information Theory*, 42(1):40–47.

Naruya Saitou and Masatoshi Nei. 1987. The neighbor-joining method: a new method for reconstructing phylogenetic trees. *Molecular biology and evolution*, 4(4):406–425.

Sergei A. Starostin. 2005. Tower of Babel: StarLing etymological databases. http://newstar.rinet.ru/.

Hannes Wettig and Roman Yangarber. 2011. Probabilistic models for alignment of etymological data. In *Proceedings of NoDaLiDa: the 18th Nordic Conference on Computational Linguistics*, Riga, Latvia.

Hannes Wettig, Suvi Hiltunen, and Roman Yangarber. 2011. MDL-based Models for Alignment of Etymological Data. In *Proceedings of RANLP: the 8th Conference on Recent Advances in Natural Language Processing*, Hissar, Bulgaria.

Hannes Wettig, Kirill Reshetnikov, and Roman Yangarber. 2012. Using context and phonetic features in models of etymological sound change. In *Proc. EACL Workshop on Visualization of Linguistic Patterns and Uncovering Language History from Multilingual Resources*, pages 37–44, Avignon, France.

Hannes Wettig, Javad Nouri, Kirill Reshetnikov, and Roman Yangarber. 2013. Information-theoretic modeling of etymological sound change. In Lars Borin and Anju Saxena, editors, *Approaches to measuring linguistic differences*, volume 265 of *Trends in Linguistics*, pages 507–531. de Gruyter Mouton.

Martijn Wieling and John Nerbonne. 2011. Measuring linguistic variation commensurably. In *Dialectologia Special Issue II: Production, Perception and Attitude*, pages 141–162.

Martijn Wieling and John Nerbonne. 2015. Advances in dialectometry. In *Annual Review of Linguistics*, volume 1. To appear.

Martijn Wieling, Jelena Prokić, and John Nerbonne. 2009. Evaluating the pairwise string alignment of pronunciations. In *Proceedings of the EACL 2009 Workshop on Language Technology and Resources for Cultural Heritage, Social Sciences, Humanities, and Education*, pages 26–34, Athens, Greece.

# Towards Universal Syntactic Processing of Natural Language (invited talk)

**Slav Petrov**
Google Inc.
76 9th Avenue
New York, NY 10011
slav@google.com

## 1 Abstract

In this talk I will first describe some techniques for projecting syntactic information across language boundaries, allowing us to build models for languages with no labeled training data. I will then present some ongoing work towards a universal representation of morphology and syntax that makes it possible to model language phenomena across language boundaries in a consistent way. Finally, I will highlight some examples of how we have successfully used syntax at Google to improve downstream applications like question answering and machine translation.

## 2 Author's Biography

Slav Petrov is a researcher in Google's New York office, leading a team that works on syntactic parsing and its applications to information extraction, question answering and machine translation. He holds a PhD degree from UC Berkeley, where he worked with Dan Klein. Before that he completed a Master's degree at the Free University of Berlin and was a member of the FU-Fighters team that won the RoboCup world championship in 2004. His work on fast and accurate multilingual syntactic analysis has been recognized with best paper awards at ACL 2011 and NAACL 2012. Slav also teaches Statistical Natural Language Processing at New York University.



*Language Technology for Closely Related Languages and Language Variants (LT4CloseLang)*, page 66,
October 29, 2014, Doha, Qatar. 

# Proper Name Machine Translation from Japanese to Japanese Sign Language

**Taro Miyazaki, Naoto Kato, Seiki Inoue, Shuichi Umeda, Makiko Azuma, Nobuyuki Hiruma**
NHK Science & Technology Research Laboratories
Tokyo, Japan
{miyazaki.t-jw, katou.n-ga, inoue.s-li, umeda.s-hg, azuma.m-ia, hiruma.n-dy}@nhk.or.jp

**Yuji Nagashima**
Faculty of Information, Kogakuin University
Tokyo, japan
nagasima@cc.kogakuin.ac.jp

## Abstract

This paper describes machine translation of proper names from Japanese to Japanese Sign Language (JSL). "Proper name transliteration" is a kind of machine translation of proper names between spoken languages and involves character-to-character conversion based on pronunciation. However, transliteration methods cannot be applied to Japanese-JSL machine translation because proper names in JSL are composed of words rather than characters. Our method involves not only pronunciation-based translation, but also sense-based translation, because kanji, which are ideograms that compose most Japanese proper names, are closely related to JSL words. These translation methods are trained from parallel corpora.

The sense-based translation part is trained via phrase alignment in sentence pairs in a Japanese and JSL corpus. The pronunciation-based translation part is trained from a Japanese proper name corpus and then post-processed with transformation rules. We conducted a series of evaluation experiments and obtained 75.3% of accuracy rate, increasing from baseline method by 19.7 points. We also developed a Japanese-JSL proper name translation system, in which the translated proper names are visualized with CG animations.

## 1 Introduction

Sign language is a visual language in which sentences are created using the fingers, hands, head, face, and lips. For deaf people, sign language is easier to understand than spoken language because it is their mother tongue. To convey the meaning of sentences in spoken language to deaf people, the sentences need to be translated into sign language.

To provide more information with sign language, we have been studying machine translation from Japanese to Japanese Sign Language (JSL). As shown in Figure 1, our translation system automatically translates Japanese text into JSL computer graphics (CG) animations. The system consists of two major processes: text translation and CG synthesis. Text translation translates word sequences in Japanese into word sequences in JSL. CG synthesis generates seamless motion transitions between each sign word motion by using a motion interpolation technique. To improve the machine translation system, we have been tackling several problems with translating in JSL. In this paper, we focus on the problem of proper name translation, because proper names occur frequently in TV news programs and are hard to translate with conventional methods.

Proper name translation is one of the major topics of machine translation. In particular, there are many methods that work with spoken language, such as "proper name transliteration," which means character-to-character conversion based on pronunciation (Knight et al., 1998; Goto et al., 2003; Virga et al., 2003; Li et al., 2004; Finch et al., 2010; Sudoh et al., 2013). However, transliteration methods cannot be applied to Japanese-JSL proper name translation because proper names in JSL are not composed of characters but rather of sign words. To translate proper names using sign words, sense-based translation is required. Sense-based translation trans-



*Language Technology for Closely Related Languages and Language Variants (LT4CloseLang)*, pages 67–75,
October 29, 2014, Doha, Qatar. 

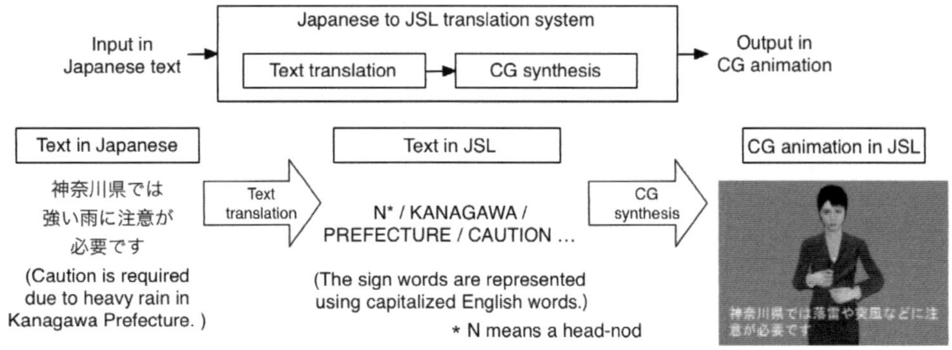


Figure 1: Japanese-JSL translation system overview

lates kanji, which are ideograms that compose most Japanese proper names, into closely related JSL words. Moreover, although several methods have been proposed to translate sentences in sign language, there is as yet no method to translate proper names (Massó et al., 2010; San-Segundo et al., 2010; Morrissey, 2011; Stein et al., 2012; Mazzei, 2012; Lugaresi et al., 2013).

This paper describes proper name translation from Japanese into JSL. The method involves sense-based translation and pronunciation-based translation. Both conversions are based on a statistical machine translation framework. The sense-based translation is a sense-based character-wise translation learned from phrase pairs in a Japanese-JSL corpus. The pronunciation-based translation is a pronunciation-based character-wise translation learned from a Japanese proper name corpus and is post-processed with transformation rules. We conducted a series of evaluation experiments and obtained good results. We also developed a proper name translation system from Japanese to JSL, in which the translated proper names are visualized with CG-animations.

## 2 Proper Names in JSL

### 2.1 Types of proper name in JSL

In JSL, proper name representations are classified into four types, as follows.

**Type 1: sense-based case**

Here, each character in Japanese proper names is translated into sign words in JSL. Most characters that make up Japanese proper names are kanji. Kanji are ideograms, i.e., each kanji representing concept, so they can be translated into words with the concepts in JSL.

For example, in the Japanese place name "香川 (Kagawa)," the kanji-characters "香 (aroma)" and "川 (river)" are respectively translated into sign words "AROMA[1]" and "RIVER." Accordingly, the translation of "香川 (Kagawa)" is "AROMA / RIVER" in JSL.

**Type 2: Pronunciation-based case**

Here, the pronunciations of the kanji are transliterated into the Japanese kana alphabet. The kana are visualized by fingerspelling[2]. The transliteration in this case is not a spelling-based transformation from the source language because kanji are not phonograms[3].

For example, in the Japanese personal name "茂木" (Motegi, written in kana as "モテギ"), the two kanji "茂" and "木" are respectively transliterated into the kana "モテ (mote)" and "ギ (gi)."

Each of the three kana, "モ (mo)," "テ (te)" and "ギ (gi)," is fingerspelled in JSL.

**Type 3: Mixed case**

This type includes Type 1 and Type 2. That is, some of the characters in the proper names are translated into sign words and the others are transliterated into kana and then visualized by fingerspelling. For example, regarding the Japanese place name "長野" (Nagano, written in kana as "ナガノ"), the kanji "長" is translated into the sign word "LONG" and "野" is transliterated into the kana "ノ (no)."

[1]The words in JSL are represented using capitalized English words. This notation method is called "glosses" in the sign language research community.

[2]All of the kana can be visualized by fingerspelling in JSL.

[3]For example, the character "木" is pronounced "ki," "gi," "moku," "boku" etc. The decision as to which pronunciation should be used is by context, meanings or idiom.

Table 1: Analysis of proper name types

| | | |
|---|---|---|
| Place name | Type 1 | 43% |
| | Type 2 | 3% |
| | Type 3 | 10% |
| | Type 4 | 44% |
| Persons' name | Type 1 | 60% |
| | Type 2 | 14% |
| | Type 3 | 21% |
| | Type 4 | 21% |

**Type 4: Idiomatic case**

These proper names are traditionally defined as fixed representations in JSL.

### 2.2 Analysis of Proper Name Types in Corpora

To investigate the frequencies of these four types in corpora, we analyzed a geographical dictionary (JFD, 2009) of place names and our corpus (mentioned in section 4.2.1) of persons' names. Table 1 shows the results of the analysis.

Proper names of Types 1, 2 and 3 needed to be translated, while those of Type 4 needed to be registered in an idiomatic translation dictionary of proper names. Furthermore, the proper name translations of Type 1, 2 and 3 reduce to sense-based translations and/or pronunciation-based translations.

Our translation method performs sense-based translation and pronunciation-based translation on the basis of statistical machine translation (SMT) methods. The next section describes this method.

## 3 Our translation method

### 3.1 Sense-based translation

#### 3.1.1 Basic method (baseline)

The sense-based translation uses SMT, and the translation probabilities (i.e. a lexicon model in SMT) are trained on our news corpus consisting of sentence pairs in Japanese and JSL. The basic method of training the lexicon model uses the corpus in a sentence-by-sentence manner (Figure 2-(a)). It segments the sentences into characters in Japanese and into words in JSL. Then, the model is trained on the characters of the Japanese sentences and the words of the JSL sentences. Regarding Sentence 1 below, the method segments it into Sentence 2 in Japanese and trains the model.

**Sentence 1**

**JP** 香川は朝から晴れるでしょう

(It will be fine from the morning in Kagawa)

**JSL** AROMA / RIVER / MORNING / FROM / FINE / DREAM

**Sentence 2**

**JP** 香/川/は/朝/か/ら/晴/れ/る/で/し/ょ/う

(It will be fine from the morning in Kagawa)

**JSL** AROMA / RIVER / MORNING / FROM / FINE / DREAM

We took the basic method above to be the baseline method for the evaluations.

#### 3.1.2 Our method

Our method uses the corpus in a phrase-by-phrase manner. To use the phrase-segmented corpus, the method is composed of two steps. The first step aligns Japanese phrases to JSL phrases in each of the sentence pairs in the corpus by using many-to-many word alignment. Using the results of the alignment, each sentence pair is divided into phrase pairs. The second step segments the phrases into characters in Japanese and trains the sense-based translation part on the phrase pairs (Figure 2-(b)).

Let us illustrate our method using Sentence 1. The first step is dividing a sentence into phrase pairs. We use alignment pairs, the result of the many-to-many word alignment, as the phrase pairs. The alignment pairs are combined into phrase pairs, as shown in Phrase 1 below.

**Phrase 1**

**JP1** 香川 / は (in Kagawa)

**JSL1** AROMA / RIVER

**JP2** 朝 / から (from the morning)

**JSL2** MORNING / FROM

**JP3** 晴れる / でしょ / う (it will be fine)

**JSL3** FINE / DREAM

Alignment pairs that consist of many more or fewer sign words than Japanese words are discarded as alignment errors. In this paper, we regard the alignment pair as the alignment error when $n_{sign} > (N_{JP} + \alpha)$ or $(n_{sign} + \alpha) < n_{JP}$. Here, $n_{sign}$ means the number of sign words in

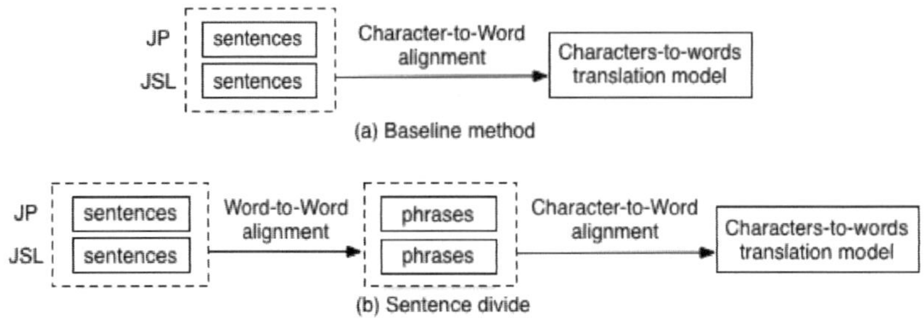


Figure 2: Two ways of learning translation models

the alignment pair, and $n_{JP}$ means the number of Japanese words in the alignment pair. We chose $\alpha$ to be 5, on the basis of preliminary experiment.

The second step segments Phrase 1 into characters in Japanese, as in Phrase 2 below.

**Phrase 2**

**JP1** 香/川/は (in Kagawa)

**JSL1** AROMA / RIVER

**JP2** 朝/か/ら (from the morning)

**JSL2** MORNING / FROM

**JP3** 晴/れ/る/で/し/ょ/う (It will be fine)

**JSL3** FINE / DREAM

Then, as shown in Example 1, the sense-based translation is trained on the corpus of phrase pairs.

**Example 1**

香 → AROMA

川 → RIVER

は → (null)

⋮

Our method can reduce the combinations of alignments between Japanese characters and JSL words, because it segments sentences into phrases in which the number of words is less than that in the sentences. Therefore, it improves the alignment accuracy.

### 3.2 Pronunciation-based translation

The pronunciation-based translation is not transliteration but translation, because kanji do not represent their pronunciation. Therefore, the translation probabilities are also trained on a Japanese proper name corpus as a lexicon model in the SMT training step.

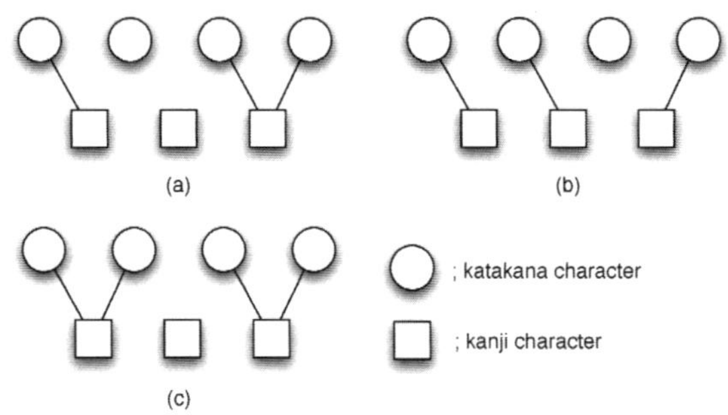


Figure 3: Patterns that cannot be aligned

Using the trained lexicon model, a decoder aligns the kana with the kanji. However, some of the kanji and kana are not aligned because of the sparse data problem. Such non-aligned cases are as follows.

**Pattern (a)** Aligned on neither the kanji nor the kana side (Fig.3-(a)).

**Pattern (b)** Insertion occurred (Fig.3-(b)).

**Pattern (c)** Deletion occurred (Fig.3-(c)).

The kanji-to-kana alignment is generally many-to-many, but we restricted the alignment to one-to-many.

To improve the result of these cases, we devised transformation rules that use the word's context, as follows.

**Rule (a)** Align all of the non-aligned kana with the non-aligned kanji.

**Rule (b)** Align the non-aligned kana to the kanji with the lower probability by comparing the translation probability of the left aligned kanji with the translation probability of the right aligned kanji.

**Rule (c)** Align the non-aligned kanji to the kana with the lower probability and un-align the

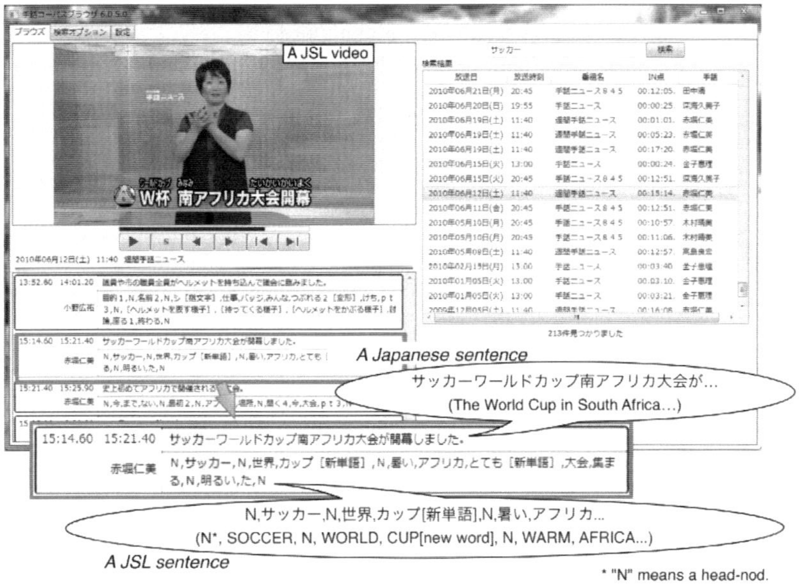


Figure 4: Japanese-JSL news corpus

old aligned kanji with the lower one by comparing the translation probability of the left aligned kana with the translation probability of the rightaligned kana.

Using these rules, our methods can align kanji to kana even if the kanji and/or kana are not in the training data. It has the advantage of robustness to the data sparse problem unlike conventional transliteration methods such as in (Finch et al., 2010; Knight et al., 1998). There are many different family names in Japan[4], so these characteristics are important for translating Japanese proper names.

Our method applies these rules to the non-aligned kanji and kana from the beginning character in the sentences after the sense-based translation.

### 3.3 Combining sense-based and pronunciation-based translation

In our proper name translation, sense-based translation is first applied to a Japanese proper name and then pronunciation-based translation is applied to the characters that were not converted into sign words. Such characters occur in the following cases.

- The character does not appear in the training data of the sense-based translation.
- The character is translated into kana because the character is often translated into Kana in the training data of sense-based translation.

In these cases, our system translates the character into kana by using pronunciation-based translation.

## 4 Experiments and Results

### 4.1 Experimental setting

Our method uses GIZA++ and "grow-diag-final-and" (Och et al., 2003) as the model training and Moses (Koehn et al., 2007) as the decoding; it does not use a language model because word context and reordering are useless in proper name translation from Japanese to JSL.

The training sets were our Japanese-JSL news corpus (including 21,995 sentence pairs) for sense-based translation and a human-name corpus (including 34,202 personal names) for pronunciation-based translation. These corpora are described below.

The test set consisted of persons' names and place names. Regarding the persons' names, the candidates for the test set were first randomly sampled from a Japanese family name database[5]. The 100 sampled names were translated by three native signers and if two or three of the signers gave the same translation, the sample was added to the test

[4]There are over 300,000 family names in Japan(Power, 2008).

[5]http://www.douseidoumei.net/prof.html

Table 2: Results of evaluation

| | Person | Place | Total | Type 1 | Type 2 | Type 3 | Type 4 |
|---|---|---|---|---|---|---|---|
| # in the test set | 96 | 82 | 178 | 123 | 16 | 32 | 7 |
| Baseline | 61<br>(63.5%) | 37<br>(46.3%) | 99<br>(55.6%) | 86<br>(69.9%) | 2<br>(12.5%) | 9<br>(28.1%) | 2<br>(28.6%) |
| Pialign | 75<br>(78.1%) | 41<br>(51.3%) | 118<br>(66.3%) | 97<br>(78.9%) | 3<br>(18.8%) | 15<br>(46.9%) | 3<br>(42.9%) |
| Proposed (sense-based) | 77<br>(80.2%) | 43<br>(53.8%) | 121<br>(68.0%) | 95<br>(77.2%) | 3<br>(18.8%) | 20<br>(62.5%) | 3<br>(42.9%) |
| Baseline<br>+ pronunciation-based | 69<br>(71.9%) | 44<br>(55.0%) | 114<br>(64.0%) | 86<br>(69.9%) | 5<br>(31.3%) | 21<br>(65.6%) | 2<br>(28.6%) |
| Pialign<br>+ pronunciation-based | 74<br>(77.1%) | 47<br>(58.8%) | 123<br>(69.1%) | 97<br>(78.9%) | 5<br>(31.3%) | 18<br>(56.3%) | 3<br>(42.9%) |
| Proposed (sense-based)<br>+ pronunciation-based | 80<br>(83.3%) | 53<br>(66.3%) | 134<br>(75.3%) | 95<br>(77.2%) | 8<br>(0.50%) | 28<br>(87.5%) | 3<br>(42.9%) |

set. This procedure produced a test set consisting of 96 names. The test set for place names was produced in the same way and amounted to 82 names. The total number of names used in our evaluation experiments was thus 178.

## 4.2 Training Corpora

### 4.2.1 Japanese-JSL corpus

We have been building up a Japanese-JSL news corpus to study Japanese-to-JSL machine translation. The corpus was collected from daily NHK Sign Language News programs, which are broadcast on NHK TV with Japanese narration and JSL signs.

The corpus consists of Japanese transcriptions, their JSL transcriptions, and their JSL movies. The Japanese transcriptions are transcribed by revising the speech recognition results of the news programs. The transcriptions are carried out by changing the sign gestures of the newscasters into sequences of JSL words. The JSL movies are manually extracted from the program by referring to the time intervals of the transcribed JSL transcriptions. The corpus currently includes about 22,000 sentence pairs taken from broadcasts running from April 2009 to August 2010. Our bilingual corpus is larger than other recent sign language corpora built in various sign language research projects (Bungeroth et al., 2006; Schembri, 2008; Johnston, 2009; Balvet et al., 2010; Matthes et al., 2012; Mesch et al., 2012). Figure 4 shows an example of our corpus.

### 4.2.2 Human Name Corpus

The human-name corpus was constructed by extracting personal names written in both kanji and kana from the IPADIC dictionary[6].

## 4.3 Evaluation and Discussion

We conducted a series of experiments to evaluate our method. Table 2 shows the translation accuracies for proper names. The tested methods were as follows.

**Baseline** A simple baseline method (mentioned in 3.1.1)

**Pialign** The conventional character-based translation method (Neubig et al., 2012)

**Proposed (sense-based)** Our method for sense-based translation (described in 3.1.2)

**Pronunciation-based** Our method for pronunciation-based translation (described in 3.2)

Our overall method is "Proposed (sense-based) + pronunciation-based." The upper row of each cell in the table shows the number of the correct words, whereas the lower row of each cell is the accuracy.

The table indicates that compared with the baseline, our method is higher in accuracy by 19.7 points in total, 19.8 points on persons' name, and 19.6 points on place names. It is higher in accuracy than the baseline for each type of translation. The sense-based translation is effective at the raising total translation accuracy, whereas

[6]http://code.google.com/p/mecab/downloads

the pronunciation-based translation increases the translation accuracy Types 2 and 3.

Each method had lower accuracy for place names than for persons' names. The reasons are as follows. One problem is that some of the characters in the place names are used only in place names, and though they appear in the test set, they do not appear in the training set. This is the out-of-vocabulary problem, which is a major issue with the corpus-based method. To tackle this problem, we will make our corpus larger by using Japanese-JSL place name dictionary. The other problem is that some of the place names have ambiguous Japanese-JSL translations. In this regard, the rate of agreement of the signers making was lower for place names (i.e. 82) than for personal names (i.e. 96).

The sense-based translation method is more accurate than pialign especially in translating type 2 and 3. This is because our discard process is able to delete infrequently used kanji in the corpus from the training data. Infrequently used kanji are often translated using their pronunciation because native signers cannot imagine the sign word that well represents the kanji.

Some of the type 4 words that occurred frequently in the training data were translated with the phrase-based method, however, the accuracy was low. An idiomatic translation dictionary is required for this purpose.

A Japanese-JSL place name dictionary would also improve the character-to-word conversion. For example, our method mistranslated the character "神 (god)" in a personal family name "神谷 (Kamiya)" into "KOBE (Kobe)." The cause of this error is that our method trains the character-to-word conversion "神 (god) → KOBE(Kobe)" from Phrase 3.

**Phrase 3**

**JP** 神戸 (Kobe)

**JSL** KOBE

Our method would be able to avoid such a conversion error by deleting from the training set phrase pairs such as Phrase 3 that are registered in the place dictionary.

## 5 Proper Name Translation System

Using our translation method, we developed a proper name translation system from Japanese to JSL. This system visualizes the translated proper names as computer graphics (CG) animations.

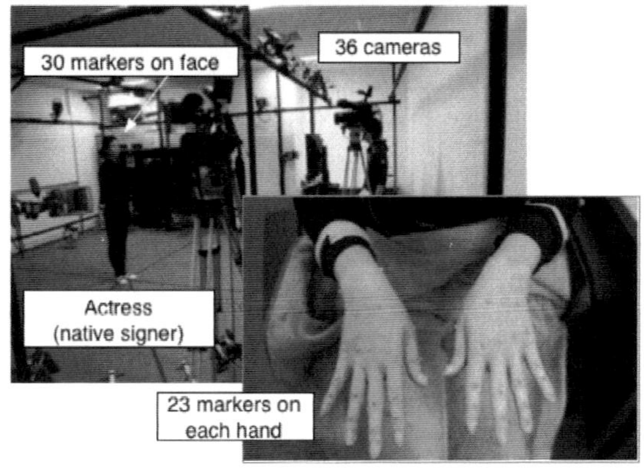


Figure 5: Motion capture system

The CG animation is a high-quality 3D model of human hands and fingers, and the model is controlled using motion-capture (MoCap) data. The data is captured with an optical MoCap system in which many markers are attached to fingers to pick up their movements precisely. Figure5 shows the MoCap system. The CG-model has about 100 joints with three rotation angles. The CG-animation is rendered from scripts written in TVML (TM program Making Language[7]), which is a scripting language developed by NHK to describe full TV programs (Kaneko et al., 2010).

Figure 6 shows an example of the Japanese-to-JSL proper name translation system. When a proper name in Japanese is entered, a corresponding sign language animation is created and shown in the system. The translation system will be used in subjective evaluation of proper name translations.

## 6 Conclusion

We presented a Japanese-JSL proper name machine translation method. The method involves sense-based translation and pronunciation-based translation, both of which are based on statistical machine translation. We conducted a series of evaluation experiments and obtained 75.3% of accuracy, increasing from baseline method by 19.7 points.

We will incorporate our method of proper name translation from Japanese to JSL in our machine translation system.

[7] http://www.nhk.or.jp/strl/tvml/english/player2/index.html

Figure 6: Japanese-JSL proper name translation system

## Acknowledgements

The authors would like to express our deep gratitude to Hirokazu Kosugi for implementing the experimental system for translating sign word sequences into sign language CG animations. They would also like to express their gratitude to Hideki Tanaka, Ichiro Yamada, Tadashi Kumano, Isao Goto, and the anonymous reviewers for their valuable comments and suggestions.

## References

Antonio Balvet, Cyril Courtin, Dominique Boutet, Christian Cuxac, Ivani Fusellier-Souza, Brigitte Garcia, Marie-Thérèse L'Huillier and Marie-Anne Sallandre. 2010. The Creagest Project: a Digitized and Annotated Corpus for French Sign Language (LSF) and Natural Gestural Languages. *International Conference on Language Resources and Evaluation (LREC 2010)*: 469–475.

Jan Bungeroth, Daniel Stein, Philippe Dreuw, Morteza Zahedi and Hermann Ney. 2006. A German Sign Language corpus of the domain weather report. *International Conference on Language Resources and Evaluation (LREC 2006)*: 2000–2003.

Andrew Finch, Keiji Yasuda, Hideo Okuma, Eiichiro Sumita and Satoshi Nakamura. 2011. A Bayesian Model of Transliteration and Its Human Evaluation when Integrated into a Machine Translation System. *IEICE transactions on Information and Systems*: Vol. E94–D, No. 10, pp.1889–1900.

Isao Goto, Naoto Kato, Noriyoshi Uratani and Terumasa Ehara. 2003. Transliteration considering context information based on the maximum entropy method. *The 9th Machine Translation Summit*: 125–132.

Japanese Federation of the Deaf (JFD). 2009. Place names map in Japanese Sign Language in Japan (in Japanese, "全国地名手話マップ") Japanese Federation of the Deaf Press.

Trevor Johnston. 2009. Creating a corpus of Auslan within an Australian national corpus. *Selected Proceedings of the 2008 HCSNet Workshop on Designing the Australian National Corpus: Mustering Languages.*

Hiroyuki Kaneko, Narichika Hamaguchi, Mamoru Doke and Seiki Inoue. 2010. Sign language animation using TVML. *9th ACM SIGGRAPH International Conference on Virtual-Reality Continuum and Its Applications in Industry (VRCAI 2010)*, ACM 2010:289–292.

Kevin Knight, Jonathan Graehl. 1998. Machine transliteration. *Computer Linguistics*, 24: 599–612.

Philipp Koehn, Hieu Hoang, Alexandra Birch, Chris Callison-Burch, Marcello Federico, Nicola Bertoldi, Brooke Cowen, Wade Shen, Christine Moran, Richard Zens, Chris Dyer, Ondřej Bojar, Alexandra Constantin and Evan Herbst. 2007. Moses: Open source toolkit for statistical machine translation. *Annual meeting of the Association for Computational Linguistics (ACL 2007)*, demonstration session.

Li Haizhou, Zhang Min, Su Jian. 2004 A joint source-channel model for machine transliteration. *Proceedings of the 42nd Annual Meeting on Association for Computational Linguistics (ACL '04).* Article No. 159.

Camillo Lugaresi and Barbara Di Eugenio. 2013. Translating Italian connectives into Italian Sign Language. *Proceedings of the 51st Annual Meeting of the Association for Computational Linguistics (ACL 2013)*, pp 270–280. Sofia, Bulgaria, August.

Guillem Massó and Toni Badia. 2010. Dealing with sign language morphemes in statistical machine translation. *4th workshop on the representation and processing of sign language: interactions between corpus and lexicon at LREC 2010*: 154–157.

Silke Matthes, Thomas Hanke, Anja Regan, Jakob Storz, Satu Worseek, Eleni Efthimiou, Athanasia-Lida Dimou, Annelies Braffort, John Glauert and Eva Safar. 2012. Dicta-Sign – Building a multilingual sign language corpus. *5th workshop on the representation and processing of sign language: interactions between corpus and lexicon at LREC 2012*: 117–122.

Alessandro Mazzei. 2012. Sign language generation with expert systems and ccg. *Proceedings of the Seventh International Natural Language Generation Conference (INLG '12)*: 105–109.

Johanna Mesch, Lars Wallin and Thomas Björkstrand. 2012. Sign language resources in Swedes: dictionary and corpus. *5th workshop on the representation and processing of sign language: interactions between corpus and lexicon at LREC 2012*: 127–130.

Sara Morrissey. 2011. Assessing three representation methods for sign language machine translation and evaluation. *15th annual meeting of the European Association for Machine Translation (EAMT 2011)*: 137–144.

Graham Neubig, Taro Watanabe, Shinsuke Mori and Tatsuya Kawahara. 2012. Machine Translation without Words through Substring Alignment. *Proceedings of the 50th Annual Meeting of the Association for Computational Linguistics (ACL2012)* : 165–174.

Franz Josef Och and Hermann Ney. 2003. A systematic comparison of various statistical alignment models. *Computational Linguistics*,29: 19–51.

John Power. 2008. Japanese Names. *The Indexer*, Volume 26, No 2, pp. C4-2–C4-8.

Rubén San-Segundo, Verónica López, Raquel Martín, David Sánchez, Adolfo García. 2010. Language resources for Spanish – Spanish Sign Language (LSE) translation. *The 4th workshop on the representation and processing of sign languages: corpora and sign language technologies at LREC 2010*: 208–211.

Adam Schembri. 2008. British Sign Language corpus project: open access archives and the observer's paradox. *3rd workshop on the representation and processing of sign languages at LREC 2008.*

Daniel Stein, Christoph Schmidt and Hermann Ney. 2012. Analysis, preparation, and optimization of statistical sign language machine translation. *Machine Translation* 26: 325-357.

Katsuhito Sudoh, Shinsuke Mori and Masaaki Nagata. 2013. Noise-aware Character Alignment for Bootstrapping Statistical Machine Translation from Bilingual Corpora. *Proceedings of the 2013 Conference on Empirical Methods in Natural Language Processing (EMNLP 2013)*: 204–209.

Paola Virga, Senjeev Khudanpur. 2003. Transliteration of proper names in cross-lingual information retrieval. *MultiNER '03 Proceeding of the ACL 2003 workshop on multilingual and mixed-language named entity recognition* Volume 15, pp 57–64.

# Exploring cross-language statistical machine translation for closely related South Slavic languages

**Maja Popović**
DFKI Berlin, Germany
maja.popovic@dfki.de

**Nikola Ljubešić**
University of Zagreb, Croatia
nikola.ljubesic@ffzg.hr

**Abstract**

This work investigates the use of cross-language resources for statistical machine translation (SMT) between English and two closely related South Slavic languages, namely Croatian and Serbian. The goal is to explore the effects of translating from and into one language using an SMT system trained on another. For translation into English, a loss due to cross-translation is about 13% of BLEU and for the other translation direction about 15%. The performance decrease for both languages in both translation directions is mainly due to lexical divergences. Several language adaptation methods are explored, and it is shown that very simple lexical transformations already can yield a small improvement, and that the most promising adaptation method is using a Croatian-Serbian SMT system trained on a very small corpus.

## 1 Introduction

Statistical machine translation has become widely used over the last decade – open source tools such as Moses (Koehn et al., 2007) make it possible to build translation systems for any language pair within days, or even hours. However, the prerequisite is that appropriate bilingual training data is available, which is actually one of the most severe limitations of the statistical approach – large resources are only available for a few language pairs and domains. Therefore exploiting language closeness can be very convenient if there are no appropriate corpora containing the desired language, but it is possible to acquire corpora containing a closely related one. Croatian and Serbian are very close languages, and both[1] are under-resourced in terms of free/open-source language resources and tools, especially in terms of parallel bilingual corpora. On the other hand, Croatian has recently become the third official South Slavic language in the EU[2], and Serbian[3] is the official language of a candidate member state. Therefore investigating cross-language translation for these two languages can be considered very useful.

Both languages belong to the South-Western Slavic branch. As Slavic languages, they have a free word order and are highly inflected. Although they exhibit a large overlap in vocabulary and a strong morphosyntactic similarity so that the speakers can understand each other without difficulties, there is a number of small, but notable and frequently occurring differences between them.

In this paper, we investigate the impact of these differences on cross-language translation. The main questions are:

- How much will the translation performance decrease if a Serbian-English SMT system is used for translation from and into Croatian? (and the other way round)
- What are the possibilities for diminishing this performance decrease?

### 1.1 Related work

First publications dealing with statistical machine translation systems for Serbian-English (Popović et al., 2005) and for Croatian-English (Ljubešić et al., 2010) are reporting results of first steps on small bilingual corpora. Recent work on Croatian-English pair describes building a parallel corpus in the tourism domain by automatic web harvesting (Esplà-Gomis et al., 2014) and results of a SMT system built on this parallel corpus which yielded significant improvement (10%

[1] as well as other South Slavic languages

[2] together with Slovenian and Bulgarian

[3] together with Bosnian and Montenegrin



*Language Technology for Closely Related Languages and Language Variants (LT4CloseLang)*, pages 76–84,
October 29, 2014, Doha, Qatar. 

BLEU) over the Google baseline in the tourism domain (Toral et al., 2014). A rule-based Apertium system (Peradin et al., 2014) has been recently developed for translation from and into Slovenian (also closely related language, but more distant).

Techniques simpler than general SMT such as character-level translation have been investigated for translation between various close language pairs, where for the South Slavic group the Bulgarian-Macedonian pair has been explored (Nakov and Tiedemann, 2012). Character-based translation has also been used for translating between Bosnian and Macedonian in order to build pivot translation systems from and into English (Tiedemann, 2012).

Developing POS taggers and lemmatizers for Croatian and Serbian and using Croatian models on Serbian data has been explored in (Agić et al., 2013).

To the best of our knowledge, a systematic investigation of cross-language translation systems involving Croatian and Serbian, thereby exploiting benefits from the language closeness and analyzing problems induced by language differences has not been carried out yet.

## 2 Language characteristics

### 2.1 General characteristics

Croatian and Serbian, as Slavic languages, have a very rich inflectional morphology for all word classes. There are six distinct cases affecting not only common nouns but also proper nouns as well as pronouns, adjectives and some numbers. Some nouns and adjectives have two distinct plural forms depending on the number (less than five or not). There are also three genders for the nouns, pronouns, adjectives and some numbers leading to differences between the cases and also between the verb participles for past tense and passive voice.

As for verbs, person and many tenses are expressed by the suffix, and the subject pronoun (e.g. I, we, it) is often omitted (similarly as in Spanish and Italian). In addition, negation of three quite important verbs, "biti" (to be, auxiliary verb for past tense, conditional and passive voice), "imati" (to have) and "ht(j)eti" (to want, auxiliary verb for the future tense), is formed by adding the negative particle to the verb as a prefix.

As for syntax, both languages have a quite free word order, and there are no articles.

### 2.2 Differences

The main differences between the languages are illustrated by examples in Table 1.

The largest differences between the two languages are in the vocabulary. Months have Slavic-derived names in Croatian whereas Serbian uses standard set of international Latin-derived names. A number of other words are also completely different (1), and a lot of words differ only by one or two letters (2). In addition, Croatian language does not transcribe foreign names and words, whereas phonetical transcriptions are usual in Serbian although original writing is allowed too (3).

Apart from lexical differences, there are also structural differences mainly concerning verbs. After modal verbs such as "morati" (to have to) or "moći" (can) (4), the infinitive is prescribed in Croatian ("moram raditi"), whereas the construction with particle "da" (that/to) and present tense ("moram da radim") is preferred in Serbian. An inspection of the Croatian and Serbian web corpora[4] (Ljubešić and Klubička., 2014) shows the prescription being followed by identifying 1286 vs. 29 occurrences of the two phrases in the Croatian and 40 vs. 322 occurrences in the Serbian corpus. It is important to note that the queried corpora consist of texts from the Croatian and Serbian top-level web domain and that the results in discriminating between Croatian and Serbian language applied to these corpora are not used at this point.

The mentioned difference partly extends to the future tense (5), which is formed in a similar manner to English, using present of the verb "ht(j)eti" as auxiliary verb. The infinitive is formally required in both variants, however, when "da"+present is used instead, it can additionally express the subject's will or intention to perform the action. This form is frequent in Serbian ("ja ću da radim"), whereas in Croatian only the infinitive form is used ("ja ću raditi"). This is, again, followed by corpus evidence with 0 vs. 71 occurrences of the phrases in the Croatian corpus and 13 vs. 22 occurrences in the Serbian corpus. Another difference regarding future tense exists when the the auxiliary and main verb are reversed (5b): in Croatian the final "i" of the infinitive is removed ("radit ću"), whereas in Serbian the main and the auxiliary verb merge into a single word ("radiću").

[4]the corpora can be queried via `http://nl.ijs.si/noske/`

| | | Croatian | Serbian | English |
|---|---|---|---|---|
| vocabulary | | | | |
| 1) | word level | gospodarstvo | ekonomija | economy |
| | | tjedan | nedelja | week |
| | | tisuća | hiljada | one thousand |
| | months | siječanj | januar | January |
| 2) | character level | točno | tačno | accurate |
| | | Europa | Evropa | Europe |
| | | vjerojatno | verovatno | probably |
| | | vijesti | vesti | news |
| | | terorist | terorista | terrorist |
| 3) | transcription | Washington | Vašington | Washington |
| structure (verbs) | | | | |
| 4) | modal verbs | moram raditi | moram da radim | I have to work |
| | | mogu raditi | mogu da radim | I can work |
| 5) | future tense a) | ja ću raditi | ja ću da radim | I will work |
| | b) | radit ću | radiću | I will work |
| 6) | "trebati" = should a) | trebam raditi | treba da radim | I should work |
| | | trebaš raditi | treba da radiš | you should work |
| | = need b) | trebam posao | treba mi posao | I need a job |
| | | Petar treba knjige | Petru trebaju knjige | Petar needs books |

Table 1: Examples of main differences between Croatian and Serbian.

Corpus evidence follows this as well with 611 vs. 9 occurrences in the Croatian corpus and 4 vs. 103 occurrences in the Serbian one. A very important difference concerns the verb "trebati" (to need, should) (6). In Croatian, the verb takes the tense according to the subject and it is transitive as in English. In Serbian, when it means "should" (6a) it is impersonal followed by "da" and the present of the main verb ("treba da radim"). When it means "to need" (6b), the verb is conjugated according to the needed object ("treba" (job), "trebaju" (books)), and the subject which needs something (I, Petar) is an indirect grammatical object in dative case ("meni", "Petru").

Apart from the described differences, there is also a difference in scripts: Croatian uses only the Latin alphabet whereas Serbian uses both Latin and Cyrillic scripts[5]. However, this poses no problem regarding corpora because a Cyrillic Serbian text can be easily transliterated into Latin.

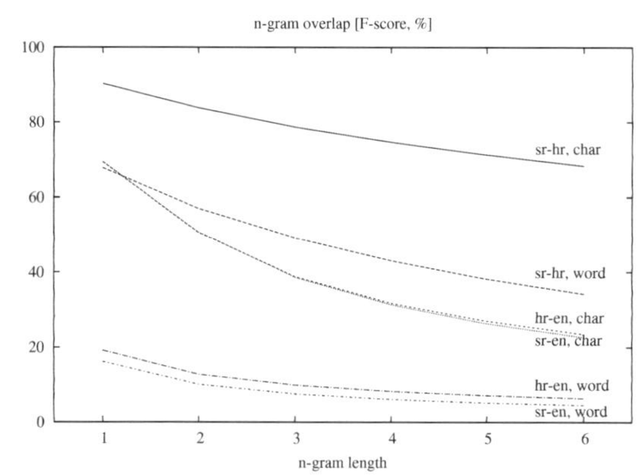


Figure 1: n-gram overlap on word level and on character level between Croatian-Serbian, Croatian-English and Serbian-English.

The idea of Figure 1 is to illustrate the closeness and the differences between the two close languages of interest by numbers: overlapping of

[5]During the compilation process of the Serbian web corpus (Ljubešić and Klubička., 2014), 16.7% of retrieved text was written in the Cyrillic script.

word level and character level $n$-grams for $n = 1, ...6$ in training, development and test corpora together is presented via the F-score. In order to give a better insight, overlaps with English are calculated as well. It can be seen that the Croatian-Serbian overlap on character level is very high, and still rather high on the word level. Character overlaps with English are below the Croatian-Serbian overlap on the word level, whereas the word level overlaps with English are very low.

## 3 Translation experiments

In order to explore effects of the described language differences on cross-language SMT, four translation systems have been built: Croatian→English, Serbian→English, English→Croatian and English→Serbian. For the sake of brevity and clarity, we will use the terms "corresponding source/output" when the test language is same as the language used for training, and "other source/output" when the cross-language translation is performed. For translation into English, the translation outputs of the other source text and its adapted variants are compared to the translation output of the corresponding source test with respect to the English reference. For translation from English, the other translation output and its adapted versions are compared to the corresponding output with respect to the corresponding reference. The investigated adaptation methods are described in the next section.

### 3.1 Language adaptation methods

The following methods were investigated for adaptation of the test set in the other language:

- lexical conversion of the most frequent words (*conv*);

  The most frequent[6] different words together with simple morphological variations are replaced by the words in the corresponding language. This method is simple and fast, however it is very basic and also requires knowledge of the involved languages to be set up. It can be seen as a very first step towards the use of a rule-based Croatian-Serbian system.

- Croatian-Serbian translation system trained on three thousand parallel sentences (*3k*);

  This method does not require any language knowledge, and a small bilingual corpus is often not very difficult to acquire. It is even not very difficult to create it manually from a monolingual corpus by translating it, although in that case the language knowledge is needed.

- Croatian-Serbian translation system trained on the large parallel corpus (*200k*);

  This method is interesting in order to see the upper limits of the adaptation, however it is not realistic – if a large in-domain corpus is available in both languages, there is no need for cross-language translation, but pivoting or synthetic corpora can be used.

The language adaptation is performed in the following way: for translation into English, the other language test set is first preprocesssed, i.e. converted or translated into the corresponding language, and then translated. For the other translation direction, the English test is translated into the other language and then converted/translated into the corresponding one.

In addition, training a system using the converted corpus has also been investigated for all translation directions.

## 4 Experimental set-up

The enhanced version[7] of the SEtimes corpus (Tyers and Alperen, 2010) is used for translation experiments. The corpus is based on the content published on the SETimes.com news portal which publishes "news and views from Southeast Europe" in ten languages: Bulgarian, Bosnian, Greek, English, Croatian, Macedonian, Romanian, Albanian and Serbian. We used the parallel trilingual Croatian-English-Serbian part of the corpus. The detailed corpus statistic is shown in Table 2. The Croatian language is further referred to as *hr*, Serbian as *sr* and English as *en*.

The translation system used is the phrase-based Moses system (Koehn et al., 2007). The evaluation metrics used for assessment of the translations are the BLEU score (Papineni et al., 2002) and the F-score, which also takes recall into account and generally better correlates with human rankings which has been shown in (Melamed et al., 2003) and confirmed in (Popović, 2011). For

[6]occurring $\geq$ 1000 times in the training corpus

[7]http://nlp.ffzg.hr/resources/corpora/setimes/

| | | Croatian (hr) | Serbian (sr) | English (en) |
|---|---|---|---|---|
| Train | sentences | | 197575 | |
| | avg sent length | 22.3 | 22.5 | 23.9 |
| | running words | 4410721 | 4453579 | 4731746 |
| | vocabulary | 149416 | 144544 | 76242 |
| Dev | sentences | | 995 | |
| | avg sent length | 22.2 | 22.5 | 24.0 |
| | running words | 22125 | 22343 | 23896 |
| | running OOVs | 1.7% | 1.6% | 0.8% |
| Test | sentences | | 1000 | |
| | avg sent length | 22.3 | 22.4 | 23.8 |
| | running words | 22346 | 22428 | 23825 |
| | running OOVs | 1.5% | 1.4% | 0.7% |

Table 2: Corpus statistics

translation into Croatian and Serbian, F-scores on character level are also calculated.

## 5 Results

### 5.1 Croatian↔Serbian language adaptation

This section presents the results of conversion and translation between Croatian and Serbian in order to better understand advantages and disadvantages of each of the adaptation methods. The effects of each method on translation into and from English will be reported in the next section.

Table 3 shows the BLEU and F-scores as well as the percentage of running OOVs for each adaptation method. If no adaptation is performed (first row), the word level scores are about 40%, CHARF score is close to 75% , and a large number of OOVs is present – 13% of running words are unseen. A large portion of these words differ only by one or two characters, and for a standard SMT system there is no difference between such words and completely distinct ones.

The *conv* method, i.e. simple replacement of a set of words, already makes the text more close: it reduces the number of OOVs by 3-5% and improves the scores by 3%. The best results are obtained, as it can be expected, by *200k* adaptation, i.e. translation using the large Croatian-Serbian training corpus; the amount of OOVs in the adapted text is comparable with the text in the corresponding language (presented in Table 2). The *3k* translation system, being the most suitable for "real-word" tasks and improving significantly the text in the other language (almost 10% reduction of OOVs and 13% increase of scores) seems to be the most promising adaptation method.

### 5.2 Croatian/Serbian↔English translation

The translation results into and from English are presented in Table 4. It can be seen that the BLEU/WORDF loss induced by cross-language translation is about 12-13% for translation into English and about 13-15% for the other direction. The effects of language adaptation methods are similar for all translation directions: the simple lexical conversion *conv* slightly improves the translation outputs, and the best option is to use the *200k* translation system. The small training corpus achieves, of course, less improvement than the large corpus. On the other hand, taking into account the significant improvement over the original of the text of the other language (about 9%) and the advantages of the method discussed in Sections 3.1 and 5.1, this performance difference is actually not too large. Future work should explore techniques for improvement of such systems.

Last two rows in each table represent the results of the additional experiment, namely using the converted other language corpus for training. However, the results do not outperform those obtained by (much faster) conversion of the source/output, meaning that there is no need for retraining the translation system – it is sufficient to adapt only the test source/output.

### Translation examples

Table 5 presents two translation examples: the source/reference sentence in all three languages, the cross-language translation output, the trans-

| direction | method | BLEU | WORDF | CHARF | OOV |
|---|---|---|---|---|---|
| | none | 40.1 | 43.1 | 74.7 | 13.3 |
| hr→sr | conv | 43.7 | 46.3 | 76.4 | 10.7 |
| | 3k | 54.8 | 55.9 | 80.8 | 4.6 |
| | 200k | 64.3 | 65.4 | 85.2 | 1.4 |
| sr→hr | conv | 43.5 | 46.1 | 76.3 | 8.5 |
| | 3k | 54.0 | 55.9 | 80.9 | 4.3 |
| | 200k | 64.1 | 65.3 | 85.1 | 1.4 |

Table 3: BLEU and F-scores for Croatian-Serbian conversion and translation used for adaptation.

lation outputs of adapted sources, as well as the translation output of the corresponding source. The examples are given only for translation into English, and the effects for the other translation direction can be observed implicitly. Generally, the main source of errors are OOV words, but structural differences also cause problems.

For the first sentence (1), the *conv* method is sufficient for obtaining a perfect cross-translation output: the obstacles are three OOV words, all of them being frequent and thus converted. The outputs obtained by *3k* and *200k* methods as well as the output for the corresponding language are exactly the same and therefore not presented.

The second sentence (2) is more complex: it contains three OOV words, two of which are not frequent and thus not adapted by *conv*, and one future tense i.e. a structural difference. The OOV words do not only generate lexical errors (untranslated words) but also incorrect word order ("from 17 dječjih kazališta"). The *conv* method is able to repair only the month name, whereas other errors induced by language differences[8] are still present. The *3k* translation system resolves one more OOV word ("theater") together with its position, as well as the future tense problem, but the third OOV word "children's" is still untranslated and in the wrong position. This error is fixed only when *200k* translation system is used, since the word occurs in the large corpus but not in the small one. It should be noted that the word is, though, an OOV only due to the one single letter and probably could be dealt with by character-based techniques (Nakov and Tiedemann, 2012) which should be investigated in future work.

[8]It should be noted that errors not related to the language differences are out of the scope of this work.

## 6 Conclusions

In this work, we have examined the possibilities for using a statistical machine translation system built on one language and English for translation from and into another closely related language. Our experiments on Croatian and Serbian showed that the loss by cross-translation is about 13% of BLEU for translation into English and 15% for translation from English.

We have systematically investigated several methods for language adaptation. It is shown that even a simple lexical conversion of limited number of words yields improvements of about 2% BLEU, and the Croatian-Serbian translation system trained on three thousand sentences yields a large improvement of about 6-9%. The best results are obtained when the translation system built on the large corpus is used; however, it should be taken into account that such scenario is not realistic.

We believe that the use of a small parallel corpus is a very promising method for language adaptation and that the future work should concentrate in improving such systems, for example by character-based techniques. We also believe that a rule-based Croatian-Serbian system could be useful for adaptation, since the translation performance has been improved already by applying a very simple lexical transfer rule. Both approaches will be investigated in the framework of the ABU-MATRAN project[9].

Depending on the availability of resources and tools, we plan to examine texts in other related languages such as Slovenian, Macedonian and Bulgarian (the last already being part of ongoing work in the framework of the QTLEAP project[10]), and also to do further investigations on the Croatian-Serbian language pair.

[9]http://abumatran.eu/

[10]http://qtleap.eu/

(a) translation into English

| training | source | BLEU | WORDF |
|---|---|---|---|
| sr→en | hr | 29.8 | 34.1 |
| | hr-sr.conv | 32.3 | 36.4 |
| | hr-sr.3k | 37.6 | 41.1 |
| | hr-sr.200k | 42.3 | 45.6 |
| | sr | 42.9 | 46.0 |
| hr→en | sr | 31.4 | 35.5 |
| | sr-hr.conv | 32.8 | 36.8 |
| | sr-hr.3k | 37.2 | 40.8 |
| | sr-hr.200k | 41.7 | 44.9 |
| | hr | 43.2 | 46.3 |
| sr-hr.conv→en | hr | 32.2 | 36.2 |
| hr-sr.conv→en | sr | 33.5 | 37.4 |

(b) translation from English

| reference | output | BLEU | WORDF | CHARF |
|---|---|---|---|---|
| hr | sr | 20.6 | 25.4 | 62.7 |
| | sr-hr.conv | 22.8 | 27.4 | 64.2 |
| | sr-hr.3k | 29.3 | 33.4 | 68.5 |
| | sr-hr.200k | 33.5 | 37.2 | 71.2 |
| | hr | 35.5 | 38.9 | 72.1 |
| sr | hr | 20.3 | 25.3 | 62.7 |
| | hr-sr.conv | 22.6 | 27.4 | 64.2 |
| | hr-sr.3k | 29.8 | 33.7 | 68.4 |
| | hr-sr.200k | 34.0 | 37.5 | 71.3 |
| | sr | 35.3 | 38.5 | 72.1 |
| sr | en→hr-sr.conv | 22.6 | 27.4 | 64.2 |
| hr | en→sr-hr.conv | 23.2 | 27.7 | 64.2 |

Table 4: BLEU, WORDF and CHARF scores for translation (a) into English; (b) from English.

## Acknowledgments

This work has been supported by the QTLEAP project – EC's FP7 (FP7/2007-2013) under grant agreement number 610516: "QTLEAP: Quality Translation by Deep Language Engineering Approaches" and the ABU-MATRAN project – EC's FP7 (FP7/2007-2013) under grant agreement number PIAP-GA-2012-324414: "ABU-MATRAN: Automatic building of Machine Translation".

## References

Željko Agić, Nikola Ljubešić and Danijela Merkler. 2013. Lemmatization and Morphosyntactic Tagging of Croatian and Serbian, In *Proceedings of the 4th Biennial International Workshop on Balto-Slavic Natural Language Processing*, pages 48–57, Sofia, Bulgaria, August.

Miquel Esplà-Gomis and Filip Klubička and Nikola Ljubešić and Sergio Ortiz-Rojas and Vassilis Papavassiliou and Prokopis Prokopidis 2014. Comparing Two Acquisition Systems for Automatically Building an English-Croatian Parallel Corpus from Multilingual Websites, In Proceedings of the 9th International Conference on Language Resources and Evaluation (LREC), Reykjavik, Iceland, May.

Nikola Ljubešić and Filip Klubička 2014. {bs,hr,sr}WaC – Web corpora of Bosnian, Croatian and Serbian, In Proceedings of the 9th Web as Corpus Workshop (WaC-9), Gothenburg, Sweden, April.

Philipp Koehn, Hieu Hoang, Alexandra Birch, Chris Callison-Burch, Marcello Federico, Nicola Bertoldi, Brooke Cowan, Wade Shen, Christine Moran,

| | | |
|---|---|---|
| | sr | Pregled poslovnih i **ekonomskih vesti** sa Balkana od 15. **avgusta**. |
| 1) | hr | Pregled poslovnih i **gospodarskih vijesti** s Balkana od 15. **kolovoza**. |
| | en | A review of business and economic news from the Balkans since 15 **August**. |
| training: | sr→en | |
| source: | hr | A review of business and **gospodarskih vijesti** from the Balkans since 15 **kolovoza** . |
| | hr-sr.conv | A review of business and economic news from the Balkans since 15 August . |

| | | |
|---|---|---|
| | sr | Srpski grad Subotica *biće* domaćin 16. izdanja Međunarodnog festivala **dečjih pozorišta** od 17. do 23. **maja**. |
| 2) | hr | Subotica u Srbiji *bit će* domaćin 16 . Međunarodnog festivala **dječjih kazališta** od 17. do 23. **svibnja**. |
| | en | Subotica, Serbia, *will host* the 16th edition of the International Festival of **Children's Theatres** from **May** 17th to **May** 23rd . |
| training: | sr→en | |
| source: | hr | Subotica in Serbia *will be will host* the 16th International Festival from 17 **dječjih kazališta** to 23 **svibnja**. |
| | hr-sr.conv | Subotica in Serbia *will be will host* the 16th International Festival from 17 **dječjih kazališta** to 23 May. |
| | hr-sr.3k | Subotica in Serbia will host the 16th International Theatre Festival from 17 **dječjih** to 23 May. |
| | hr-sr.200k | Subotica in Serbia will host the 16th International Children's Theatre Festival from 17 to 23 May. |
| | sr | The Serbian town of Subotica will host the 16th edition of the International Children's Theatre Festival from 17 to 23 May. |

Table 5: Two examples of cross-translation of Croatian source sentence into English using Serbian→English translation system.


Richard Zens, Chris Dyer, Ondřej Bojar, Alexandra Constantin, and Evan Herbst. 2007. Moses: open source toolkit for statistical machine translation, In *Proceedings of the 45th Annual Meeting of the ACL on Interactive Poster and Demonstration Sessions*, pages 177–180, Prague, Czech Republic, June.

Nikola Ljubešić, Petra Bago and Damir Boras. 2010. Statistical machine translation of Croatian weather forecast: How much data do we need?, In *Proceedings of the ITI 2010 32nd International Conference on Information Technology Interfaces*, pages 91–96, Cavtat, Croatia, June.

I.Dan Melamed, Ryan Green and Joseph P. Turian. 2003. Precision and Recall of Machine Translation. In *Proceedings of the Human Language Technology Conference (HLT-NAACL)*, pages 61–63, Edmonton, Canada, May/June.

Preslav Nakov and Jörg Tiedemann. 2012. Combining word-level and character-level models for machine translation between closely-related languages, In *Proceedings of the 50th Annual Meeting of the Association of Computational Linguistics (ACL)*, pages 301–305, Jeju, Republic of Korea, July.

Kishore Papineni, Salim Roukos, Todd Ward and Wie-Jing Zhu. 2002. BLEU: a method for automatic evaluation of machine translation, In *Proceedings of the 40th Annual Meeting of the Association for Computational Linguistics (ACL)*, pages 311–318, Philadelphia, PA, July.

Hrvoje Peradin, Filip Petkovski and Francis Tyers. 2014. Shallow-transfer rule-based machine translation for the Western group of South Slavic languages, In *Proceedings of the 9th SaLTMiL Workshop on Free/open-Source Language Resources for the Machine Translation of Less-Resourced Languages*, pages 25–30, Reykjavik, Iceland, May.

Maja Popović, David Vilar, Hermann Ney, Slobodan Jovičić and Zoran Šarić. 2005. Augmenting a Small Parallel Text with Morpho-syntactic Language Resources for Serbian–English Statistical Machine Translation In *Proceedings of the ACL-05 Workshop on Building and Using Parallel*

*Texts: Data-Driven Machine Translation and Beyond*, pages 119–124, Ann Arbor, MI, June.

Maja Popović. 2011. Morphemes and POS tags for n-gram based evaluation metrics, In *Proceedings of the Sixth Workshop on Statistical Machine Translation (WMT 2011)*, pages 104–107, Edinburgh, Scotland, July.

Jörg Tiedemann. 2012. Character-based pivot translation for under-resourced languages and domains, In *Proceedings of the 13th Conference of the European Chapter of the Association for Computational Linguistics (EACL)*, pages 141–151, Avignon, France, April.

Antonio Toral, Raphael Rubino, Miquel Esplà-Gomis, Tommi Pirinen, Andy Way and Gema Ramirez-Sanchez 2014. Extrinsic Evaluation of Web-Crawlers in Machine Translation: a Case Study on Croatian–English for the Tourism Domain, In *Proceedings of the 17th Conference of the European Association for Machine Translation (EAMT)*, pages 221–224, Dubrovnik, Croatia, June.

Francis M. Tyers and Murat Alperen. 2010. South-East European Times: A parallel corpus of the Balkan languages, In *Proceedings of the LREC Workshop on Exploitation of Multilingual Resources and Tools for Central and (South-) Eastern European Languages*, pages 49–53, Valetta, Malta, May.

# Exploring System Combination approaches for Indo-Aryan MT Systems

**Karan Singla[1], Nishkarsh Shastri[2], Megha Jhunjhunwala[2], Anupam Singh[3], Srinivas Bangalore[4], Dipti Misra Sharma[1]**

[1]LTRC IIIT Hyderabad, [2]IIT-Kharagpur, [3]NIT-Durgapur,[4]AT&T Labs-Research

## Abstract

Statistical Machine Translation (SMT) systems are heavily dependent on the quality of parallel corpora used to train translation models. Translation quality between certain Indian languages is often poor due to the lack of training data of good quality. We used triangulation as a technique to improve the quality of translations in cases where the direct translation model did not perform satisfactorily. Triangulation uses a third language as a pivot between the source and target languages to achieve an improved and more efficient translation model in most cases. We also combined multi-pivot models using linear mixture and obtained significant improvement in BLEU scores compared to the direct source-target models.

## 1 Introduction

Current SMT systems rely heavily on large quantities of training data in order to produce good quality translations. In spite of several initiatives taken by numerous organizations to generate parallel corpora for different language pairs, training data for many language pairs is either not yet available or is insufficient for producing good SMT systems. Indian Languages Corpora Initiative (ILCI) (Choudhary and Jha, 2011) is currently the only reliable source for multilingual parallel corpora for Indian languages however the number of parallel sentences is still not sufficient to create high quality SMT systems.

This paper aims at improving SMT systems trained on small parallel corpora using various recently developed techniques in the field of SMTs. Triangulation is a technique which has been found to be very useful in improving the translations when multilingual parallel corpora are present. Triangulation is the process of using an intermediate language as a pivot to translate a source language to a target language. We have used phrase table triangulation instead of sentence based triangulation as it gives better translations (Utiyama and Isahara, 2007). As triangulation technique explores additional multi parallel data, it provides us with separately estimated phrase-tables which could be further smoothed using smoothing methods (Koehn et al. 2003). Our subsequent approach will explore the various system combination techniques through which these triangulated systems can be utilized to improve the translations.

The rest of the paper is organized as follows. We will first talk about the some of the related works and then we will discuss the facts about the data and also the scores obtained for the baseline translation model. Section 3 covers the triangulation approach and also discusses the possibility of using combination approaches for combining triangulated and direct models. Section 4 shows results for the experiments described in previous section and also describes some interesting observations from the results. Section 5 explains the conclusions we reached based on our experiments. We conclude the paper with a section about our future work.

## 2 Related Works

There are various works on combining the triangulated models obtained from different pivots with the direct model resulting in increased confidence score for translations and increased coverage by (Razmara and Sarkar, 2013; Ghannay et al., 2014; Cohn and Lapata, 2007). Among these techniques we explored two of the them. The first one is the technique based on the confusion matrix (dynamic) (Ghannay et al., 2014) and the other one is based on mixing the models as explored by (Cohn and Lapata, 2007). The paper also discusses the better choice of combination technique



*Language Technology for Closely Related Languages and Language Variants (LT4CloseLang)*, pages 85–91, October 29, 2014, Doha, Qatar. 

among these two when we have limitations on training data which in our case was small and restricted to a small domain (Health & Tourism).

As suggested in (Razmara and Sarkar, 2013), we have shown that there is an increase in phrase coverage when combining the different systems. Conversely we can say that out of vocabulary words (OOV) always decrease in the combined systems.

## 3 Baseline Translation Model

In our experiment, the baseline translation model used was the direct system between the source and target languages which was trained on the same amount of data as the triangulated models. The parallel corpora for 4 Indian languages namely Hindi (hn), Marathi (mt), Gujarati (gj) and Bangla (bn) was taken from Indian Languages Corpora Initiative (ILCI) (Choudhary and Jha, 2011) . The parallel corpus used in our experiments belonged to two domains - health and tourism and the training set consisted of 28000 sentences. The development and evaluation set contained 500 sentences each. We used MOSES (Koehn et al., 2007) to train the baseline Phrase-based SMT system for all the language pairs on the above mentioned parallel corpus as training, development and evaluation data. Trigram language models were trained using SRILM (Stolcke and others, 2002). Table 1 below shows the BLEU score for all the trained pairs.

| Language Pair | BLEU Score |
|---|---|
| bn-mt | 18.13 |
| mt-bn | 21.83 |
| bn-gj | 22.45 |
| gj-mt | 23.02 |
| gj-bn | 24.26 |
| mt-gj | 25.5 |
| hn-mt | 30.01 |
| hn-bn | 32.92 |
| bn-hn | 34.99 |
| mt-hn | 36.82 |
| hn-gj | 40.06 |
| gj-hn | 43.48 |

Table 1: BLEU scores of baseline models

## 4 Triangulation: Methodology and Experiment

We first define the term *triangulation* in our context. Each source phrase `s` is first translated to an intermediate (pivot) language `i`, and then to a target language `t`. This two stage translation process is termed as triangulation.

Our basic approach involved making triangulated models by triangulating through different pivots and then interpolating triangulated models with the direct source-target model to make our combined model.

In line with various previous works, we will be using multiple translation models to overcome the problems faced due to data sparseness and increase translational coverage. Rather than using sentence translation (Utiyama and Isahara, 2007) from source to pivot and then pivot to target, a phrase based translation model is built.

Hence the main focus of our approach is on phrases rather than on sentences. Instead of using combination techniques on the output of several translation systems, we constructed a combined phrase table to be used by the decoder thus avoiding the additional inefficiencies observed while merging the output of various translation systems. Our method focuses on exploiting the availability of multi-parallel data, albeit small in size, to improve the phrase coverage and quality of our SMT system.

Our approach can be divided into different steps which are presented in the following sections.

### 4.1 Phrase-table triangulation

Our emphasis is on building an enhanced phrase table that incorporates the translation phrase tables of different models. This combined phrase table will be used by the decoder during translation.

Phrase table triangulation depends mainly on phrase level combination of the two different phrase based systems mainly source (src) - pivot (pvt) and pivot (pvt) - target (tgt) using pivot language as a basis for combination. Before stating the mathematical approach for triangulation, we present an example.

#### 4.1.1 Basic methodology

Suppose we have a Bengali-Hindi phrase-table ($T_{BH}$) and a Hindi-Marathi phrase-table ($T_{HM}$). From these tables, we have to construct a Bengali-Marathi phrase-table ($T_{BM}$). For that we need

| Triangulated System | Full-Triangulation (phrase-table length) | Triangulation with top 40 (Length of phrase table) | Full Triangulation (BLEU Score) | Triangulation with top 40 (BLEU SCORE) |
|---|---|---|---|---|
| gj - hn - mt | 3,585,450 | 1,086,528 | 24.70 | 24.66 |
| gj - bn - mt | 7,916,661 | 1,968,383 | 20.55 | 20.04 |

Table 2: Comparison between triangulated systems in systems with full phrase table and the other having top 40 phrase-table entries

to estimate four feature functions: phrase translation probabilities for both directions $\phi(\bar{b}|\bar{m})$ and $\phi(\bar{m}|\bar{b})$, and lexical translation probabilities for both directions $lex(\bar{b}|\bar{m})$ and $lex(\bar{m}|\bar{b})$ where $\bar{b}$ and $\bar{m}$ are Bengali and Marathi phrases that will appear in our triangulated Bengali-Marathi phrase-table $T_{BM}$.

$$\phi(\bar{b}|\bar{m}) = \sum_{\bar{h} \in T_{BH} \cap T_{HM}} \phi(\bar{b}|\bar{h})\phi(\bar{h}|\bar{m}) \quad (1)$$

$$\phi(\bar{m}|\bar{b}) = \sum_{\bar{h} \in T_{BH} \cap T_{HM}} \phi(\bar{m}|\bar{h})\phi(\bar{h}|\bar{b}) \quad (2)$$

$$lex(\bar{b}|\bar{m}) = \sum_{\bar{h} \in T_{BH} \cap T_{HM}} lex(\bar{b}|\bar{h})lex(\bar{h}|\bar{m}) \quad (3)$$

$$lex(\bar{m}|\bar{b}) = \sum_{\bar{h} \in T_{BH} \cap T_{HM}} lex(\bar{m}|\bar{h})lex(\bar{h}|\bar{b}) \quad (4)$$

In these equations a conditional independence assumption has been made that source phrase $\bar{b}$ and target phrase $\bar{m}$ are independent given their corresponding pivot phrase(s) $\bar{h}$. Thus, we can derive $\phi(\bar{b}|\bar{m}), \phi(\bar{m}|\bar{b}), lex(\bar{b}|\bar{m}), lex(\bar{m}|\bar{b})$ by assuming that these probabilities are mutually independent given a Hindi phrase $\bar{h}$.

The equation given requires that all phrases in the *Hindi-Marathi* bitext must also be present in the *Bengali-Hindi* bitext. Clearly there would be many phrases not following the above requirement. For this paper we completely discarded the missing phrases. One important point to note is that although the problem of missing contextual phrases is uncommon in multi-parallel corpora, as it is in our case, it becomes more evident when the bitexts are taken out from different sources.

In general, wider range of possible translations are found for any source phrase through triangulation. We found that in the direct model, a source phrase is aligned to three phrases then there is high possibility of it being aligned to three phrases in intermediate language. The intermediate language phrases are further aligned to three or more phrases in target language. This results in increase in number of translations of each source phrase.

#### 4.1.2 Reducing the size of phrase-table

While triangulation is intuitively appealing, it suffers from a few problems. First, the phrasal translation estimates are based on noisy automatic word alignments. This leads to many errors and omissions in the phrase-table. With a standard source-target phrase-table these errors are only encountered once, however with triangulation they are encountered twice, and therefore the errors are compounded. This leads to much noisier estimates than in the source-target phrase-table. Secondly, the increased exposure to noise means that triangulation will omit a greater proportion of large or rare phrases than the standard method. An alignment error in either of the source-intermediate bitext or intermediate-target bitext can prevent the extraction of a source-target phrase pair.

As will be explained in the next section, the second kind of problem can be ameliorated by using the triangulated phrase-based table in conjunction with the standard phrase based table referred to as direct *src-to-pvt* phrase table in our case.

For the first kind of problem, not only the compounding of errors leads to increased complexity but also results in an absurdly large triangulated phrase based table. To tackle the problem of unwanted phrase-translation, we followed a novel approach.

A general observation is that while triangulating between *src-pvt* and *pvt-tgt* systems, the resultant src-tgt phrase table formed will be very large since for a translation $\bar{s}$ to $\bar{i}$ in the *src-to-pvt* table there may be many translations from $\bar{i}$ to $\bar{t}1, \bar{t}2...\bar{t}n$. For example, the Bengali-Hindi phrase-table($T_{BH}$) consisted of 846,106 translations and Hindi-Marathi phrase-table($T_{HM}$) consisted of 680,415 translations and after triangulating these two tables our new Bengali-Marathi triangulated table($T_{BM}$) consisted of 3,585,450 translations as shown in Table 2. Tuning with such a large phrase-table is complex and time-consuming. To reduce the complexity of the phrase-table, we used only the top-40 translations (translation with 40 maximum values of $P(\bar{f}|\bar{e})$ for every source phrase in our triangulated phrase-table($T_{BM}$) which reduced the phrase table to 1,086,528 translations.

We relied on $P(\bar{f}|\bar{e})$(inverse phrase translation probability) to choose 40 phrase translations for each phrase, since in the direct model, MERT training assigned the most weight to this parameter.

It is clearly evident from Table 2 that we have got a massive reduction in the length of the phrase-table after taking in our phrase table and still the results have no significant difference in our output models.

### 4.2 Combining different triangulated models and the direct model

Combining Machine translation (MT) systems has become an important part of Statistical MT in the past few years. There have been several works by (Rosti et al., 2007; Karakos et al., 2008; Leusch and Ney, 2010);
We followed two approaches

1. A system combination based on confusion network using open-source tool kit **MANY** (Barrault, 2010), which can work dynamically in combining the systems

2. Combine the models by linearly interpolating them and then using MERT to tune the combined system.

#### 4.2.1 Combination based on confusion matrix

MANY tool was used for this and initially it was configured to work with TERp evaluation matrix, but we modified it to work using METEOR-Hindi (Gupta et al., 2010), as it has been shown by (Kalyani et al., 2014), that METEOR evaluation metric is closer to human evaluation for morphologically rich Indian Languages.

#### 4.2.2 Linearly Interpolated Models

We used two different approaches while merging the different triangulated models and direct src-tgt model and we observed that both produced comparable results in most cases. We implemented the linear mixture approach, since linear mixtures often outperform log-linear ones (Cohn and Lapata, 2007). Note that in our combination approaches the reordering tables were left intact.

1. Our first approach was to use linear interpolation to combine all the three models (Bangla-Hin-Marathi, Bangla-Guj-Marathi and direct Bangla-Marathi models) with uniform weights, i.e 0.3 each in our case.

2. In the next approach, the triangulated phrase tables are combined first into a single triangulated phrase-table using uniform weights. The combined triangulated phrase-table and direct src-tgt phrase table is then combined using uniform weights. In other words, we combined all the three systems, Ban-Mar, Ban-Hin-Mar, and Ban-Guj-Mar with 0.5, 0.25 and 0.25 weights respectively. This weight distribution reflects the intuition that the direct model is less noisy than the triangulated models.

In the experiments below, both weight settings produced comparable results. Since we performed triangulation only through two languages, we could not determine which approach would perform better. An ideal approach will be to train the weights for each system for each language pair using standard tuning algorithms such as MERT (Zaidan, 2009).

#### 4.2.3 Choosing Combination Approach

In order to compare the approaches on our data, we performed experiments on Hindi-Marathi pair following both approaches discussed in Section 4.2.1 and 4.2.2. We also generated triangulated models through Bengali and Gujarati as pivot languages.

Also, the approach presented in section 4.2.1 depends heavily on LM (Language Model).In order to study the impact of size, we worked on training Phrase-based SMT systems with subsets of data in sets of 5000, 10000, 150000 sentences and LM was trained for 28000 sentences for comparing these approaches. The combination results were compared following the approach mentioned in 4.2.1 and 4.2.2.

Table 3, shows that the approach discussed in 4.2.1 works better if there is more data for LM but we suffer from the limitation that there is no other in-domain data available for these languages. From the Table, it can also be seen that combining systems with the approach explained in 4.2.2 can also give similar or better results if there is scarcity of data for LM. Therefore we followed the

| #Training | #LM Data | Comb-1 | Comb-2 |
|---|---|---|---|
| 5000 | 28000 | 21.09 | 20.27 |
| 10000 | 28000 | 24.02 | 24.27 |
| 15000 | 28000 | 27.10 | 27.63 |

Table 3: BLEU scores for Hindi-Marathi Model comparing approaches described in 3.2.1(Comb-1) and 3.2.2(Comb-2)

approach from Section 4.2.2 for our experiments on other language pairs.

## 5 Observation and Resuslts

Table 4, shows the BLEU scores of triangulated models when using the two languages out of the 4 Indian languages Hin, Guj, Mar, Ban as source and target and the remaining two as the pivot language. The first row mentions the BLEU score of the direct src-tgt model for all the language pairs. The second and third rows provide the triangulated model scores through pivots which have been listed. The fourth and fifth rows show the BLEU scores for the combined models (triangulated+direct) with the combination done using the first and second approach respectively that have been elucidated in the Section 4.2.2

As expected, both the combined models have performed better than the direct models in all cases.

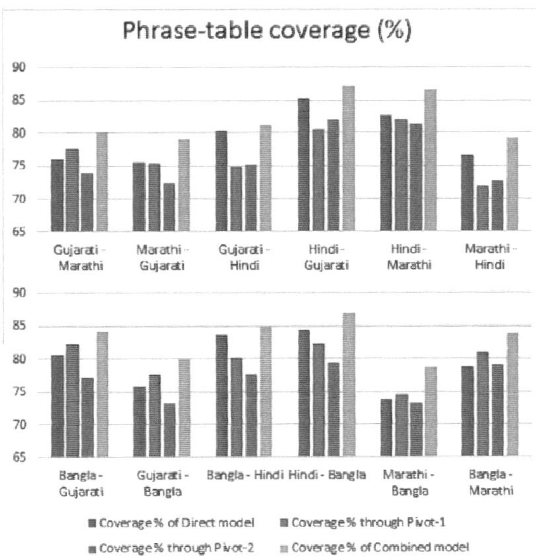


Figure 1: Phrase-table coverage of the evaluation set for all the language pairs

Figure 1, shows the phrase-table coverage of the evaluation set for all the language pairs. Phrase-table coverage is defined as the percentage of unigrams in the evaluation set for which translations are present in the phrase-table. The first bar corresponds to the direct model for each language pair, the second and third bars show the coverage for triangulated models through the 2 pivots, while the fourth bar is the coverage for the combined model (direct+triangulated). The graph clearly shows that even though the phrase table coverage may increase or decrease by triangulation through a single pivot the combined model (direct+triangulated) always gives a higher coverage than the direct model.

Moreover, there exists some triangulation models whose coverage and subsequent BLEU scores for translation is found to be better than that of the direct model. This is a particularly interesting observation as it increases the probability of obtaining better or at least comparable translation models even when direct source-target parallel corpus is absent.

## 6 Discussion

Dravidian languages are different from Indo-aryan languages but they are closely related amongst themselves. So we explored similar experiments with Malayalam-Telugu pair of languages with similar parallel data and with Hindi as pivot.

The hypothesis was that the direct model for Malayalam-Telegu would have performed better due to relatedness of the two languages. However the results via Hindi were better as can be seen in Table 5.

As Malayalam-Telegu are comparatively closer than compared to Hindi, so the results via Hindi should have been worse but it seems more like a biased property of training data which considers that all languages are closer to Hindi, as the translation data was created from Hindi.

## 7 Future Work

It becomes increasingly important for us to improve these techniques for such languages having rare corpora. The technique discussed in the paper is although efficient but still have scope for improvements.

As we have seen from our two approaches of combining the phrase tables and subsequent interpolation with direct one, the best combination among the two is also not fixed. If we can find the

| BLEU scores | gj-mt | | mt-gj | | gj-hn | | hn-gj | | hn-mt | | mt-hn | |
|---|---|---|---|---|---|---|---|---|---|---|---|---|
| **Direct model** | 23.02 | | 25.50 | | 43.48 | | 40.06 | | 30.01 | | 36.82 | |
| **Triangulated through pivots** | **hn** | 24.66 | **hn** | 27.09 | **mt** | 36.76 | **mt** | 33.69 | **gj** | 29.27 | **gj** | 33.86 |
| | **bn** | 20.04 | **bn** | 22.02 | **bn** | 35.07 | **bn** | 32.66 | **bn** | 26.72 | **bn** | 31.34 |
| **Mixture-1** | 26.12 | | **27.46** | | 43.23 | | 39.99 | | 33.09 | | **38.50** | |
| **Mixture-2** | **26.25** | | 27.32 | | **44.04** | | **41.45** | | **33.36** | | 38.44 | |

(a)

| BLEU scores | bn-gj | | gj-bn | | bn-hn | | hn-bn | | mt-bn | | bn-mt | |
|---|---|---|---|---|---|---|---|---|---|---|---|---|
| **Direct model** | 22.45 | | 24.26 | | 34.99 | | 32.92 | | 21.83 | | 18.13 | |
| **Triangulated through pivots** | **hn** | 23.97 | **hn** | 26.26 | **gj** | 31.69 | **gj** | 29.60 | **hn** | 23.80 | **hn** | 21.04 |
| | **mt** | 20.70 | **mt** | 22.32 | **mt** | 28.96 | **mt** | 27.95 | **gj** | 22.41 | **gj** | 18.15 |
| **Mixture-1** | **25.80** | | **27.45** | | **35.14** | | 34.77 | | **24.99** | | 22.16 | |
| **Mixture-2** | 24.66 | | 27.39 | | 35.02 | | **34.85** | | 24.86 | | **22.75** | |

(b)

Table 4: Table (a) & (b) show results for all language pairs after making triangulated models and then combining them with linear interpolation with the two approaches described in 3.2.2. In *Mixture-1*, uniform weights were given to all three models but in *Mixture-2*, direct model is given 0.5 weight relative to the other models (.25 weight to each)

| System | Blue Score |
|---|---|
| Direct Model | 4.63 |
| Triangulated via Hindi | 14.32 |

Table 5: Results for Malayalam-Telegu Pair for same data used for other languages

best possible weights to be assigned to each table, then we can see improvement in translation. This can be implemented by making the machine learn from various iterations of combining and adjusting the scores accordingly.(Nakov and Ng, 2012) have indeed shown that results show significant deviations associated with different weights assigned to the tables.

## References


Loïc Barrault. 2010. Many: Open source machine translation system combination. *The Prague Bulletin of Mathematical Linguistics*, 93:147–155.

Narayan Choudhary and Girish Nath Jha. 2011. Creating multilingual parallel corpora in indian languages. In *Proceedings of Language and Technology Conference*.

Trevor Cohn and Mirella Lapata. 2007. Machine translation by triangulation: Making effective use of multi-parallel corpora. In *ANNUAL MEETING-ASSOCIATION FOR COMPUTATIONAL LINGUISTICS*, volume 45, page 728. Citeseer.

Sahar Ghannay, France Le Mans, and Loıc Barrault. 2014. Using hypothesis selection based features for confusion network mt system combination. In *Proceedings of the 3rd Workshop on Hybrid Approaches to Translation (HyTra)@ EACL*, pages 1–5.

Ankush Gupta, Sriram Venkatapathy, and Rajeev Sangal. 2010. Meteor-hindi: Automatic mt evaluation metric for hindi as a target language. In *Proceedings of ICON-2010: 8th International Conference on Natural Language Processing*.

Aditi Kalyani, Hemant Kumud, Shashi Pal Singh, and Ajai Kumar. 2014. Assessing the quality of mt systems for hindi to english translation. *arXiv preprint arXiv:1404.3992*.

Damianos Karakos, Jason Eisner, Sanjeev Khudanpur, and Markus Dreyer. 2008. Machine translation system combination using itg-based alignments. In *Proceedings of the 46th Annual Meeting of the Association for Computational Linguistics on Human Language Technologies: Short Papers*, pages 81–84. Association for Computational Linguistics.

Philipp Koehn, Hieu Hoang, Alexandra Birch, Chris Callison-Burch, Marcello Federico, Nicola Bertoldi, Brooke Cowan, Wade Shen, Christine Moran, Richard Zens, et al. 2007. Moses: Open source toolkit for statistical machine translation. In *Proceedings of the 45th Annual Meeting of the ACL on Interactive Poster and Demonstration Sessions*, pages 177–180. Association for Computational Linguistics.

Gregor Leusch and Hermann Ney. 2010. The rwth system combination system for wmt 2010. In *Proceedings of the Joint Fifth Workshop on Statistical*

*Machine Translation and MetricsMATR*, pages 315–320. Association for Computational Linguistics.

Preslav Nakov and Hwee Tou Ng. 2012. Improving statistical machine translation for a resource-poor language using related resource-rich languages. *Journal of Artificial Intelligence Research*, 44(1):179–222.

Majid Razmara and Anoop Sarkar. 2013. Ensemble triangulation for statistical machine translation. In *Proceedings of the Sixth International Joint Conference on Natural Language Processing*, pages 252–260.

Antti-Veikko I Rosti, Spyridon Matsoukas, and Richard Schwartz. 2007. Improved word-level system combination for machine translation. In *ANNUAL MEETING-ASSOCIATION FOR COMPUTATIONAL LINGUISTICS*, volume 45, page 312. Citeseer.

Andreas Stolcke et al. 2002. Srilm-an extensible language modeling toolkit. In *INTERSPEECH*.

Masao Utiyama and Hitoshi Isahara. 2007. A comparison of pivot methods for phrase-based statistical machine translation. In *HLT-NAACL*, pages 484–491.

Omar Zaidan. 2009. Z-mert: A fully configurable open source tool for minimum error rate training of machine translation systems. *The Prague Bulletin of Mathematical Linguistics*, 91:79–88.

# A Comparison of MT Methods for Closely Related Languages: a Case Study on Czech – Slovak Language Pair *

**Vladislav Kuboň**[1]
[1]Institute of Formal and Applied Linguistics
Faculty of Mathematics and Physics
Charles University in Prague
vk@ufal.mff.cuni.cz

**Jernej Vičič**[2,3]
[2]FAMNIT
University of Primorska,
[3]Fran Ramovš Institute of the
Slovenian Language, SRC SASA,
jernej.vicic@upr.si

## Abstract

This paper describes an experiment comparing results of machine translation between two closely related languages, Czech and Slovak. The comparison is performed by means of two MT systems, one representing rule-based approach, the other one representing statistical approach to the task. Both sets of results are manually evaluated by native speakers of the target language. The results are discussed both from the linguistic and quantitative points of view.

## 1 Introduction

Machine translation (MT) of related languages is a specific field in the domain of MT which attracted the attention of several research teams in the past by promising relatively good results through the application of classic rule-based methods. The exploitation of lexical, morphological and syntactic similarity of related languages seemed to balance the advantages of data-driven approaches, especially for the language pairs with smaller volumes of available parallel data.

This simple and straightforward assumption have led to the construction of numerous rule-based translation systems for related (or similar) natural languages. The following list (ordered alphabetically) includes several examples of those systems:

- (Altintas and Cicekli, 2002) for Turkic languages.
- Apertium (Corbi-Bellot et al., 2005) for Romance languages.
- (Dyvik, 1995; Bick and Nygaard, 2007; Ahrenberg and Holmqvist, 2004) for Scandinavian languages.
- Česílko (Hajič et al., 2000), for Slavic languages with rich inflectional morphology, mostly language pairs with Czech language as a source.
- Ruslan (Oliva, 1989) full-fledged transfer based RBMT system from Czech to Russian.
- (Scannell, 2006) for Gaelic languages; Irish (Gaeilge) and Scottish Gaelic (G'aidhlig).
- (Tyers et al., 2009) for the North Sami to Lule Sami language pair.
- Guat (Vičič, 2008) for Slavic languages with rich inflectional morphology, mostly language pairs with Slovenian language.

Many of the systems listed above had been created in the period when it was hard to obtain a good quality data-driven system which would enable comparison against these systems. The existence of Google Translate[1] which nowadays enables the automatic translation even between relatively small languages made it possible to investigate advantages and disadvantages of both approaches. This paper introduces the first step in this direction - the comparison of results of two different systems for two really very closely related languages - Czech and Slovak.

## 2 State of the art

There has already been a lot of research in Machine Translation evaluation. There are quite a few conferences and shared tasks devoted entirelly to this problem such as NIST Machine Translation Evaluation (NIST, 2009) or Workshop on Statistical Machine Translation (Bojar et al., 2013). (Weijnitz et al., 2004) presents a research on how systems from two different MT paradigms cope with a new domain. (Kolovratnık et al., 2009) presents a research on how relatedness of languages influences the translation quality of a SMT sytem.

The novelty of the presented paper is in the focus on machine translation for closely related languages and in the comparison of the two mostly used paradigms for this task: shallow parse and transfer RBMT and SMT paradigms.

## 3 Translation systems

The translation systems selected for the experiment are:

- Google Translate

* This work has been using language resources developed and/or stored and/or distributed by the LINDAT-Clarin project of the Ministry of Education of the Czech Republic (project LM2010013).

[1]Google Translate: `https://translate.google.com/`.



*Language Technology for Closely Related Languages and Language Variants (LT4CloseLang)*, pages 92–98,
October 29, 2014, Doha, Qatar. 

- Česílko (Hajič et al., 2003)

Google Translate was selected as the most used translation system. Česílko belongs to the shallow-parse and shallow-transfer rule based machine translation paradigm which is by many authors the most suitable for translation of related languages.

Česílko (Hajič et al., 2003) was used as a representative of rule-based MT systems, the translation direction from Czech to Slovak was naturally chosen because this is the only direction this system supports for this particular language pair.

The on-line publicly available versions of the systems sere used in the experiment to ensure the reproducibility of the experiment. All the test data is publicly available at the language technologies server of the University of Primorska[2].

Let us now introduce the systems in a more detail.

### 3.1 Google Translate

This system is currently probably the most popular and most widely used MT system in the world. It belongs to the Statistical Machine Translation – SMT paradigm. SMT is based on parametric statistical models, which are constructed on bilingual aligned corpora (training data). The methods focus on looking for general patterns that arise in the use of language instead of analyzing sentences according to grammatical rules. The main tool for finding such patterns is counting a variety of objects – statistics. The main idea of the paradigm is to model the probability that parts of a sentence from the source language translate into suitable parts of sentence in the target language.

The system takes advantage of the vast parallel resources which Google Inc. has at their disposal and it is therefore able to translate a large number of language pairs. Currently (July 2014), this system offers automatic translation among 80 languages. This makes it a natural candidate as a universal quality standard for MT, especially for pairs of smaller (underrepresented) languages for which there are very few MT systems.

### 3.2 Česílko

One of the first systems which fully relied on the similarity of related languages, Česílko (Hajič et al., 2003), had originally a very simple architecture. Its first implementation translated from Czech to Slovak. It used the method of direct word-for-word translation (after necessary morphological processing). More precisely, it translated each lemma obtained by morphological analysis and morphological tag provided by a tagger to a lemma and a corresponding tag in the target language. For the translation of lemmas it was necessary to use a bilingual dictionary, the differences in morphology of both languages, although to a large extent regular, did not allow to use a simple transliteration. The translation of lemmas was necessary due to differences in tagsets of the source and target language.

The syntactic similarity of both languages allowed the omission of syntactic analysis of the source language and syntactic synthesis of the target one, therefore the dictionary phase of the system had been immediately followed by morphological synthesis of the target language. No changes of the word order were necessary, the target language order of words preserved the word order of the source language.

Later versions of the system experimented with the architecture change involving the omission of the source language tagger and the addition of a stochastic ranker of translation hypothesis at the target language side. The purpose of this experiment was to eliminate tagging errors at the beginning of the translation process and to enable more variants of translation from which the stochastic ranker chose the most probable hypothesis. This change has been described for example in (Homola and Kuboň, 2008). For the purpose of our experiment we are using the original version of the system which has undergone some minor improvements (better tagger, improved dictionary etc.) and which is publicly available for testing at the website of the LINDAT project[3]. The decision to use this version is natural, given the fact that this is the only publicly available version of the system.

## 4 Methodology

In the planning phase of our experiment it was necessary to make a couple of decisions which could cause certain bias and invalidate the results obtained. First of all, the choice of the language pair (Czech to Slovak) was quite natural. These languages show very high degree of similarity at all levels (morphological, syntactic, semantic) and thus they constitute an ideal language pair for the development of simplified rule-based architecture. We are of course aware that for a complete answer to this question it would be necessary to test more systems and more language pairs, but in this phase of our experiments we do not aim at obtaining a complete answer, our main goal is to develop a methodology and to perform some kind of pilot testing showing the possible directions of future research.

The second important decision concerned the method of evaluation. Our primary goal was to set up a method which would be relatively simple and fast, thus allowing to manually (the reasons for manual evaluation are given in 4.2.1 subsection) process reasonable volume of results. The second goal concerned the endeavor to estimate evaluator's confidence in their judgments.

### 4.1 Basic properties of the language pair

The language pair used in our experiment belongs to western Slavic language group. We must admit that

[2] Test data: http://jt.upr.si/research_projects/related_languages/

[3] Česílko: http://lindat.mff.cuni.cz/services/cesilko/

the reason for choosing this language group was purely pragmatic – there is an extensive previous experience with the translation of several language pairs from this group, see, e.g. (Hajič et al., 2003), (Homola and Kuboň, 2008) or (Homola and Vičič, 2010). On top of that, the availability of the Česílko demo in the LINDAT repository for the free translation of up to 5000 characters naturally led to the decision to use this system (although it is in fact the original version of the system with very simple architecture).

Czech and Slovak represent the closest language pair among the western Slavic languages. Their morphology and syntax are very similar, their lexicons slightly differ, their word order is free (and also similar). In the former Czechoslovakia it was quite common that people understood both languages very well, but after the split of the country the younger people who don't have regular contact with the other language experience certain difficulties because the number of the words unknown to them is not negligible.

However, the greatest challenge for the word-for-word translation approach is not the lexicon (the differences in the lexicon can be handled by a bilingual dictionary), but the ambiguity of word forms. These are typically not part-of-speech ambiguities, they are quite rare although they do exist (*stát* [to stay/the state], *žena* [woman/chasing] or *tři* [three/rub(imper.)]), however, the greatest challenge is the ambiguity of gender, number and case (for example, the form of the adjective *jarní* [spring] is 27-way ambiguous). Resolving this ambiguity is very important for translation because Czech has very strict requirements on agreement (not only subject - predicate agreement, but also agreement in number, gender and case in nominal groups). Even though several Slavic languages including Slovak exhibit similar richness of word forms, the morphological ambiguity is not preserved at all or it is preserved only partially, it is distributed in a different manner and the "form-for-form" translation is not applicable.

For example, if we want to translate the Czech expression *jarní louka* [a spring meadow] into Slovak word for word, it is necessary to disambiguate the adjective which has the same form in Czech for all four genders (in Czech, there are two masculine genders - animate and inanimate) while in Slovak, there are three different forms for masculin, feminin and neutral gender - *jarný, jarná, jarné*. The disambiguation is performed by a state-of-the art stochastic tagger. Although this brings a stochastic factor into the system, we still consider Česílko to be primarily rule based system.

## 4.2 Experiment outline

The aim of the experiment was double: to show the quality of the simple RBMT methods (shallow-parse and shallow transfer RBMT) in comparison to the state-of-the-art SMT system. The second part of the experiment was to outline the most obvious and most challenging errors produced by each translation paradigm.

### 4.2.1 Translation quality evaluation

This part of the experiment relied on the methodology similar to that used in the 2013 Workshop on Statistical Machine Translation (Bojar et al., 2013). We conducted manual evaluation of both systems' outputs consisting of ranking individual translated sentences according to the translation quality (the evaluators had access to the original sentence). Unlike the ranking of the SMT Workshop which worked always with 5 translations, our task was much simpler and the ranking naturally consisted of ranking translated sentences of both systems. The evaluator indicated which of the two systems is better, having also the chance to indicate that both translations are identical, because the systems produced relatively large number of identical results - see section 5).

The reason why we didn't automatic measures of translation quality was quite natural. After a period of wide acceptance of automatic measures like BLEU (Papineni et al., 2001) or NIST (NIST, 2009), recent MT evaluation experiments seem to prefer manual methods. Many papers such as Callison-Burch et al. (2006) and authors of workshops such as WMT 2013 (Bojar et al., 2013) contend that automatic measures of machine translation quality are an imperfect substitute for human assessments, especially when it is necessary to compare different systems (or, even worse, the systems based on different paradigms).

### 4.2.2 Test data

Our evaluation is based upon a small, yet relevant, test corpus. Because one of the systems undergoing the evaluation has been developed by Google, the creation of the test set required special attention. We could not use any already existing on-line corpus as Google regularly enhances language models with new language data. Any on-line available corpus could have already been included in the training data of Google Translate, thus the results of the evaluation would have been biased towards the SMT system. Therefore we have decided to use fresh newspaper texts which cannot be part of any training data set used by Google.

We have selected 200 sentences from fresh newspaper articles of the biggest Czech on-line daily newspapers. Several headline news were selected in order to avoid author bias although the the domain remained daily news. We have selected articles from "iDnes"[4], "Lidovky"[5] and "Novinky"[6]. The test set was created from randomly selected articles on the dates between *14.7.2014* and *18.7.2014*.

All the test-data is publicly available at the language technologies server of the University of Primorska[2].

This part of the experiment consisted in manually examining the translated data from the translation quality evaluation task (described in section 4.2.1). As we have

[4] iDnes: `http://www.idnes.cz/`

[5] Lidovky: `http://www.lidovky.cz/`

[6] Novinky: `http://www.novinky.cz/`

expected, the most common errors of Česílko were out of the vocabulary errors. The dictionary coverage of the system has apparently been inadequate for a wide variety of topics from daily news. The results are presented in section 5.1.

## 5 Results

The results of our experiment are summarized in Table 1. The evaluation has been performed by 5 native speakers of Slovak, the sentences have been randomized so that no evaluator could know which of the two systems produced which translation. The evaluators were asked to mark which translation they consider to be better. Ties were not allowed, but the evaluators were also asked to mark identical sentences. This requirement served also as a kind of thoroughness check, too many unrecognized identical sentences could indicate that the evaluator lost concentration during the task.

| | Sent. count | Percentage |
|---|---|---|
| Identical sentences | 43 | 21.5% |
| Clear win of RBMT | 10 | 5% |
| Clear win of SMT | 59 | 29.5% |
| Win by voting - RBMT | 23 | 11.5% |
| Win by voting - SMT | 62 | 31% |
| Draw | 3 | 1.5% |
| Total | 200 | 100% |

Table 1: Evaluation of results

The rows of Table 1 marked as *Clear win* of one of the systems represent the sentences where none of the evaluators marked the other system as the *better one*. Win by voting does not distinguish how many evaluators were against the system marked by the majority as being the better of the two. The 3 sentences in the Draw row represent the cases when 1 or 3 evaluators mistakenly marked the pair of translations as being identical and there was no majority among the remaining ones.

The results clearly indicate that the quality of Google Translate is better, although it clearly dominates in less than one third of translations. The large number of identical sentences also means that although Česílko produced only 5% of translations which were clearly better than those of Google, it reached absolutely identical quality of translation in yet another 21.5%. This actually means that the top quality translations have been achieved in 26.5% by Česílko and in 51% by Google Translate. According to our opinion, this ratio (approximately 2:1 in favor of the SMT approach) more realistically describes the difference in quality than the ratio of clear wins (approx. 6:1 for Google Translate).

### 5.1 Errors

This section presents the most obvious errors detected in the evaluation of both systems.

First of all, before we'll look at individual types of errors of both systems, it is necessary to mention one very surprising fact concerning the translations. Although we have expected substantial differences between the corresponding sentences, the translations produced by both systems are surprisingly similar, 21.5% of them being absolutely identical. On top of that, when we have compared the first 100 translated sentences, we have discovered that the edit distance between the two sets is only 493 elementary operations. Given that the translations produced by Google Translate contain 9.653 characters in the first 100 sentences of the test set, this actually represents only about 5% difference.

This looks much more like the results of two variants of the same system than the results of two different systems based upon two completely different paradigms. Because no details about the Google translate for this language pair have been published, it is impossible to judge the reasons for such a similarity. The following example demonstrates this similarity, it represents quite typical example of a long sentence with very few differences between both translations. Errors in translations are stressed by a bold font.

**Example 1.**

Source: *"V momentě, kdy by třeba Praha chtěla převést systém na Plzeňskou kartu či kartu Českých drah, musela by porušit autorský zákon, protože jedině autor může se softwarem nakládat," vysvětluje mluvčí EMS.*
Google: "V momente, kedy by **potrebné** Praha chcela previesť systém na Plzeňskú kartu či kartu Českých dráh, musela by porušiť autorský zákon, pretože jedine autor môže so softvérom **zaobchádzať**," vysvetľuje hovorca EMS.
Česílko: "V momente, kedy by napríklad Praha chcela previesť systém na Plzenskú **karta** či **karta Český** dráh, musela by porušiť autorský zákon, pretože **jedině** autor môže so softwarom **nakladať**," vysvetľuje hovorca EMS.
English translation: *"In the moment when Prague would like for example to transfer the system to Pilsen card or the Czech railways card, it would have to violate the copyright law, because the author is the only person which can modify the software," explains the speaker of the EMS.*

Even more suspicious are translated sentences which are identical, incorrect and both contain the same error. If something like that happens in a school, the teacher has all reasons to think that one of the two pupils is cheating and that he copied from his neighbor. The systems had no chance to cheat, what makes identical results as in the following example very weird. It would be very interesting to perform more detailed tests in the future and to investigate the reasons for such behavior of two completely different systems. The straightforward explanation that both languages are so similar that these identical errors simply happen, seems to be too simplistic. Example 2 clearly shows that both systems misinterpreted the Czech adjective *právní* (legal) in the context which allowed reading the first three words of the source sentence as "It is legal" without the regard to the context of the rest of the sentence.

**Example 2.**

Source: *Je to právní, ale i technologický problém.*
Both systems: Je to **právne**, ale aj technologický problém.
English: *It is a legal, but also a technological problem.*

Let us now look at individual categories of errors.

**Lexical errors**

The most frequent lexical errors are untranslated words. This happens solely in the translations performed by the RBMT system Česílko due to inadequate coverage of the wide domain of newspaper articles. Some of the cases of untranslated words may have escaped the evaluatorś attention simply because Česílko leaves out-of-the-vocabulary words unchanged. Because Czech and Slovak are really very close also at the lexical level, some of the word forms used in both languages are identical, and thus they fit into the target sentence. Increasing the coverage of the bilingual dictionary (it currently contains about 40,000 lemmas) would definitely improve the translation quality.

Another lexical error produced entirely by the RBMT system is a wrong translation of some irregular words, as in the following example.

**Example 3.**

Source: *Mnozí lidé si téměř neumějí představit, že by zapomněli svůj rodný jazyk.*
Google: Mnohí **ľudia** si takmer nevedia predstaviť, že by zabudli svoj rodný jazyk.
Česílko: Mnohí **človek** si takmer nevedia představit, že by zabudli svoj rodný jazyk.
English translation: *Many people cannot imagine that they could forget their native language.*

The plural of *člověk* [human] is irregular in Czech (*lidé* [people]). Although this error looks like a lexical error, it is more likely caused by the conceptual differences between the morphological analysis of Czech (which recognizes the form as a plural of the lemma *člověk*) and the synthesis of Slovak which uses two lemmas instead of one, one for singular (*človek*) and one for plural (*ľudia*). The Czech plural word form is then never correctly translated to the Slovak plural form.

Much more serious errors are mistranslated words produced by Google Translate. Such errors are quite typical for phrase-based SMT systems. Let us present an example which appeared a couple of times in our test corpus.

**Example 4.**

Source: *Česká veřejnost si na omezení zvykla a většinou je respektuje.*
Google: **Slovenská** verejnosť si na obmedzenie zvykla a väčšinou je rešpektuje.
Česílko: **Český** verejnosť si na obmedzenie zvykla a väčšinou ich rešpektuje.
English translation: *Czech public got used to the limits and mostly accepts them.*

The incorrect translation of the adjective *Česká* [Czech] as *Slovenská* [Slovak] has most probably been caused by the language model based upon target language text where the occurrences of the adjective Slovak probably vastly outnumber the occurrences of the word Czech. The same incorrect translations appeared also in different contexts in other sentences of the test corpus.

**Morphological errors**

Both languages are very similar also with regard to the number of inflected word forms derived from one lemma. This property seems to cause certain problems to both systems, as we can see in the Example 5, where both systems use an incorrect (but different) form of the same adjective. It is interesting that in this specific case the correct translation actually means no translation at all because the correct Czech and Slovak forms are identical in this context.

**Example 5.**

Source: *V březnu malajsijské aerolinky přišly o Boeing 777 s 239 lidmi na palubě, který se ztratil z leteckých radarů cestou z Kuala Lumpuru do Pekingu.*
Google: V marci **malajzijského** aerolinky prišli o Boeing 777 s 239 ľuďmi na palube, ktorý sa stratil z leteckých radarov cestou z Kuala Lumpur do Pekingu.
Česílko: V marci **malajsijský** aerolinky prišli o Boeing 777 s 239 človek na palube, ktorý sa stratil z leteckých radarov cestou z Kuala Lumpuru do Pekingu.
English translation: *In March, Malaysian Airlines lost Boeing 777 with 239 people on board, which got lost from air radars on the way from Kuala Lumpur to Beijing.*

Although the morphological errors have a negative influence on automatic measures like BLEU or NIST (incorrect form of a correct word influences the score to the same extent as completely incorrect word), they usually do not change the meaning of the translated sentence and the speakers of the target language can easily reconstruct their correct form and understand the translation. From this point of view both systems perform very well because the relatively low number of incorrect word forms produced by both systems doesn't reach the threshold when the sentence as a whole would be unintelligible.

**Word order**

Both systems follow very strictly the order of words

of source sentences. This is not surprising in the case of the RBMT system, because its simple architecture is exploiting the fact that the word order of both languages is extremely similar. As we have already mentioned in the section 3, Česílko translates word by word. The strict correspondence of the word order of source and target sentences is a bit more surprising in the case of the SMT system, whose language model is probably based on a large volume of texts with a wide variety of word order variants. Czech and Slovak languages both have very few restrictions on the order of words and thus we have supposed that the translated sentences might have an altered word order compared to the source sentences. The only difference in the order of words appeared in the sentence presented below, where the RBMT system followed the original word order strictly, while the SMT system made changes (acceptable ones) to the order of clitics.

**Example 6.**

Source: *Ačkoli vyšetřovatelé už jsou si jisti, že stroj se odklonil ze své trasy a zřítil se pravděpodobně po dlouhém letu nad Indickým oceánem, nevědí dodnes, co bylo příčinou nehody a nenašli ani trosky stroje.*
Google: Hoci vyšetrovatelia **sú si už** istí, že stroj sa odklonil zo svojej trasy a zrútil sa pravdepodobne po dlhom lete nad Indickým oceánom, nevedia dodnes, čo bolo príčinou nehody a nenašli ani trosky stroja.
Česílko: Bárs vyšetrovatelia **už sú si** istí, že stroj sa odklonil zo svojej trasy a zrútil sa pravdepodobne po dlhom lete nad Indickým oceánom, nevedia dodnes, čo bolo príčinou nehody a nenašli ani trosky stroja.
English translation: *Although the investigators are now sure that the plane swerved from its path and fell down probably after a long flight over the Indian ocean, they didn't find out till today what was the cause of the accident and they even didn't find any remains of the plane.*

**Syntactic errors**

There are no errors which could be classified as purely violating the syntax of the target language. The use of an incorrect form of direct or indirect object can be attributed to the category of morphological errors, because neither of the two systems deals with syntax directly. The RBMT system ignores syntax on the basis of the fact that both languages are syntactically very similar; the SMT system probably primarily relies on phrases discovered in large volumes of training data and thus it takes the syntactic rules into account only indirectly.

**Errors in meaning**

There were very few errors in incorrectly translated meaning of the source sentence into the target one. Although some SMT systems are infamous for issues related to the preservation of negated expressions, the only two examples of such errors were produced by the RBMT system in our tests. The sentence which was affected by this error to a greater extent is listed below. No other errors in the translation of the original meaning have been encountered in our tests.

Source: *Vedení školy odpovídá na některé oficiální dotazy rodičů až po opakované urgenci a chování ředitelky Kozohorské je podle slov rodičů alibistické, nevstřícné a nezřídka arogantní.*
Google: Vedenie školy odpovedá na niektoré oficiálne otázky rodičov až po opakovanej urgencii a správanie riaditeľky Kozohorský je podľa slov rodičov alibistické, *nevstřícné a nezriedka* arogantný.
Česílko: Vedenie školy odpovedá na niektorých oficiálne otázky rodičov až po opakovanej urgencii a chovaní ředitelka Kozohorský je podľa slov rodičov alibistické, **vstřícný a zriedka** arogantní.
English translation: *The school management answers some official questions of parents after repeated reminders and the behavior of director Kozohorská is, in the words of parents, buck-passing, unresponsive and often arrogant.*

The sentence produced by Česílko has lost two negations making the behavior of the director *responsive and seldom arrogant*. This is probably caused by the fact that both the positive and negative forms have the same lemma - the negation constitutes only a small part of the morphological tag[7] and thus it may easily be forgotten or lost in the process of transfer of a Czech tag into a Slovak one (a different system of tags is used for Slovak).

## 6 Conclusions and further work

Although our experiment represents only the first step in systematic evaluation of machine translation results between closely related languages, it has already brought very interesting results. It has shown that contrary to a popular belief that RBMT methods are more suitable for MT of closely related languages, Google Translate outperforms the RBMT system Česílko. The similarity of source and target language apparently not only allows much simpler architecture of the RBMT system, it also improves the chances of SMT systems to generate good quality translation, although this results need further examination.

The most surprising result of our experiment is the high number of identical translations produced by both systems not only for short simple sentences, but also for some of the long ones, as well as very similar results produced for the rest of the test corpus. The minimal differences between two systems exploiting different paradigms deserve further experiments. These experiments will involve a phrase-based SMT system based on Moses (in this way we are going to guarantee that we are really comparing two different paradigms) and we will investigate its behavior on the same language pair. A second interesting experimental direction will

[7]Česílko exploits a positional system of morphological tags with 15 fixed positions, the negation marker occupies only one of these positions.

be the investigation whether the results for another pair of languages related not so closely as Czech and Slovak would confirm the results obtained in this experiment.

## References


Lars Ahrenberg and Maria Holmqvist. 2004. Back to the Future? The Case for English-Swedish Direct Machine Translation. In *Proceedings of The Conference on Recent Advances in Scandinavian Machine Translation*. University of Uppsala.

Kemal Altintas and Ilyas Cicekli. 2002. A Machine Translation System between a Pair of Closely Related Languages. In *Proceedings of the 17th International Symposium on Computer and Information Sciences (ISCIS 2002)*, page 5. CRC Press.

Eckhard Bick and Lars Nygaard. 2007. Using Danish as a CG Interlingua: A Wide-Coverage Norwegian-English Machine Translation System. In *Proceedings of NODALIDA, Tartu*. University of Tartu.

Ondřej Bojar, Christian Buck, Chris Callison-Burch, Christian Federmann, Barry Haddow, Philipp Koehn, Christof Monz, Matt Post, Radu Soricut, and Lucia Specia. 2013. Findings of the 2013 Workshop on Statistical Machine Translation. In *2013 Workshop on Statistical Machine Translation*, pages 1–44.

Chris Callison-Burch, Miles Osborne, and Philipp Koehn. 2006. Re-evaluating the role of BLEU in machine translation research. In *Proceedings of EACL*, pages 249–256. Association for Computational Linguistics.

Antonio M Corbi-Bellot, Mikel L Forcada, and Sergio Ortiz-Rojas. 2005. An open-source shallow-transfer machine translation engine for the Romance languages of Spain. In *Proceedings of the EAMT conference*, pages 79–86. HITEC e.V.

Helge Dyvik. 1995. Exploiting Structural Similarities in Machine Translation. *Computers and Humanities*, 28:225–245.

Jan Hajič, Jan Hric, and Vladislav Kuboň. 2000. Machine translation of very close languages. In *Proceedings of the 6th Applied Natural Language Processing Conference*, pages 7–12. Association for Computational Linguistics.

Jan Hajič, Petr Homola, and Vladislav Kuboň. 2003. A simple multilingual machine translation system. In Eduard Hovy and Elliott Macklovitch, editors, *Proceedings of the MT Summit IX*, pages 157–164, New Orleans, USA. AMTA.

Petr Homola and Vladislav Kuboň. 2008. A method of hybrid MT for related languages. In *Proceedings of the IIS*, pages 269–278. Academic Publishing House EXIT.

Petr Homola and Jernej Vičič. 2010. Combining MT Systems Effectively. In *Proceedings of the 23th International Florida-Artificial-Intelligence-Research-Society Conference (FLAIRS 2010)*, pages 198–203, Daytona Beach, Florida, USA. Florida {AI} Research Society, Florida AI Research Society.

David Kolovratnık, Natalia Klyueva, and Ondrej Bojar. 2009. Statistical machine translation between related and unrelated languages. In *Proceedings of the Conference on Theory and Practice on Information Technologies*, pages 31–36.

NIST. 2009. NIST 2009 Open Machine Translation Evaluation (MT09). Technical report, NIST.

Karel Oliva. 1989. *A Parser for Czech Implemented in Systems Q*. MFF UK Prague.

Kishore Papineni, Salim Roukos, Todd Ward, and Wei-Jing Zhu. 2001. BLEU: a method for automatic evaluation of machine translation. Technical report, IBM.

Kevin P Scannell. 2006. Machine translation for closely related language pairs. In *Proceedings of the Workshop Strategies for developing machine translation for minority languages*, pages 103–109. Genoa, Italy.

Francis M Tyers, Linda Wiechetek, and Trond Trosterud. 2009. Developing prototypes for machine translation between two Sámi languages. In *Proceedings of EAMT*. HITEC e.V.

Jernej Vičič. 2008. Rapid development of data for shallow transfer RBMT translation systems for highly inflective languages. In *Language technologies: proceedings of the conference*, pages 98–103. Institut Jožef Stefan, Ljubljana.

Per Weijnitz, Eva Forsbom, Ebba Gustavii, Eva Pettersson, and Jorg Tiedemann. 2004. MT goes farming: Comparing two machine translation approaches on a new domain. In *LREC*, pages 1–4.

# Handling OOV Words in Dialectal Arabic to English Machine Translation

**Maryam Aminian, Mahmoud Ghoneim, Mona Diab**
Department of Computer Science
The George Washington University
Washington, DC
{aminian,mghoneim,mtdiab}@gwu.edu

## Abstract

Dialects and standard forms of a language typically share a set of cognates that could bear the same meaning in both varieties or only be shared homographs but serve as *faux amis*. Moreover, there are words that are used exclusively in the dialect or the standard variety. Both phenomena, faux amis and exclusive vocabulary, are considered out of vocabulary (OOV) phenomena. In this paper, we present this problem of OOV in the context of machine translation. We present a new approach for dialect to English Statistical Machine Translation (SMT) enhancement based on normalizing dialectal language into standard form to provide equivalents to address both aspects of the OOV problem posited by dialectal language use. We specifically focus on Arabic to English SMT. We use two publicly available dialect identification tools: AIDA and MADAMIRA, to identify and replace dialectal Arabic OOV words with their modern standard Arabic (MSA) equivalents. The results of evaluation on two blind test sets show that using AIDA to identify and replace MSA equivalents enhances translation results by 0.4% absolute BLEU (1.6% relative BLEU) and using MADAMIRA achieves 0.3% absolute BLEU (1.2% relative BLEU) enhancement over the baseline. We show our replacement scheme reaches a noticeable enhancement in SMT performance for faux amis words.

## 1 Introduction

In this day of hyper connectivity, spoken vernaculars are ubiquitously ever more present in textual social media and informal communication channels. Written (very close to the spoken) informal language as represented by dialect poses a significant challenge to current natural language processing (NLP) technology in general due to the lack of standards for writing in these vernaculars. The problem is exacerbated when the vernacular constitutes a dialect of the language that is quite distinct and divergent from a language standard and people code switch within utterance between the standard and the dialect. This is the case for Arabic. Modern Standard Arabic (MSA), as the name indicates, is the official standard for the Arabic language usually used in formal settings, while its vernaculars vary from it significantly forming dialects known as dialectal Arabic (DA), commonly used in informal settings such as the web and social media. Contemporary Arabic is a collection of these varieties. Unlike MSA, DA has no standard orthography (Salloum and Habash, 2013). Most of the studies in Arabic NLP have been conducted on MSA. NLP research on DA, the unstandardized spoken variety of Arabic, is still at its infancy. This constitutes a problem for Arabic processing in general due to the ubiquity of DA usage in written social media. Moreover, linguistic code switching between MSA and DA always happens either in the course of a single sentence or across different sentences. However this intrasentential code switching is quite pervasive (Elfardy et al., 2013). For instance 98.13% of sentences crawled from Egyptian DA (EGY) discussion forums for the COLABA project (Diab et al., 2010) contains intrasentential code switching.

MSA has a wealth of NLP tools and resources compared to a stark deficiency in such resources for DA. The mix of MSA and DA in utterances constitutes a significant problem of Out of Vocabulary (OOV) words in the input to NLP applications. The OOV problem is two fold: completely unseen words in training data, and homograph OOVs where the word appears in the training data but with a different sense. Given these issues, DA



*Language Technology for Closely Related Languages and Language Variants (LT4CloseLang)*, pages 99–108,
October 29, 2014, Doha, Qatar. 

NLP and especially DA statistical machine translation (SMT) can be seen as highly challenging tasks and this illustrates the need for conducting more research on DA.

MSA has a wealth of resources such as parallel corpora and tools like morphological analyzers, disambiguation systems, etc. On the other hand, DA still lacks such tools and resources. As an example, parallel DA to English (EN) corpora are still very few and there are almost no MSA-DA parallel corpora. Similar to MSA, DA has the problem of writing with optional diacritics. It also lacks orthographic standards. Hence, translating from DA to EN is challenging as there are impediments posed by the nature of the language coupled with the lack of resources and tools to process DA (Salloum and Habash, 2013).

MSA and DA are significantly different on all levels of linguistic representation: phonologically, morphologically, lexically, syntactically, semantically and pragmatically. The morphological differences between MSA and DA are most noticeably expressed by using some clitics and affixes that do not exist in MSA. For instance, the DA (Egyptian and Levantine) future marker clitic *H*[1] is expressed as the clitic *s* in MSA (Salloum and Habash, 2013). On a lexical level, MSA and DA share a considerable number of faux amis where the lexical tokens are homographs but have different meanings. For instance the word *yEny* in MSA means 'to mean', but in DA, it is a pragmatic marker meaning 'to some extent'. We refer to this phenomenon as sense OOV (SOOV). This phenomenon is in addition to the complete OOV (COOV) that exist in DA but don't exist in MSA. These issues constitute a significant problem for processing DA using MSA trained tools. This problem is very pronounced in machine translation.

In this paper, we present a new approach to build a DA-to-EN MT system by normalizing DA words into MSA. We focus our investigation on the Egyptian variety of DA (EGY). We leverage MSA resources with robust DA identification tools to improve SMT performance for DA-to-EN SMT. We focus our efforts on replacing identified DA words by MSA counterparts. We investigate the replacement specifically in the decoding phase of the SMT pipeline. We explore two state of the art DA identification tools for the purposes of our study. We demonstrate the effects of our replacement scheme on each OOV type and show that normalizing DA words into their equivalent MSA considerably enhances SMT performance in translating SOOVs.

The remainder of this paper is organized as follows: Section 2 overviews related work; Section 3 details our approach; Section 4 presents the results obtained on standard data sets; in Section 5, we discuss the results and perform error analysis; finally we conclude with some further observations in Section 6.

## 2 Related Work

Leveraging MSA resources and tools to enrich DA for NLP purposes has been explored in several studies. Chiang, et. al. (2006) exploit the relation between Levantine Arabic (LEV) and MSA to build a syntactic parser on transcribed spoken LEV without using any annotated LEV corpora.

Since there are no DA-to-MSA parallel corpora, rule-based methods have been predominantly employed to translate DA-to-MSA. For instance, Abo Bakr et al. (2008) introduces a hybrid approach to transfer a sentence from EGY into a diacritized MSA form. They use a statistical approach for tokenizing and tagging in addition to a rule-based system for constructing diacritized MSA sentences. Moreover, Al-Sabbagh and Girju (2010) introduce an approach to build a DA-to-MSA lexicon through mining the web.

In the context of DA translation, Sawaf (2010) introduced a hybrid MT system that uses statistical and rule-based approaches for DA-to-EN MT. In his study, DA words are normalized to the equivalent MSA using a dialectal morphological analyzer. This approach achieves 2% absolute BLEU enhancement for Web texts and about 1% absolute BLEU improvement over the broadcast transmissions. Furthermore, Salloum and Habash (2012) use a DA morphological analyzer (ADAM) and a list of hand-written morphosyntactic transfer rules (from DA to MSA) to improve DA-to-EN MT. This approach improves BLEU score on a blind test set by 0.56% absolute BLEU (1.5% relative) on the broadcast conversational and broadcast news data. Test sets used in their study contain a mix of Arabic dialects but Levantine Arabic constitutes the majority variety.

Zbib et al. (2012) demonstrate an approach to ac-

[1]We use the Buckwalter Transliteration as represented in www.qamus.com for Romanized Arabic representation throughout the paper.

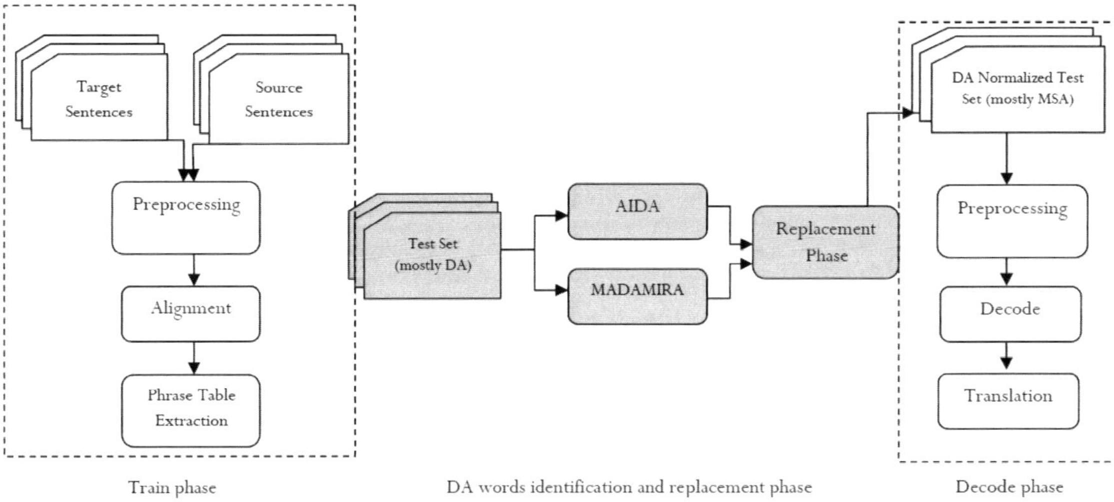


Figure 1: Block diagram of the proposed system for enhancing DA-to-EN SMT via normalizing DA

quire more DA-to-EN data to improve DA SMT performance by enriching translation models with more DA data. They use Amazon Mechanical Turk to create a DA-to-EN parallel corpus. This parallel data is augmented to the available large MSA-to-EN data and is used to train the SMT system. They showed that their trained SMT model on this DA-to-EN data, can achieve 6.3% and 7% absolute BLEU enhancement over an SMT system trained on MSA-to-EN data when translating EGY and LEV test sets respectively. Habash (2008) demonstrates four techniques for handling OOV words through modifying phrase tables for MSA. He also introduces a tool which employs these four techniques for online handling of OOV in SMT (Habash, 2009).

Habash et al. (2013) introduces MADA-ARZ, a new system for morphological analysis and disambiguation of EGY based on an MSA morphological analyzer MADA (Habash and Rambow, 2005). They evaluate MADA-ARZ extrinsically in the context of DA-to-EN MT and show that using MADA-ARZ for tokenization leads to 0.8% absolute BLEU improvement over the baseline which is simply tokenized with MADA. In this paper, we use MADAMIRA (Pasha et al., 2014), a system for morphological analysis and disambiguation for both MSA and DA (EGY), to identify DA words and replace MSA equivalents. Our approach achieves 0.6% absolute BLEU improvement over the scores reported in (Habash et al., 2013).

## 3 Approach

In the context of SMT for DA-to-EN, we encounter a significant OOV rate between test and training data since the size of the training data is relatively small. On the other hand, we have significant amounts of MSA-to-EN parallel data to construct rich phrase tables. MSA and DA, though divergent, they share many phenomena that can be leveraged for the purposes of MT. Hence, if we combine training data from MSA with that from DA, and then at the decode time normalize OOV DA words into their equivalent MSA counterparts we should be able to overcome the resource challenges in the DA-to-EN SMT context, yielding better overall translation performance. The OOV problem is two fold: complete OOV (COOV) and sense OOV (SOOV). The COOV problem is the standard OOV problem where an OOV in the input data is not attested at all in the training data. The SOOV problem is where a word is observed in the training data but with a different usage or sense, different from that of the test data occurrence. To our knowledge, our research is the first to address the SOOV directly in the context of SMT. To that end, we employ two DA identification tools: a morphological tagger, as well as a full-fledged DA identification tool to identify and replace DA words with their equivalent MSA lemmas in the test data at decoding time.

Accordingly, the ultimate goal of this work is to assess the impact of different DA identification and replacement schemes on SMT overall performance and overall OOV (both types) reduction. It is worth noting that we focus our experiments on the decoding phase of the SMT system. Figure1 shows the block diagram of the proposed system. We exploit the following tools and resources:

- **MADAMIRA:** A system for morphological analysis and disambiguation for both MSA and DA (EGY). MADAMIRA indicates whether a word is EGY or MSA based on its underlying lexicon which is used to generate an equivalent EN gloss. However, for EGY words, MADAMIRA does not generate the equivalent MSA lemma (Pasha et al., 2014);
- **AIDA:** A full-fledged DA identification tool which is able to identify and classify DA words on the token and sentence levels. AIDA exploits MADAMIRA internally in addition to more information from context to identify DA words (Elfardy and Diab, 2013). AIDA provides both the MSA equivalent lemma(s) and corresponding EN gloss(es) for the identified DA words;
- **THARWA:** A three-way lexicon between EGY, MSA and EN (Diab et al., 2014).

To evaluate effectiveness of using each of these resources in OOV reduction, we have exploited the following replacement schemes:

- AIDA identifies DA words in the context and replaces them with the most probable equivalent MSA lemma;
- MADAMIRA determines whether a word is DA or not. If the word is DA, then EN gloss(es) from MADAMIRA are used to find the most probable equivalent MSA lemma(s) from THARWA.

As all of these DA identification resources (MADAMIRA, AIDA and THARWA) return MSA equivalents in the lemma form, we adopt a factored translation model to introduce the extra information in the form of lemma factors. Therefore, DA replacement affects only the lemma factor in the factored input. We consider the following setups to properly translate replaced MSA lemma to the the corresponding inflected form (lexeme):[2]

- Generated lexeme-to-lexeme translation (Glex-to-lex): To derive inflected MSA lexeme from MSA replaced lemma and POS, we construct a generation table on the factored data to map lemma and POS factors into lexeme. This table is generated using Moses toolkit (Koehn et al., 2007) generation scripts and provides a list of generated lexemes for each lemma-POS pair. An MSA lexeme language model (LM) is then used to decode the most probable sequence of MSA lexemes given these generated lexemes for each word in the sentence.
- lemma+POS-to-lexeme translation (lem+POS-to-lex): In this path source lemma and POS are translated into the appropriate target lexeme. We expect this path provides plausible translations for DA words that are not observed in the phrase tables.
- lexeme-to-lexeme;lemma+POS-to-lexeme translation (lex-to-lex;lem+POS-to-lex): The first path translates directly from a source lexeme to the target lexeme. So it provides appropriate lexeme translations for the words (MSA or DA) which have been observed in the trained model. It is worth noting that lex-to-lex translation path does not contain any replacement or normalization. Therefore, it is different from the first path (Glex-to-lex). The second path is similar to the lem+POS-to-lex path and is used to translate DA words that do not exist in the trained model.

### 3.1 Data Sets

For training translation models we use a collection of MSA and EGY texts created from multiple LDC catalogs[3] comprising multiple genres (newswire, broadcast news, broadcast conversations, newsgroups and weblogs).The train data contains 29M MSA and 5M DA tokenized words. We use two test sets to evaluate our method on both highly DA and MSA texts: For DA test data, we selected 1065 sentences from LDC2012E30, which comprises 16177 tokenized words (BOLT-arz-test); For MSA, we use the NIST MTEval 2009 test set (LDC2010T23), which contains

[2] We use the term lexeme to indicate an inflected tokenized uncliticized form of the lemma. A lemma in principle is a lexeme but it is also a citation form in a dictionary.

[3] 41 LDC catalogs including data prepared for GALE and BOLT projects. Please contact the authors for more details.

1445 sentences corresponding to 40858 tokenized words (MT09-test). As development set (dev set), we randomly select 1547 sentences from multiple LDC catalogs (LDC2012E15, LDC2012E19, LDC2012E55) which comprises 20780 tokens.

The following preprocessing steps are performed on the train, test and dev sets: The Arabic side of the parallel data is Alef/Ya normalized and tokenized using MADAMIRA v1. according to Arabic Treebank (ATB) tokenization scheme (Maamouri et al., 2004); Tokenization on the EN side of the parallel data is performed using Tree Tagger (Schmid, 1994).

### 3.2 Language Modeling

We create a 5-gram language model (LM) from three corpora sets: a) The English Gigaword 5 (Graff and Cieri, 2003); b) The English side of the BOLT Phase1 parallel data; and, c) different LDC English corpora collected from discussion forums (LDC2012E04, LDC2012E16, LDC2012E21, LDC2012E54). We use SRILM (Stolcke., 2002) to build 5-gram language models with modified Kneser-Ney smoothing.

### 3.3 SMT System

We use the open-source Moses toolkit (Koehn et al., 2007) to build a standard phrase-based SMT system which extracts up to 8 words phrases in the Moses phrase table. The parallel corpus is word-aligned using GIZA++ (Och and Ney, 2003). Feature weights are tuned to maximize BLEU on the dev set using Minimum Error Rate Training (MERT) (Och, 2003). To account for the instability of MERT, we run the tuning step three times per condition with different random seeds and use the optimized weights that give the median score on the development set. As all our DA identification resources (MADAMIRA, AIDA and THARWA) are lemma-based, we adopt a factored translation model setup to introduce the extra information in the form of a lemma factor. As lemma only is not enough to generate appropriate inflected surface (lexeme) forms, we add a POS factor with two main translation paths: (i) direct translation from a source lexeme to the target lexeme; and (ii) translation from source lemma and POS to the appropriate target lexeme. Therefore, the first path should provide plausible translations for the words that have been seen before in the phrase tables while we expect that the second path provides feasible translations for DA words that are not seen in the trained model.

## 4 Experimental Results

### 4.1 Baseline Results

For each experimental condition mentioned in Section 3, we define a separate baseline with similar setup. These baselines use the SMT setup described in Section 3.3 and are evaluated on the two test sets mentioned in Section 3.1. To assess effectiveness of normalizing DA into MSA on the overall performance of MT system, the dev and test sets are processed through the similar steps to generate factored data but without any replacement of the DA words with MSA correspondents. We believe this to be a rigorous and high baseline as data contains some morphological information useful for DA-to-EN translation in the form of lemma and POS factors. We started with a baseline trained on the 29M words tokenized MSA training set and 5M words tokenized DA set separately. We created the baseline trained on the 34M words MSA+DA train data. Our objective of splitting train data based on its dialectal variety is to assess the role of DA words existing in the train set in the performance of our approach.

Table 1 illustrates baseline BLEU scores on BOLT-arz and MT09-test sets with three different training conditions: MSA+DA, MSA only, and DA only.

### 4.2 Replacement Experimental Results

We run the SMT pipeline using the feature weights that performed best during the tuning session on our dev set. Then the SMT pipeline with these tuned weights is run on two blind test sets. To account for statistical significance tests we used bootstrapping methods as detailed in (Zhang and Vogel, 2010). Table 2 shows BLEU scores of different DA identification and replacement schemes exploited in different setups on the test sets.

As we can see in Table 2, both AIDA and MADAMIRA replacement schemes outperform the baseline scores using MSA+DA trained models and lem+POS-to-lex;lex-to-lex setup. AIDA reaches 0.4% absolute BLEU (1.6% relative BLEU) improvement and MADAMIRA achieves 0.3% absolute BLEU (1.2% relative BLEU) enhancement over the corresponding baselines. This is while the same enhancement in BLEU scores can not be captured when we exploit the model

| Test Set | Train Set | lex-to-lex | lem+POS-to-lex | lex-to-lex:lem+POS-to-lex |
|---|---|---|---|---|
| BOLT-arz-test | MSA+DA | 26.2 | 25.4 | 25.5 |
| | MSA | 21.8 | 21.2 | 21.8 |
| | DA | 24.3 | 24.6 | 24.8 |
| MT09-test | MSA+DA | 48.2 | 46.9 | 47.3 |
| | MSA | 44.4 | 45.4 | 44.6 |
| | DA | 35.6 | 36.1 | 34.2 |

Table 1: Baseline BLUE scores for each setup on two test sets: BOLT-arz-test and MT09-test. Results are reported for each training input language variety separately.

| Test Set | Train Set | Glex-to-lex | | lem+POS-to-lex | | lex-to-lex:lem+POS-to-lex | |
|---|---|---|---|---|---|---|---|
| | | AIDA | MADAMIRA | AIDA | MADAMIRA | AIDA | MADAMIRA |
| BOLT-arz-test | MSA+DA | 24.4 | 25.1 | 22.6 | 24.1 | **25.9** | 25.8 |
| | MSA | 20.6 | 21.0 | 20.1 | 20.3 | 21.7 | 22.0 |
| | DA | 24.3 | 23.7 | 21.3 | 23.1 | 24.5 | 24.8 |
| MT09-test | MSA+DA | 45.9 | 45.8 | 45.4 | 44.6 | 47.1 | 47.3 |
| | MSA | 42.7 | 42.4 | 45.2 | 43.7 | 44.5 | 44.6 |
| | DA | 35.6 | 34.0 | 36.1 | 34.5 | 34.1 | 34.3 |

Table 2: BLEU scores of AIDA and MADAMIRA replacement for the different setups on BOLT-arz-test and MT09-test. Results are reported for each training language variety separately.

which is trained on MSA or DA parallel data solely. This indicates that normalizing DA into MSA can reach its best performance only when we enrich the training model with DA words at the same time. Therefore, we note that acquiring more DA data to enrich phrase tables at the training phase and normalizing DA at the decoding step of SMT system would yield the best DA-to-EN translation accuracy.

Regardless of the replacement scheme we use to reduce the OOV rate (AIDA or MADAMIRA), BLEU scores on the MT09 are much higher than those on the BOLT-arz because the amount of MSA words in the training data is much more than DA words. Therefore, SMT system encounters less OOVs at the decode time on MSA texts such as MT09. Overall we note that adding AIDA or MADAMIRA to the setup at best has no impact on performance on the MT09 data set since it is mostly MSA. However, we note a small impact for using the tools in the lex-to-lex:lem+POS-to-lex path in the MSA+DA experimental setting.

Comparing results of different setups indicates that adding lex-to-lex translation path to the lem+POS-to-lex increases both AIDA and MADAMIRA performance on two test sets significantly. As Table 2 demonstrates adding lex-to-lex path to the lem+POS-to-lex translation using the model trained on MSA+DA data leads to 3.3% and 1.7% BLEU improvement using AIDA and MADAMIRA, respectively on the BOLT-arz set. Similar conditions on the MT09-test gives us 1.7% and 0.7% absolute improvement in the BLEU scores using AIDA and MADAMIRA respectively. This happens because lex-to-lex path can provide better translations for the words (MSA or DA) which have been seen in the phrase tables and having both these paths enables the SMT system to generate more accurate translations. Our least results are obtained when we use lem+POS-to-lex translation path solely either using AIDA or MADAMIRA which mainly occurs due to some errors existing in the output of morphological analyzer that yields to the erroneous lemma or POS.

| | BOLT-arz | MT09 |
|---|---|---|
| Sent. | 1065 | 1445 |
| Types | 4038 | 8740 |
| Tokens | 16177 | 40858 |
| COOV (type) | 126 (3%) | 169 (2%) |
| COOV (token) | 134 (0.82%) | 187 (0.45%) |

Table 3: Number of sentences, types, tokens and COOV percentages in each test set

| Reference | not private , i mean like buses and the metro and trains ... etc . |
|---|---|
| **Baseline** | mc mlkyp xASp yEny AqSd **zy** AlAtwbys w+ Almtrw w+ AlqTAr . . . Alx |
| **Baseline translation** | privately , i mean , i mean , i do not like the bus and metro and train , etc . |
| **Replacement** | mc mlkyp xASp yEny AqSd **mvl** AlAtwbys w+ Almtrw w+ AlqTAr . . . Alx |
| **Replacement translation** | not a private property , i mean , i mean , like the bus and metro and train , etc . |

Table 4: Example of translation enhancement by SOOV replacement

## 5 Error Analysis

To assess the rate of OOV reduction using different replacement methodologies, we first identify OOV words in the test sets. Then, out of these words, cases that our approach has led to an improvement in the sentence BLEU score over the baseline is reported. Table 3 shows the number of sentences, types and tokens for each test set as well as the corresponding type and token OOV counts. As we can see in this table, 0.82% of tokens in BOLT-arz and 0.45% of tokens in MT09-test sets are OOV. These cover the complete OOV cases (COOV).

In addition to these cases of COOV that are caused by lack of enough training data coverage, there are sense OOV (SOOV). SOOV happens when a particular word appears in both DA and MSA data but have different senses as faux amis. For instance the Arabic word *qlb* occurs in both MSA and DA contexts but with a different set of senses due to the lack of diacritics. In the specific MSA context it means 'heart' while in DA it means either 'heart' or 'change'. Therefore, in addition to the cases that word sense is triggered by DA context, other levels of word sense ambiguity such as homonymy and polysemy are involved in defining an SOOV word. Hence, SOOV identification in the test set needs additional information such as word equivalent EN gloss.

We determine SOOV as the words that (i) are observed as MSA word in the training data and considered a DA word in the test set once processed by AIDA and MADAMIRA; and, (ii) MSA and DA renderings have different non-overlapped equivalent EN glosses as returned by our AIDA and MADAMIRA. We assume that words with different dialectal usages in the train and test will have completely different EN equivalents, and thereby will be considered as SOOV. One of the words that this constraint has recognized as SOOV is the word *zy* with English equivalent 'uniform' or 'clothing' in MSA and 'such as' or 'like' in DA. Replacement of this SOOV by the MSA equivalent 'mvl' yields better translation as shown in Table 4.

Among all COOV words, our approach only targets COOV which are identified as DA. Table 5 and 6 report the number of COOV words (type and token) which have been identified as DA by AIDA or MADAMIRA in BOLT-arz and MT09 test sets, respectively. Second column in these tables represent number of SOOV (type and token) in each set. Last columns show percentage of sentences which have had at least one COOV or SOOV word and our replacement methodology has improved the sentence BLEU score over the baseline for each setup, respectively. Percentages in these columns demonstrate the ratio of enhanced sentences to the total number of sentences which have been determined to have at least one COOV or SOOV word. These percentages are reported on the MSA+DA data to train the SMT system condition.

While Table 5 and 6 show enhancements through DA COOV replacements, our manual assessment finds that most of these enhancements are actually coming from SOOVs present in the same sentences. For example, when we examined the 21 types identified by AIDA as DA COOV in BOLT-arz we found 9 typos, 5 MSAs, one foreign word and only 6 valid DA types. Moreover, none of the replacements over these 6 DA types yield an enhancement.

Although Table 5 shows that MADAMIRA achieves more success enhancing BLEU score of sentences which contain SOOV words on BOLT-arz test set, results of our investigation show that AIDA deteriorated performance on SOOV happens due to the noise that its MSA replacements add to the non-SOOV proportion of data. To assess this hypothesis we ran the best experimental setup (decoding:lex-to-lex:lem+POS-to-lex, training: MSA+DA) on the proportion of sentences in BOLT-arz which contain at least one SOOV

| Replacement Scheme | DA COOV | | SOOV | setup | Enhanced Sentences DA COOV | Enhanced Sentences SOOV |
|---|---|---|---|---|---|---|
| AIDA Replacement | type | 21 | 712 | lex-to-lex | 40% | 58% |
| | | | | lem+POS-to-lex | **60%** | 35% |
| | token | 26 | 1481 | lex-to-lex:lem+POS-to-lex | 55% | 57% |
| MADAMIRA Replacement | type | 9 | 194 | lex-to-lex | 34% | 55% |
| | | | | lem+POS-to-lex | 34% | 47% |
| | token | 9 | 281 | lex-to-lex:lem+POS-to-lex | 45% | **62%** |

Table 5: Columns from left to right: number of DA COOV, SOOV and percentages of enhanced sentences for BOLT-arz set.

| Replacement Scheme | DA COOV | | SOOV | setup | Enhanced Sentences DA COOV | Enhanced Sentences SOOV |
|---|---|---|---|---|---|---|
| AIDA Replacement | type | 6 | 376 | lex-to-lex | 67% | 44% |
| | | | | lem+POS-to-lex | **84%** | 35% |
| | token | 6 | 499 | lex-to-lex:lem+POS-to-lex | 50% | **61%** |
| MADAMIRA Replacement | type | 7 | 559 | lex-to-lex | 29% | 40% |
| | | | | lem+POS-to-lex | 27% | 34% |
| | token | 7 | 852 | lex-to-lex:lem+POS-to-lex | 43% | 48% |

Table 6: Similar to Table 5 for MT09 set.

word as processed using AIDA and MADAMIRA (the intersection subset). It is worth noting that compared to the baseline BLEU score of 23.8 on this subset, AIDA achieves a BLEU score of 24.4 while MADAMIRA only achieves a lower BLEU score of 24.0. This implicitly demonstrates that AIDA provides better MSA equivalents even for DA words which have MSA homographs with different meanings (faux amis cases). Overall, we note that the same results can be captured from Table 2 that shows AIDA outperforming MADAMIRA in identifying and replacing DA words.

## 6 Conclusion and Future Work

We presented a new approach to enhance DA-to-EN machine translation by reducing the rate of DA OOV words. We employed AIDA and MADAMIRA to identify DA words and replace them with the corresponding MSA equivalent.
We showed our replacement scheme reaches a noticeable enhancement in SMT performance for SOOVs. This can be considered one of the contributions of this work which was not addressed in the previous studies before. The results of evaluation on two blind test sets showed that using AIDA to identify and replace MSA equivalents enhances translation results by 0.4% absolute BLEU (1.6% relative BLEU) and using MADAMIRA achieves 0.3% absolute BLEU (1.2% relative BLEU) enhancement over the baseline on two blind test sets. One of the interesting ideas to extend this project in the future is to combine AIDA and MADAMIRA top choices in a confusion network and feeding this confusion network to the SMT system. Acquiring more DA-to-EN parallel data to enrich translation models is another work which we intend to pursue later. Moreover, evaluating possible effects of different genres and domains on the framework efficiency provides another path to extend this work in future.

## Acknowledgments

This work was supported by the Defense Advanced Research Projects Agency (DARPA) Contract No. HR0011-12-C-0014, the BOLT program with subcontract from Raytheon BBN. We would like to acknowledge the useful comments by three anonymous reviewers who helped in making this publication more concise and better presented.

## References

Abhaya Agarwal, and Alon Lavie. 2008. Meteor, m-bleu and m-ter: Evaluation metrics for high-correlation with human rankings of machine translation output. In *Proceedings of the Third Workshop on Statistical Machine Translation,* pp. 115-118,

Rania Al-Sabbagh and Roxana Girju. 2010. Mining the Web for the Induction of a dialectal Arabic Lexicon. In *Proceedings of the Language Resources and Evaluation Conference (LREC),*

David Chiang, Mona Diab, Nizar Habash, Owen Rambow, and Safiullah Shareef. 2006. Parsing Arabic Dialects. In *Proceedings of EACL 2006,*

Mona Diab, Mohamed Al-Badrashiny, Maryam Aminian, Mohammed Attia, Pradeep Dasigi, Heba Elfardy, Ramy Eskander, Nizar Habash, Abdelati Hawwari and Wael Salloum. 2014. Tharwa: A Large Scale Dialectal Arabic - Standard Arabic - English Lexicon. In *Proceedings of LREC 2014,* Reykjavik, Iceland.

Mona Diab, Nizar Habash, Owen Rambow, Mohamed Altantawy and Yassin Benajiba. 2010. Colaba: Arabic dialect annotation and processing. In *Proceedings of LREC Workshop on Semitic Language Processing,* pp. 6674.

Heba Elfardy and Mona Diab. 2013. Sentence level dialect identification in Arabic. In *Proceedings of ACL 2013,* Sofia, Bulgaria.

Heba Elfardy, Mohamed Al-Badrashiny and Mona Diab. 2013. Code Switch Point Detection in Arabic. In Natural Language Processing and Information Systems, Springer Berlin Heidelberg, pp. 412-416.

David Graff and Christopher Cieri. 2003. English Gigaword, LDC Catalog No.: LDC2003T05 Linguistic Data Consortium, University of Pennsylvania.

Nizar Habash and Owen Rambow. 2005. Arabic tokenization, part-of-speech tagging and morphological disambiguation in one fell swoop. In *Proceedings of ACL 2005,*

Nizar Habash. 2009. REMOOV: A tool for online handling of out-of-vocabulary words in machine translation.. In *Proceedings of the 2nd International Conference on Arabic Language Resources and Tools (MEDAR),* Cairo, Egypt.

Nizar Habash. 2008. Four Techniques for Online Handling of Out-of-Vocabulary Words in Arabic-English Statistical Machine Translation. In *Proceedings of ACL 2008: HLT, Short Papers,* Columbus, Ohio.

Nizar Habash, Ryan Roth, Owen Rambow, Ramy Eskander and Nadi Tomeh. 2013. Morphological analysis and disambiguation for dialectal Arabic. In *Proceedings of NAACL 2013:HLT,* pp. 426-432.

Philipp Koehn, Hieu Hoang, Alexandra Birch, Christopher Callison-Burch, Marcello Federico, Nicola Bertoldi, Brooke Cowan, Wade Shen, Christine Moran, Richard Zens, Christopher Dyer, Ondrej Bojar, Alexandra Constantin, and Evan Herbst. 2007. Moses: open source toolkit for statistical machine translation. In *Proceedings of ACL 2007, Demo and Poster Sessions.* Prague, Czech Republic.

Mohamed Maamouri, Ann Bies, Tim Buckwalter, and Wigdan Mekki. 2004. The Penn Arabic Treebank: Building a Large-Scale Annotated Arabic Corpus. In *NEMLAR Conference on Arabic Language Resources and Tools,* Cairo, Egypt.

Franz Josef Och. 2003. Minimum Error Rate Training for Statistical Machine Translation. In *Proceedings of ACL 2003,* pages 160-167 Sapporo, Japan.

Franz Josef Och and Hermann Ney. 2003. A systematic comparison of various statistical alignment models. Computational linguistics. Vol. 29. pp. 19-51.

Kishore Papineni, Salim Roukos, Todd Ward, and Wei-Jing Zhu. 2002. BLEU: a Method for Automatic Evaluation of Machine Translation. In *Proceedings of ACL 2002,* pages 311318, Philadelphia, PA.

Arfath Pasha, Mohamed Al-Badrashiny, Mona Diab, Ahmed El Kholy, Ramy Eskander, Nizar Habash, Manoj Pooleery, Owen Rambow and Ryan M. Roth. 2014. MADAMIRA: A Fast, Comprehensive Tool for Morphological Analysis and Disambiguation of Arabic. In *Proceedings of LREC 2014,* Reykjavik, Iceland.

Wael Salloum and Nizar Habash. 2013. Dialectal Arabic to English Machine Translation: Pivoting through Modern Standard Arabic. In *Proceedings of NAACL 2013:HLT,* Atlanta, Georgia.

Wael Salloum and Nizar Habash. 2012. Elissa: A Dialectal to Standard Arabic Machine Translation System. In *Proceedings of COLING 2012,* Denver, Colorado.

Hassan Sawaf. 2010. Arabic dialect handling in hybrid machine translation. In *Proceedings of AMTA 2010,* Denver, Colorado.

Helmut Schmid. 1994. Probabilistic part-of-speech tagging using decision trees. In *Proceedings of international conference on new methods in language processing,* pp. 44-49.

Matthew Snover, Bonnie Dorr, Richard Schwartz, Linnea Micciulla, and John Makhoul. 2006. A study of translation edit rate with targeted human annotation. In *Proceedings of AMTA 2006,* pp. 223-231.

Andreas Stolcke. 2002. SRILM an Extensible Language Modeling Toolkit. In *Proceedings of the International Conference on Spoken Language Processing,*

Ying Zhang and Stephan Vogel. 2010. Significance Tests of Automatic Machine Translation Evaluation Metrics. In Machine Translation, Vol. 24, Issue 1, pages 51-65.

Rabih Zbib, Erika Malchiodi, Jacob Devlin, David Stallard, Spyros Matsoukas, Richard Schwartz, John Makhoul, Omar F. Zaidan, and Chris Callison-Burch. 2012. Machine translation of Arabic dialects. In *Proceedings of NAACL 2012:HLT,*

# Author Index

**Association for Computational Linguistics**
209 N. Eighth Street
Stroudsburg, Pennsylvania 18360

CURRAN ASSOCIATES INC
proceedings.com